Body and Soul

Body and Soul

A SYMPATHETIC
HISTORY OF AMERICAN
SPIRITUALISM

Robert S. Cox

Donna!
Best wishes for your
interesting project

RC

University of Virginia Press
Charlottesville & London

UNIVERSITY OF VIRGINIA PRESS

© 2003 by the Rector and Visitors of the University of Virginia

All rights reserved

Printed in the United States of America on acid-free paper

First published 2003

1 3 5 7 9 8 6 4 2

Library of Congress Cataloging-in-Publication Data

Cox, Robert S., 1958–

  Body and soul : a sympathetic history of American spiritualism /
Robert S. Cox.

    p.   cm.

Includes bibliographical references and index.

  ISBN 0-8139-2230-5 (alk. paper)

  1. Spiritualism—United States—History—19th century. 2. United
States—Race relations—United States—History—19th century.
I. Title.

BF1242.U6 C69 2003

133.9' 0973—dc21   2003001842

CONTENTS

ILLUSTRATIONS

. . . .

ACKNOWLEDGMENTS

PRODDED BY HIS PUBLISHER to produce, Kenneth Graeme defended himself by claiming to be "a spring, and not a pump." As the epitome of a spring, I owe a debt of gratitude to several individuals not only for bringing out my artesian tendencies but for clarifying the emissions. Susan Juster, Regina Morantz-Sanchez, Joel Howell, and William Ian Miller, were truly the ideal critics, sharp and perceptive in comment, warm in support, and packing a stick just large enough for a proper and timely rap on the snout. At various points my sympathetic community at the University of Michigan was enriched by exchanges with David Scobey, David Bien, W. Andrew Achenbaum, Michael MacDonald, Jenn Rosecrans, Jon Parmenter, Stephen Hum, John and Arlene Shy, and Shawn Kimmel, and my colleagues in the Departments of Geology and Biology were no less valuable, particularly Daniel Fisher, Gerry Smith, Catherine Badgely, K. C. Lohmann, Henry Pollack, Rob Van der Voo, David Rea, Robert Carr, and Wesley Brown. Elsewhere, John Beatty's innocent comments on sympathy played a much greater role than he should have to admit; similar gratitude is due to Michael Dietrich and Jay Aronson. Colleen McDannell, Bill Pencak, David Waldstreicher, Kariann Yokota, James Delbourgo; and two anonymous reviewers should be thanked and absolved of any responsibility for the parts they played in reading or responding to portions of this work.

Without the assistance of the staffs of some dedicated manuscripts workers and librarians, I could have done very little. I am particularly grateful to the folks at the William L. Clements Library (John Dann, John Harriman, Don Wilcox, Susan Swasta, Melissa Johnson, and Kathy Koehler), the Rare Books Department of the Boston Public Library (Bill Faucon, Eugene Zepp, Roberta Zonghi, and Gunnars Rutkovskis), the University of New Orleans (Florence Jumonville), the Schlesinger Library, the Boston Athenaeum, the Massachusetts Historical Society, the Library Company of Philadelphia, the Rare Books and Manuscripts Department of the University of Pennsylvania (Michael Ryan), the American Philosophical Society, the College of Physicians of Philadelphia (Charles Greifenstein), and the University of Virginia Library. Equally critical were the timely support afforded by an Alicia Monti Fellowship at the Boston Public Library, a fellowship from the Pew Foundation for Religion and American History, and a Scott W. Turner fellowship from the Department of Geology at Michigan and support at various points from the Departments of History and Geology and the Programs in Great Books and American Culture. Richard Holway deserves special thanks for priming the pump and for generally encouraging (and useful) words, and the same can be said of Jay Stiefel, Don Falk, Stephen Falk, Liz Otwell, Wes Cowan, Doug Price, Tom Cullen, and Steve Resnick, all of whom promised to buy a copy of the book if I mentioned them. Jay's goad was particularly well placed and well timed.

Finally, if there is a special sphere reserved for the dearest and nearest (with proximity in mind), it would be populated by Peter and Kristin Onuf, Mr. F. P. B. and Miss G. P. B. Darcy, Dex Haven, our two anonymous friends, and the heliocentric Rachel, about whom all revolves and who is always right. I enjoy it, and I'm better for it.

Body and Soul

Introduction

WENDELL NEWHALL knew his feelings, having been introduced to them by an old friend. When he reminisced about the events of that evening's self-encounter to Asa Smith, a witness, a participant, and a sympathetic soul in his own right, the sensations still boiled within.

Dear Friend

Your letter of Ap 23 duly received, and you dont know how glad I was when I read your name, the thought, that I am in my old age, remembered by persons with whom I associated 30 yrs ago, stirs up my inner man, and I ask myself, who will speak of me when I pass into the great beyond? Swedenborg tell's us that spirits love to be remembered by the association left behind; and I can very readily beleive his statement. You do not misstate aught, when you say we lived that winter that you occupied the Hutchinson Cottage. It was an association of congenial minds, and what a phenomena we were a witness of, and how futile it is to talk, or tell any one of the phenomena of which we know, and with what a power it fastened itself upon me, and when I look back to the evening of the pantomime, and think how completely, in spite of all my efforts they so glibly run my tongue, so peculiar, unsought, and unthought of in that line, it will take more than one Bob Ingersoll, to get me to say that I dont know of immortality, I emphasize *that I do know.*

Asa we did live, I cannot say fast, as that term is used, but there was a fulness, a joyfulness, we reached a point of satisfaction, a demonstration that the life beyond the grave, that the christian teachers had and were talking so much about, our little company were cognizant of phenomena, that placed it beyond cavil. How completely it came home to me, Mr. Fuller would shake his sides, and laugh when talking about that evenings performance; and how laughable it was, how we all shook with laughter, so strange that a departed spirit, Mr. Rogers if it was him, should take such method of demonstration; I dont wonder at the world's incredulity, I do not dare tell folk's what I know, I shall get pookd at for my pains, and so I keep the secret in my own bosom. Just think, there was I, in full possession of all my conscious powers, and an intelligence foreign to my-self, waging my tongue, at will, making me exclaim, I have got you, I have got you; then for one breath I would say—No you havent then again seize my tongue against my will, and exclaim—Yes I have—I have got you, I have got you. And when I was relieved, how I sweat—and to have them use my own tongue, and tell me with my own breath, that my features, and my hair were like, N. P. Rodgers—Asa, what was our spiritual status that night; Oh! if we could have had our spiritual sight opened that night, what rapturous joy would have been ours, science has no method of probing this phenomena, they are without crucible, or scalpel. How glad I should be to have you visit me, try and come—and Louise is stricken, soon to leave for the parts, that together we have talked about, and tried to get a knowledge about; And Ambrose and his wife you did not write about, I trust in good health. My wife & myself are still jour-neying on, soon shall reach the goal, and be forgotten on earth, but to be re-ceived by loving companions above—Extend my love to all that I ever knew in Norwich, May 6th it will be one year since my sister Ann died. Of my fathers family I am alone.

Sincerely yours,
D. Wendell Newhall[1]

For Newhall, the voices of the 1850s spoke audibly still in 1881, a reality thirty years and another world on. The early days of spiritual investigation still captivated his tongue, still fueled memories of the grand reopening of the spiritual telegraph line, of rediscovering communion between living and dead. In yielding his body to the will of another, Newhall, like thou-sands of other Americans, discovered an experience that surpassed evan-gelical Christianity and eclipsed agnosticism and dulled the crucible and scalpel of science with its persistence of emotion. Newhall was among the first generation of converts to the "movement" known as modern Spiritu-alism, a movement—a religion—held together by the slender but powerful premise that the "forgotten on earth" could converse intimately with the dead, a movement that within a decade of its founding filled out its ranks in the millions.[2]

For many historians there is something incongruous in the "rapturous joy" Newhall felt that evening, something inexplicable in the intensely physical upwelling of emotion and the "association of congenial minds" that exerted its hold even after the lapse of thirty years. In Spiritualism the capacity of historians to parse out the intricacies of mediumistic fraud and to divine the political and social ramifications of spirit communion has never been matched by a corresponding skill in understanding the shape or function of Spiritualist emotion or the nature of Spiritualist experience. Emotion has been so alien to the historical agenda that Werner Sollors and Bret Carroll deny that it was a factor at all, insisting that the characteristic feature of Spiritualist "religiosity" was a "centrality of emotional restraint" and claiming that spirit communications were "amazingly heartless," offering "little room to the emotional contexts of speaking with the dead." In a sense, many Victorians agreed. The overwhelming majority of antebellum spirit communications, as many noted, were almost literally heartless, so excruciatingly banal that Lydia Maria Child lampooned them as "more disappointing than the golden key which unlocked *nothing;* for they are the merest mass of old rags, saw-dust, and clam-shells."[3]

But whether spirit messages were personal clamshells or political bombshells, the Newhalls of the movement suggest that they could exert a profound and enduring influence. Antebellum Spiritualists insisted that emotion was integral to their beliefs, stating that as a group they tended not only "toward freer thought" than nonbelievers but toward "freer and more kindly emotion, and freer expression of emotion in all the outward acts." The medium S. E. Park placed the "free interchange of sentiment" as the motor driving all the progressive tendencies of the spirit world, the "founder and promulgator of light, truth, and facts." Antebellum Spiritualist writings were suffused with the language of sentiment expressed through a peculiarly physical emotionality in which the interpersonal was experienced viscerally and in which affect and sensation were integrated and extended beyond the boundaries of the individual. Spiritualist sentiment became, in effect, an elaborate social physiology in which individuals were integrated holistically within the structures of society, joined in thought, affect, and sensation into the fiber of a sympathetically united nation in precisely the same way that the nerves, organs, and tissues were integrated within the organic body.[4]

In tilling the familiar soil of American Spiritualism, my primary intention has been to restore feeling to the dead, to chart the topography of the emotional cosmology of Spiritualists as it took shape in the 1850s and as it transformed slowly in the years saddling the Civil War. From the sawdust and clamshells of spirit communion, I here reconstruct the variable but coherent set of cosmological principles that emerged to give shape to their distinctive social physiology, the crossfiring of affect and physical sensation that was seen in and through the social practice of sympathy. My primary aims have been to reconstruct the conformation of the sympathetic body and its relation to spirit society and to expose the role of exchange in all its senses—sympathetic, financial, physiological—within Spiritualist praxis.

In part, too, my aim is genealogical, both in the sense of reconstructing the history of ideas and practices of American Spiritualism to relate them to broader cultural currents and in the sense of re-creating the relationships between Wendell Newhall's "forgotten on earth" themselves. If emotion has been lacking in historical accounts of the Spiritualist movement, so too has a sense of the stunning diversity of spirit voices, living and dead, and of the internal tensions and temporal dynamism that affected them. More conflicted and contradictory than has previously been recognized, the range of social and political expression in Spiritualism ran the entire mid-Victorian gamut. In turn, aspects of their sympathetic cosmology were reflected throughout American culture, informed recursively by social, medical, and economic theory, by reform, religion, and American practices of race, and helped to implant exchange at the center of American life.

Inevitably, I underplay those dimensions of Spiritualism that have already sustained intense historical scrutiny, particularly the gendered aspects of the discourse and the role of scientific language. Yet I hope nevertheless to provide room to move beyond discussions of the movement's social radicals to evaluate the less well documented voices, the conservative, the reactionary, and the conflicted among them, and to analyze the role that African Americans and Indians played as subjects and participants in spirit communion and the slow, metasomatic impact of race on the topography of emotion. The sympathetic cosmology of Spiritualists—the "abstract configuration of interlinked ideas about time, nature, human nature, and social reality"—provides a valuable tool for analyzing the relationship between spiritual and social beliefs by distinguishing ideas from their specific and often contradictory discursive functions, without, I hope, severing the link between social ideas and social power.[5]

Drawing heavily upon the existing discourses of somnambulism and mesmerism, and above all upon the praxis of sympathy, Spiritualism created affective structures through which the world was perceived and experienced as a dynamically integrated whole. From the perspective of Spiritualists like Hudson Tuttle, this cosmos was supremely ordered, one in which the "planets, sun, and worlds revolve through space in given intervals of time . . . and from year to year, from age to age, preserve their orbits." More importantly it was a cosmos in which "one condition is in exact accordance with another condition; one law with another law; one effect with another effect; so that ONE GREAT UNIT is produced." It acted as a single, sympathetically coordinated body, "a unity composed of parts." It was in this sense that when Wendell Newhall recalled his first night among the spirits, his memories were not of the grand opening of a universe of thought but rather of that rare "association of congenial minds." The portentous fact of that evening was not so much that the dead lived but that "*we* did live."[6]

SPIRITUALIST HISTORIES

Trying to determine the origins of Spiritualist thought is like trying to determine on which leg a spider stands, only with Spiritualism it is spider upon spider all the way down. Spirit communion was blessed with a polyphyletic genealogy stretching back to the radical sects of the interregnum, to the Camisard prophets, to Methodists and evangelicals, and it flowed out in turn to influence these and other sects again and again. As a form of sacred theater, according to Clarke Garrett, speaking with the divine had long served as a means of proclaiming the apocalyptic urgency of reforming the social and moral orders and for expressing concerns with spiritual direction and personal salvation. Yet the search for specific connections between Spiritualism and any individual sect, or any nonsectarian alternative for that matter, is rife with peril and frustration. Always lacking in authoritative texts or structures, Spiritualism was inherently polyvocal, and Spiritualists themselves charted disparate histories of their movement, often several at once.[7]

Regardless of how they viewed their past, most Spiritualists agreed that the flint from which their movement was sparked was quarried in Hydesville, New York, a small village near Rochester that not being "directly accessible from a railroad," as the Spiritualist Emma Hardinge wrote, had become "lonely, and unmarked by those tokens of progress that the locomotive generally leaves in its track." During the winter of 1847–48, the Hydesville home of John Fox was afflicted with a series of mysterious raps that showered from the walls and floors and even thin air, seemingly without source. Despairing, praying "if this thing was of the devil, that it might be removed from them," the Foxes became the object of public curiosity as the weeks progressed and as the raps became more insistent, and as disturbing kinetic phenomena began to punctuate their nights, including unseen hands that brushed past and furniture that bustled about on its own. Kate and Margaret, the youngest of the Fox daughters, were the frequent focal points for these manifestations, but they seemed unfazed and even amused by them all until on March 31, 1848, Kate took the occasion of some particularly loud raps to address the sounds directly. "Here Mr. Splitfoot," she cried out, snapping her fingers, "do as I do!" When more raps rained down in response, the Foxes and their growing audience realized that an intelligence lay behind the mysterious phenomena, and after posing a series of simple questions, replied to with a telegraphic code of raps to signify yes and no, the young girls ascertained that the source of the commotion was a deceased man with an uncanny knack for clairvoyantly divining the number of Fox children (dead as well as living) and for reciting the names and dates of death of all their neighbors' relatives, as well.[8]

In antebellum New York neither spirits nor specters were a rarity: there were Ichabod Cranes enough to populate any number of sleepy hamlets, and seers and seekers like Jemima Wilkinson were just as familiar. Yet unlike the holy presence that spoke through Wilkinson, the spirits who rapped for the Fox sisters were neither God nor angels but personalized beings, the shades of departed relatives and intimate friends who, as the former Universalist minister Charles Hammond attested, remained so like mortals that they rocked a cradle to indicate their "maternal care for the infant's slumbers" and whirled a spinning wheel about its axis to produce "a very natural buzz" of the spindle. From the moment that the spiritual telegraph line was first strung, the public interest in these domesticated spirits proved highly contagious. Hydesville was besieged by persons longing to hear and affirm for themselves, as Asa Newhall later did, that life did not end at death.[9]

To satisfy the demand, the Foxes soon took their raps to Rochester, demonstrating the phenomena in Corinthian Hall (the site of meetings for abolition and women's rights), and later they performed in Auburn, Buffalo, and New York City and still farther afield. Under the scrutiny of the orthodox and the derision of skeptics, the sisters performed "tests" of their powers while standing on sheets of glass, on pillows, or on other nonconductive surfaces. They elicited answers to arcane questions about the personal lives of individuals they had never known. They convinced. Although a clutch of physicians in Buffalo famously dismissed their raps as the mere cracking of knee and ankle joints and some dismissed the girls as diabolical, many others accepted the manifestations for what they purported to be and welcomed them as the arrival of a new spiritual dispensation. The girls had become spiritual "mediums," intermediaries of exchange on several levels, operating like the wires of a telegraph over which forces could act at a distance and through which impressions were conveyed to the senses.[10]

Unlike most who communed with spirits before them, the Foxes' mediumship proved contagious. Among the first witnesses to the raps, both Charles Hammond and Isaac Post, a veteran of the Hicksite schism, developed powerful mediumistic abilities, and their records of their spiritual experiences became standard fare for seekers of the 1850s. Mediumship fell as well upon the eldest Fox daughter, Leah (usually called by her adjectivally rich married names, Mrs. Fish, Brown, or Underhill), who ensconced herself in Barnum's New York Hotel and communed for the public on Horace Greeley's dime. Discoveries of such latent psychic sensitivities became an important part of the lore of Spiritualists, who maintained that while some might be more innately capable than others, mediumship was available to all who openly inquired. Inspiration was free to the masses.[11]

This Fox-centered version of the origins of Spiritualism was often coupled with a sharply different version, one that pitted the Foxes' phenomena against the "Harmonial philosophy" and visionary lineage of the "Poughkeepsie Seer," Andrew Jackson Davis (fig. 1). What Davis uniquely provided was a robust theory of spiritual action that backed the tangible, empirically verifiable phenomena of the Foxes with a thick description of the structure of the spirit world and of spiritual cause and effect. As an eighteen-year-old in 1844 (four years before Hydesville), Davis began his explorations of the afterlife when he was quite literally entranced during a lecture on mesmerism. As sleepwalkers and mesmeric somnambules were widely purported to do, in this heightened mental state Davis began to perceive the interiors of those around him, providing him with a psychological scalpel with which to diagnose bodily afflictions and poising him to become a crack clairvoyant physician. As his spiritual senses sharpened, he began to see not only the physical structures of individuals but the structures of the universe as well, as if one could be exchanged for the other.[12]

With the assistance of the spirits of Emanuel Swedenborg and Galen, Davis sketched a philosophy for what the medium Hudson Tuttle called a "perfectly democratic religion," an "emphatically . . . American religion" that perfected the tendencies that historians Nathan Hatch and Gordon Wood have seen percolating throughout antebellum American Protestantism. Although Davis's harmonialism was never rigorously or consistently defined, it usually subtended a constellation of ideas that employed the "spiritual aspirations" of men and women to bring them "into harmonial relations with each other," in order to form "one common brotherhood, where angelic wisdom and order can be freely unfolded." For Davis these aspirations involved the rejection of Christianity as it was practiced, along with "every thing which is uselessly mysterious and supernatural," replacing it with a Christian rationality that "addresses the cultivated heart through the expanded understanding." Jesus, he admitted, had appealed to the "goodness" within civilized minds, instituting an "era of Love," but the modern "age of impulse" now "demands an age of Reason," the modern world needed "a 'Philosophy' which Jesus *did not* furnish . . . a 'revelation' to the faculty of REASON, which the Bible *does not* contain."[13]

Harmonial Spiritualism—which Davis carefully distinguished from the spiritual manifestations—led to a "'Revelation' of the *Structures,* and *Laws,* and *orders,* and uses, of the material and spiritual universe." It exposed the "boundless system of Nature," with the emphasis upon boundlessness, and was "addressed to the human instincts and understanding." Recognizing that Jesus' intuition of the heart required the muscular use of reason to form a satisfying religion, Davis set harmonial philosophy upon the three legs of "NATURE, REASON, and INTUITION as the only reliable authorities on all subjects." Through its lens one came to understand "MAN as a microscope—as a miniature universe; being perpetually visited

FIG. 1. Andrew Jackson Davis. Photograph by J. Gurney, ca. 1862.
(Darcy-Haven Collection: Private Collection)

by innumerable friends from the four quarters of the firmament." As the
"HEAD of Creation," man enjoyed "the countless relationships which exist, most intimately, between him and external nature; between him and the
spiritual universe!" The integration of all creation was an essential feature
of harmonialism, which stressed not only rationalism and science but a
self-reliant questioning of authority, the value of intuition, and a comprehension of the law of progress, all as the best means to "perfectly acquire
knowledge of those harmonial ties by which all and each of the pieces and
parts of the universe are fastened together."[14]

Like most early mediums Davis "unqualifiedly" rejected "all the dogmas and sectarianisms of Christendom," resisting all attempts at centralizing spiritual authority, viewing them as "so many barriers set up by ignorance and cupidity against the spontaneous development of Nature's own Religion." Instead, he and his peers urged seekers to become spiritual empiricists, trying out the spirits against the rigors of scientific logic and, as the Christian Spiritualist Uriah Clark put it, against the individual's "Protestant right to private judgment to read and interpret for himself." Despite the centripetal effects of the "Protestant right," Davis's voluminous outpouring of print lent an inertial center and measure of coherence to the movement during the 1850s, and variations on his themes spread throughout the writings and lectures of R. P. Ambler, S. B. Brittan, Allen Putnam, Herman Snow, John Worth Edmonds, James Peebles, Robert Hare, and Hudson Tuttle, of Achsa Sprague, Cora Hatch, and Emma Hardinge, and of the editors of the *Spiritual Telegraph,* the *Banner of Light, Shekinah,* and the *Spirit Messenger.* While these authors differed on many points, sometimes significantly, most retained Davis's commitment to rationalism and scientific naturalism, arguing, as the medium G. A. Redman did, that what most distinguished Spiritualism as a system of belief was the conjunction of phenomenal proof with a strong philosophical and religious underpinning, the wedding of body and soul. The physical phenomena, according to Redman, were "the foundation of the whole philosophy," and without such empirical proofs, he feared, "we *sink* back on *faith alone,* deprived of a *tangible basis.*"[15]

Even acknowledging the biparental history of Spiritualism, however, vastly underestimates the movement's true diversity. One could continue to count spiders in the history, tracing the influence of transcendentalism, of higher criticism, or socialism, but it may suffice here to note the mutual influences of Spiritualism and other religious traditions. Spirit communion did not spring fully formed from the brains of the Foxes in 1848, nor did Davis conjure his cosmos ex nihilo. Institutionalized forms of spirit communion sprang up repeatedly within Protestant and post-Protestant sects, and Spiritualists were said to owe particular debts to three prophetic traditions, the Quaker, Shaker, and Swedenborgian, though in none of these cases was the relationship unconflicted.

The contention that Quakerism influenced early Spiritualism can be traced at least to the Spiritualist Robert Dale Owen, who lauded the Friends as "the Spiritualists of the seventeenth century," and to Giles Stebbins, who stated boldly that "Spiritualism is Quakerism enlarged and revised." Although Owen criticized modern Friends for clinging to the Bible and for rejecting spirit intercourse, he cited the inward light (that divine spark immanent within all humanity) as foundational for Spiritualist conceptions of humanity, and he claimed the Friends' rejection of clergy and ceremony and their early period of prophecy as precursors of Spiritualism. Subsequent historians have picked up these cues, noting the prominence of Quakers such as Amy and Isaac Post and George Willets among the earliest supporters of the Fox sisters and emphasizing the substantial interest in spirit communion among the politically radical Progressive Friends.[16]

Yet setting aside the thorny and essentially irresolvable issue of whether an interest in spirit communion makes one a Spiritualist, there is still the nagging problem that the Spiritualists' inward light, if it was a uniform concept at all, was not very Quakerly. Among those Spiritualists who held any notion of the inward light, it often represented little more than a generalized immanence of the divine of a sort palatable to a wide range of liberal Protestants, lacking the theological force and centrality it enjoyed in Quakerism. Believers like Owen were fond of establishing genealogies that traced Spiritualism back to the days of biblical prophesy by way of a host of liberal religions, thereby demonstrating the ancient roots of Spiritualist thought, its widespread acceptance in other cultures and at other times, and its respectability. Above all, these narratives established a historical trajectory of progress in religion and morality, rationality and reason, that culminated in modern Spiritualism. As a description of intellectual connection, however, Owen's narrative was more wishful than thinking.[17]

The Shakers present a somewhat more persuasive case for influencing the course of spirit communion. From their earliest days these "John the Baptists of Spiritualism" experienced "manifestations of spiritual presence" that closely resembled the physical phenomena of Spiritualism, and in recognition of this, the Spiritualist writer Allen Putnam hailed Ann Lee, the founder of American Shakerism, as "a very superior medium" who acted "under the special direction of a class of disembodied spirits,—not ardent spirits, but souls, who once lived in forms of flesh." While Quaker prophets communed with the divine, Shakers communed with the dead, and although such "excesses" waned after Lee's death, Theodore Johnson and others continued to communicate with spirits, most notably (like Spiritualists) with the spirits of American Indians. Although communal living and celibacy were uncommon among Spiritualists, and although many of them complained of Shaker "fanaticism" and attempts to exert magnetic control over their mediums, Spiritualists and Shakers met on several occasions in congress and expressed sympathy for one another's aims.[18]

While Shakers provided a form for spirit communion, the Swedish mystic Emanuel Swedenborg provided the cosmic seeds of a system. "Enmeshed in a world of angels," Swedenborgian thought cast a long shadow over the idiosyncratic writings of A. J. Davis, and through him and others, Swedenborg's spiritual geography and epistemology exerted an enormous influence over early Spiritualism.[19] Trained as a scientist and influenced by the occultism of Böhme, the Hermeticists, and the cabala, Swedenborg set out to use theology to provide an empirical demonstration of the immortality of the soul, to make spirit comprehensible to the external senses. In a series of visions and angelic visitations that began in the 1740s, he grasped the celestial key, discerning an elaborate set of "correspondences" between the divine and natural worlds that effectively expunged the distinction between spirit and matter. The natural, ephemeral world and the divine, eternal world were part and counterpart, "complementary and inseparable dimensions of a single and universal whole." A "savvy synthesizer of natural philosophy and immediate revelation," Swedenborg wedded the language of empirical science to a dualistic reading of Scripture, coming to the recognition that there was an absolute truth beyond the external senses and asserting that the quest for spiritual knowledge would awaken entire new realms of sensation and open the gates to the influx of celestial knowledge. "The trick," as Leigh Eric Schmidt has explained, was to ignore the material and rational in favor of transforming them into the spiritual, to see the eternal and infallible counterpart lying beyond the ephemeral and fallible part, and by so doing, to "throw open the arcana of scripture and the mysteries of the heavenly world to rational understanding and empirical report."[20]

Swedenborg's correspondential geography was a favorite of antebellum spirits, who once informed Francis H. Smith that the "spirit land is but a counterpart of earth" and that everything on earth was but "a type of all we [spirits] have. There is no condition natural, that there is not a corresponding spiritual and mental." Another spirit informed Abraham Pierce that the "physical body is but a fac-simile of the spiritual body, with all its senses and constituted parts . . . ordained and fitted to work in a physical or outward form." Spirits borrowed other ideas from Swedenborg, some less specific, some highly so: like the Swede, they initially opposed the formation of a formal church, though they eventually succumbed, and they emphasized practical piety and the enlightening power of spirit and emotion. More distinctively, they relied in detail upon Swedenborg's geography of heaven. Heaven and hell, as Swedenborg learned, were a system of seven concentric spheres inhabited by beings of increasing spiritual advancement, and the inhabitants of higher spheres were engaged in showering the lower spheres with a steady influx of spirit, illuminating mortal life and providing moral and spiritual edification. In many ways Swedenborgianism and Spiritualism were part and counterpart themselves, the ethereal, intellectualized Swedenborg paired with an earthly Spiritualism geared toward practice.[21]

Yet for all their similarities, the relationship between the two was conflicted. Initially, Swedenborgians approved of spirit communion, and publishers like Bela Marsh printed works by both. A Swedenborgian minister, George Bush, joined one of the earliest spirit circles in New York City, and in 1853 he took part in a successful experiment "to test the possibility of communicating in Hebrew through the raps," while the poet Thomas Lake Harris carried out his own experiments with spirit communion. In turn, Swedenborg's mediumship was praised by Spiritualists, and he could be found returning to the circles of Isaac Post and John W. Edmonds, where, in the latter case, he was joined by Francis Bacon to form the perfect pairing of the mystic and the rationalist.[22]

But the hierarchy of the Swedenborgian church soon shifted from support to attack, rejecting any alliance with Spiritualists and, according to James Peebles, "flippantly berat[ing]" them for having fallen prey to "demoniac possessions." In part, the venom of this response is attributable to some important points of divergence that underlay a common commitment to the centrality of spirit communion. The monotonic progressivism of Spiritualism, for example, grated against Swedenborg's declensionist claim that modern humans were the degraded descendants of a golden age in which celestial intercourse was open to all, and the Spiritualist rejection of the reality of hell, sin, and evil flew in the face of the Manichaean struggle between good and evil that Swedenborgians imagined gripped the world. Furthermore, the spirits who populated Swedenborg's cosmos were not the spirits of departed humans, and certainly not departed relatives, but angelic presences of another order. That there were good spirits and bad required the spiritual seeker to be on guard for error, but communion with the higher sort of spirit exposed certain truth. With access to the highest spirits, the most profound seers, like Swedenborg, could attain virtual infallibility.[23]

On this last point it is helpful to view the divide between Spiritualists and Swedenborgians within a larger cultural context, and particularly within the contentious history of religious enthusiasm and formalism described by Ann Taves, Leigh Eric Schmidt, and John Corrigan and the "love-hate relationship" that many sects held with immediate revelation. Elation over the potential benefits in spiritual order and authority that accrued through direct revelation was often counterbalanced by dismay over the unruliness and propensity for "popular error" that often accompanied it. Like the religious revivals described by Corrigan, the sustained practice of direct revelation stood on the razor's edge of emotional excitement and emotional control, and Spiritualism threatened the balance by pitting universal spirit communion against the authority of Swedenborg's revelations and ministers.[24]

In several cases Swedenborgian ministers resolved conflicts between Spiritualist visions and Swedenborg's simply by asserting the higher order of Swedenborg's mediumship and by attributing the differences to the intervention of evil spirits in spirit circles. When Thomas Lake Harris began to dabble in Spiritualism, he was savaged by his peers for surrendering himself "up to the spirits," making him vulnerable to evil influence. Harris responded as a proper Swedenborgian. "I cannot help seeing or hearing the inhabitants of the spiritual world," he wrote.

> Since I inhabit both worlds I believe it orderly to communicate with the inhabitants of both for ends of use. But I allow no infringement of personal freedom in my intercourse with spirits whether in the natural or spiritual sphere. I look for Absolute Truth and Goodness to our Lord alone. All spirits are fellow men

with whom it is allowable to consociate only as they are in the Lord. I never to my knowledge consociate with any spirit who does not recognize that the Lord is Divine and that the Word is the receptacle of His Truth. When spirits approach me with opposite doctrines I address myself to the Lord, when they invariably recede.[25]

Harris claimed the mantle of mental and emotional discipline, of order, even while delving into the excitement of Spiritualist communion, and discipline and order were precisely the issues. Swedenborgians were no strangers to charges of excess, having often been branded as enthusiasts, and the hard-won respectability of the New Church of the 1850s made them sensitive to pressures from within and without. Claims to authority, even inerrancy, buffered them against the corrosive effects of excess.[26]

In response Spiritualists employed the devastating charge of enthusiasm both in defense and offense. Francis Smith admitted that some of his peers fell prey to excess but asked rhetorically whether there was "anything good," any "benevolent object" at all, "that is not marred by enthusiasts, fanatics and impostors?" Some Spiritualists went too far, he suggested, but the respectable lot, himself included, were sober and disciplined. But when Swedenborgians paired allegations of enthusiasm with hints of their own inerrancy, Spiritualists waged a bitter counterattack. Elizabeth Sweet ridiculed those who accepted Swedenborg's writings as "infallible authority" and who chose to "enslave their minds to his statements" and to carry "blind, idiotic subserviency so far as to deny their reason and distrust their intuitions." Similarly, Allen Putnam admitted that Swedenborg was "permitted to behold many things that pertain to the spirit-life," but he insisted that neither Swedenborg nor any other mortal could ever be "a perfect seer, for there never was one." Spirit communion was a perpetual process of partial revelation that continued long after death, reaching perfection, if at all, only in the highest of spheres.[27]

To Spiritualists Swedenborgian stridency was a sure sign that the New Church was falling victim to the creeping specter of formalism, that other long-standing bugbear of religious experience, according to Ann Taves. Sardonically, Epes Sargent reprised the history of how Swedenborgians had changed their tune from an early acceptance of Spiritualist communications. "It so happened," he wrote, "that clairvoyants and mediums, while they confirmed in general Swedenborg's other-world revelations, contradicted him in many particulars. This was intolerable,—contradict our heavenly messenger! At once the old line of argument was abandoned. Nothing was now wickeder than converse with spirits. Intercourse with them is dangerous, disorderly, and forbidden by the Word! True, Swedenborg did talk with spirits, but he held a special license from the Lord; he warned us of its perils; and his example is no pretext for all, and sundry."[28]

Sargeant's sarcasm found support from Horatio Wood, who attributed A. J. Davis's "improvements" to Swedenborg not to consultation with superior spirits, as Swedenborgians might claim, but to the fact that Davis "was less prejudiced than Swedenborg, as his mind had not been subjected to the discipline of the strait-jacket of sectarianism, or a great degree of any species of education." Davis himself argued that he was "internally assured that the abyss between Swedenborg's Disclosures and Nature's Revelations, is well-nigh impassable," and he believed that Swedenborg's perception of hell in particular was evidence that his mind had fallen prey to religious "education, the orthodox *symbols* of theology, and the *symbols* of biblical authority." For Sargent, as for most Spiritualists, formalism and the defensive bonds of sectarianism were the downfall of the New Church. Both Swedenborgians and Spiritualists claimed the mantle of spiritual discipline, but when Swedenborgians singled out the enthusiastic excesses of Spiritualists, they highlighted their own respectability in contrast. For Spiritualists, on the other hand, formalism became the point of comparison, and to appropriate a word from the medium James Peebles, "churchianity" was the dark, secret love that destroyed from within, a worse form of excess for the soul than enthusiasm.[29]

Any set of religious or social ideas in Spiritualism turns up similar concordances and discordances, similar concord and conflict. Perhaps as a result, many historians have sensibly avoided tracing the histories of specific ideas in favor of setting Spiritualism within a more general framework, as one of the last fruits of a period of remarkable spiritual innovation that witnessed the scorched earth beneath the boots of Millerites and Mormons, perfectionists and, above all, evangelicals, as they sacralized the American landscape. The spiritual hothouse in which Spiritualism developed was in some sense a product of an unusual conjunction of social stresses, ranging from the increasing pace of geographic and social mobility and the fallout of industrialization, urbanization, immigration, "modernization," and democratization to the extension of market relations, religious diversity, and the sinuous careers of religion and science and of class, race, and gender relations. These themes pepper the work of Geoffrey K. Nelson (exploring the social factors predisposing Americans to Spiritualism), R. Laurence Moore and Janet Oppenheim (parsing its relations with scientific culture), and Bret Carroll (examining the religious dimensions), each of whom argues that Spiritualism was a key means of accommodating the individual to extraordinary social change.[30]

Whatever the ultimate wellspring of the movement, and as certain as it is that many factors conspired to compound one another, Spiritualism has come to be seen as a barometer of social adjustment, recording the distinctive cadence of life in antebellum America as seen symbolically, if not structurally, in the advent of new forms of communication, in telegraphy and trains, and in new social configurations that brought together the disparate and distant. The result was a pervasive sense of what might be called the red shift of modernity, in which one could hear the distance always receding, the body politic fraying, the individual I careening toward dissolution. Feeling keenly the separations of life, Spiritualist (or evangelical) zeal emerged as one means of reasserting the integrity of the body politic, of reclaiming the stability of self, and of crafting a stable community of believers in a shifting world.

In recent years an instrumentalist tinge has been added to the literature on antebellum Spiritualism, drawing ultimately upon the anthropologist I. M. Lewis's seminal cross-cultural study of spirit possession. Lewis concluded that possession has the capacity to challenge and, at least on a local and personal scale, to subvert the normal relations of social power, particularly with respect to gender. Spirit possession and mediumship, he argued, provide leverage for social subordinates to exert pressure upon their superiors under "circumstances of deprivation and frustration when few other sanctions are available to them," creating a form of "compensation for their exclusion and lack of authority in other spheres." Claiming injury from spirits becomes a means of exacting redress, while claiming spiritual authority provides sanction for views that otherwise would be socially proscribed. Stated most powerfully in Ann Braude's study of American Spiritualism, this argument has become so commonplace that one reviewer concludes that spirit possession might be characterized generally as "an embodied critique of colonial, national, or global hegemonies whose abrasions are deeply, but not exclusively felt by women." Possession, the argument runs, is a historically sensitive mode of "cultural resistance."[31]

Mid-Victorian spirits did evince a particular fondness for confronting and critiquing the abrasions of life—gender, race, and sectarianism in North America, class in Britain—and ever since, proponents, opponents, and historians have delighted to see in their words the popular mechanics of radical social resistance and the hope of social change. Looking particularly at trance speakers and other clairvoyant visionaries, historians have depicted the spirits as speaking regularly in the progressive stream, arguing, like the important Spiritualist writer James Peebles, that Spiritualism was the font of "all genuine reform movements, physiological, temperamental, education, parental, social, philanthropic and religious." The impression received through the writings of Braude, Logie Barrow, Diana Basham, and Barbara Goldsmith is of a movement of female reformers and social critics for whom spirits provided sanction for the expression of heterodox views. Consciously or unconsciously, in this perspective the spirits arose instrumentally from reformist desires.[32]

Yet for all its insights, the instrumentalist mode has proved unsatisfactory for explaining several of the central features of American Spiritualism. Alex Owen's perceptive work has demonstrated that as a spiritual strategy mediumship can be as limiting as it is liberating, while Vieda Skultans's study of Welsh Spiritualists in the 1970s concludes that such practices in fact may reinforce the ordinary relations of social power.[33]

Beyond efficacy, Spiritualists themselves were well aware of the instrumentalist potential of mediumship and were critical of it. G. A. Redman deprecated trance lecturers, the most highly politicized of Spiritualists (and overwhelmingly female), arguing that "every idea expressed through such channels, is tainted, more or less, with the characteristics of the brain through which it comes"; and he concluded that "without doubt we may take seven-tenths of such matter at a discount." For the same reason Napoleon Wolfe dismissed the "pretensions of trance-speakers," calling them self-deceived or fraudulent but clearly "not reliable." Distinctly uneasy with the ideas flowing from the mouths of their mediums, the short-lived New England Spiritualists' Association confessed that much of the "world's impurity" could be found "floating on the waters of *Spiritual-*

ism," even as they insisted that the "ultra doctrines" professed were no different than the "ultraisms and eccentricities" of Christianity, "for the same agitators are believers in Christianity also." However they explained it, neither Spiritualists nor their critics faced politically charged messages uncritically, and structures both within Spiritualist thought and without provided a ready means to blunt pretensions to spiritual authority and spiritual sanction.[34]

The explicit political content of spirit communications—a subject dear to the instrumental heart—may not be all that it seems at first. Historians have begun to question whether Spiritualist forms of resistance were "radical" at all, suggesting instead that they were "conservative and cautious" or perhaps both conservative and radical at the same time. Nell Irvin Painter claims that far from abetting reformist causes such as antislavery, Spiritualist ethics "mellow[ed] abolitionists' opposition to the slave power and its minions in the U.S. Congress," echoing a more general sense among historians that a focus upon the afterlife "diverted energy from the struggle," displacing, deferring, and dampening, rather than radicalizing, its adherents.[35]

Such labels, however, may be more misleading than illuminating, imputing motives to Spiritualists, much less a homogeneity of motive, that are dissociated from the common experience of spirit communion. At the very least the tendency to look for explicit social argumentation, focusing nearly exclusively upon the "radical" voices, has provided a one-dimensional view of a complex terrain. The spirits spoke in voices that spanned nearly the entire political spectrum of midcentury America, occupying positions, for example, that ran from immediate abolition to gradualism to pro-slavery, from egalitarianism to antiegalitarianism, capitalism to socialism.[36]

For Spiritualists, this was cosmological reality. Spiritualism was not the product of any single set of ideas, the child of any one religious or political tradition. Epes Sargent stated that it was "impossible to lay down any statement of theological or religious doctrines in which all Spiritualists agree," and the New England Spiritualists' Association could be admirably terse in summarizing their beliefs: "Our creed is simple, *Spirits do communicate with man*—that is the creed."[37]

Diversity was the rule even in the practice of mediumship. While early mediums like the Foxes communicated by raps of yeah and nay, they and others pioneered a variety of alphabetic codes to express more complex ideas, used unseen hands to tilt tables in response to questions, or manufactured ingenious devices to enhance communication, including the planchette, alphabetic wheels, or Robert Hare's spiritoscope. In turn, these surrendered to even more efficient, more creative phases of mediumship. Inspired by Davis and his predecessors, many mediums worked entirely clairvoyantly, psychologically communing with the dead to relay messages or visions of the afterlife, while other, more phenomenally inclined communicants specialized in producing tangible evidence of spirits, whether by automatic writing, drawing, painting, music, or a variety of objects. After about 1860 several mediums began to materialize spirits themselves, either in the séance room or in photographs. A few like G. A. Redman employed a full array of methods, communicating not only by raps and tilts but by clairvoyant visions of rebuslike spiritual symbols (a spirit pointing to a wall and bridge in succession to spell out the name Wallbridge, for example). In one of the most peculiar of his mystic hours, Redman carried out a lighthearted exchange with the spirit of a man he had dissected in medical school who delighted in indicating his presence by pelting Redman with bones materialized from thin air.[38]

By any reckoning mediumship and the physical body became inseparable. One of the best-known mediums of midcentury, the "Spiritual Postmaster" James V. Mansfield, clairvoyantly read sealed letters sent to him by clients from around the country, but his mode of response was noteworthy. Whenever spirits assumed control of Mansfield's body, his left hand went into spasm, and his finger began to tap rapidly "like the motion of a telegraph key" as he wrote out lengthy and detailed responses in whichever language was prescribed. A more adventurous medium, like the young, "uneducated" Mary Comstock, used her own body as a slate for spirit messages, which appeared as "red lines corruscated" upon her flesh that disappeared as quickly as they were inscribed. To Frederick Douglass she presented a welt in the form of a kneeling slave chained to a post, under which was scratched the phrase, "A poor old slave." To another man she spelled out the name of a deceased fraternal brother in the mystic runes of the Masonic alphabet. Such dramatically performative mediums generated enormous public interest, so much so that by the mid-1860s the line separating them from stage magicians grew perilously thin.[39]

Theories for explaining the physical basis of mediumship were no less diverse than the forms through which it was expressed. Electromagnetism, clairvoyance, or both, were offered as evidence for how spirits appeared and how they influenced the living, to which others added the effects of equally "natural" phenomena, ranging from Baron von Reichenbach's "odyllic" force to mesmerism, somnambulism, phrenology, and most importantly of all, sympathy. With this superfluity of diversity in mind, in medium and mode, theory and practice, it is here that I wish to begin: in sympathy and unconsciousness, in a lineage that draws the emotional world of Wendell Newhall back into the dark nights of the sleepwalker.[40]

I

Sleepwalking and Sympathy

ON A LATE AFTERNOON near the turn of the nineteenth century, a great whale was dragged ashore on Long Island and prepared for butchery. For a town like East Hampton, the windfall of meat and oil transformed the event into a community affair, stirring "the greater part of the people" to gather round to carve or cart the blubber, or simply "to gratify their curiosity." Yet not everyone responded. Even as the leviathan became the center of "much discourse" within the community, one resident remained apart. Believing "she had but a short time to live," the consumptive Miss H expressed her "indifference" to the affair and settled in for a quiet night's sleep.[1]

Or so it appeared. Late that night, when Miss H was startled awake by a barking dog, she discovered herself standing barefoot on a sandy path far from home. "Alone" and "covered only by her night-dress," she was "lost, bewildered, and terrified," not knowing where she was or how she had gotten there. Only in the light of morning, when neighbors tracked her footprints, was it discovered precisely what had taken place: "under the influence of [the] prevalent sentiments" of the community, Miss H had walked four miles in her sleep to view the object of collective curiosity, circling round and examining it "by a close survey." "To the satisfaction of all her friends, and of the neighbours," it was agreed "that she had been to the ocean side on a visit to the whale." Miss H recalled nothing.

Between the swan song of mesmerism in the late 1780s and its phoenix-like rebirth forty years later, somnambulists stalked the land. Sleepwalkers like Miss H rose at night to fulfill their waking desires, to share sentiments with the community, to wander, pray, or declaim, to lead ordinary lives or alternate lives, to heal the sick, find the lost, and visit neighbors, to see distant cities or distant planets. During a period in which the nature of consciousness was a persistent concern of medical, philosophical, and political discourse, the seemingly contradictory behaviors of sleepwalkers—their display of purposeful behavior in the absence of consciousness and will—promised to shed light on subjects as disparate as neural anatomy, the relation of mind and body and body and behavior, and above all, the relation of body and society. In both England and America, the diverse, sometimes contradictory actions of somnambulists were plumbed for their implications in three particular areas: community, corporeality, and conduct.

Like Miss H, I wish to inspect the somnambular whale from vent to snout and suggest that during the early national period, a protracted conversation over the nature of sleeping behavior helped to shape a set of theories regarding social cohesion through a highly distinctive practice of the body. The sources of somnambular thought were diverse and eclectic, ranging from the moral philosophy of Adam Smith, David Hume, and Dugald Stewart to mental philosophy, physiology, neuroanatomy, phrenology, and mesmerism. But rather than privilege any particular narrative of events in the history of medicine or the history of knowledge, I instead trace a limited number of themes crosscutting several of these areas of discourse. What emerges in the process is a dynamic, heterogeneous, and occasionally murky tale of a somnambular body attuned to the social and physical world in which it operated and yet irrefrangibly alien to it. The somnambulist was the literal embodiment of a moral and social theory of sympathy, but also it was the epitome of its inherent contradictions.[2]

As a point of departure in exploring these themes, I begin with an outline of the cluster of theories called sympathy, and particularly of the influential moral philosophical system of Adam Smith, sketching some of the ways in which these ideas were interpreted and altered during the early national period by the community of Anglo-American physicians and writers concerned with the corporeal basis of sympathy and more generally with sensibility and its social expression. Imparting structure on the somnambular body and somnambular character, sympathy leaves off at the same spot as Miss H: face to face with the unknowable whale.

SYMPATHY AND SOCIAL ORDER

From pulpit, print, and podium, Scots moral philosophy suffused the English-speaking world at turn of the nineteenth century. From Thomas Reid to Thomas Brown, the mainstays of the Scottish Enlightenment became standard fare for collegiate and clerical study, and the outlines, if not the subtleties, of Scots ethics, epistemology, economy, and emotion filtered into American hearths and hearts. Yet despite close historical scrutiny of this notoriously "rich and various body of thought," little attention has been directed to how the Scots' deep interest in social coherence and social order were understood in America beyond the narrowest world of intellectuals, and less attention still to how these ideas were experienced. Drawing upon both medical and literary sources, I explore some of the more diffuse ends of the Scots Enlightenment in tracing the manner in which theories of sympathy were embodied and experienced through a characteristically early national behavior, somnambulism.[3]

Without wishing to downplay the theoretical chasms separating the rationalist Reid and the intuitionist Francis Hutcheson or the devout John Gregory from the skeptical Hume, I find it easy to side with Henry May's venerable conclusion that the Scots were "united by tone and origin," if not always by "doctrine." They were united, for instance, in their opposition to idealism and their keen concern for developing a robust foundation for human knowledge; most accepted the stadial model of sociocultural change; and many were profoundly interested in identifying the principles of moral behavior as a means of achieving and maintaining a stable social order. In tracing the social life and experience of Scots moral thought, however, a few additional commonalties seem particularly prominent.[4]

At the foundation of Scottish moral thought was the conviction that sensibility—feeling or emotion—was in some sense crucial to regulating moral behavior. Philosophers vigorously debated the existence of a "moral sense" and inquired whether it was innate or acquired and whether the calipers of reason or the compass of emotion held the better measure of human lives. Although perspectives varied widely, the course of this debate firmly wedded reason and emotion as opposing end points in a continuum governing the language and practice of morality. Thus while both ends of the evangelical and antievangelical spectrum in America resisted the introduction of excessive emotion into theories of morality—a product of the contentious history of religious "enthusiasm" in Anglo-America—both could nevertheless agree with Stewart's summary of Smith that "the words *right* and *wrong* express certain agreeable and disagreeable qualities in actions, which it is not the province of reason but of feeling to perceive." Through their emotions humans perceived the distinction between right and wrong; they experienced moral judgment.[5]

In this vein the physician and popular moralist John Abercrombie proclaimed that the "truth" of fundamental moral principles could not be subjected to "to any process of reasoning" at all but only "to the conviction which forces itself upon every regulated mind." For properly disciplined minds—and discipline was essential—reason would reveal the principles "implanted in our moral constitution," yet even when leading to such desirable results, reason was impaired. Against the background of increasingly diverse and acrimonious social argumentation, Abercrombie recoiled at the "absurdity" of relying upon reason as a moral guide when reason so often produced a condition "in which different minds may arrive at different conclusions, and in regard to which many are incapable of following out any argument at all." Although reason and emotion often worked to the same end, emotion was the surer guide, the safer route to propriety.[6]

In a second sifting from Scots thought, American authors in particular pursued a moral philosophy that was eminently a social philosophy. Rather than discovering morality welling up from within the individual or spalling off from the transcendent, a distinctively American skein of writers followed in the wake of philosophers from the earl of Shaftesbury and Francis Hutcheson through David Hartley, Lord Kames, and Dugald Stewart who set morality and propriety within social relations, grasping for a means to accommodate both society and autonomous individualism. While Adam Ferguson extolled affection as the basic "principle of Union among Mankind" and Hutcheson attacked self-love with moral sense, and while Kames lobbied for the "sympathetic principle" as the "great cement of human society," in America, at least, the most influential treatment of the emotional view of society was Adam Smith's. In his *Theory of Moral Sentiments*, Smith injected sympathy—"that analogous feeling, which arises from an imaginary application to ourselves of the circumstances of him with whom we sympathize"—into the heart of society.[7]

With a pedigree extending well into antiquity, sympathy was rooted during the early national and antebellum periods in three distinct but cross-fertilizing perspectives: the occult, the social, and the physiological. For occultists, sympathy was a powerful, primal force of nature, a mutual attraction between bodies, an irreducible and "imperceivable affinity" that as Ruth Leys suggests, was "one of the forms of resemblance that made possible the knowledge of all things—an immaterial principle of affinity or movement by which even the most distant parts of the universe might be drawn together." When manifested within the human body, occult sympathies were often interpreted within the framework of biological vitalism and, as a result, often imagined as antithetical to mechanistic biology and the new natural philosophy. For physiologists like Robert Whytt, sympathies were the result of the soul acting upon the muscles through the nerves but were essentially "unrestricted by anatomical laws."[8]

But sympathies shaded as well through Hermetic and other occult traditions that flourished into the nineteenth century, influencing religious sects from the Shakers through Swedenborgians, Mormons, and all varieties of perfectionists. Like the divine spirit, occult sympathies permeated the universe, revealing the cause of astrological relations between planetary and human bodies, elucidating the alchemical transformation of elements, and the mystic relations of bodies and souls. Hermeticists managed or manipulated sympathy for its transformative potential, and occult physicians used their arcane knowledge of it to heal, but in either case occult perspectives were more than the vestiges of older beliefs; they were instead a dynamic mix of the newer sciences imported within a framework that held materialist explanation as insufficient to account for the range of natural and mental phenomena. Occult sympathy was a supremely "adaptable" and "renewable" concept," one that even materialists could accept for its utilitarian value, even if the mechanics remained obscure. Joseph Comstock, a physician who attended somnambular patients in the 1830s, gladly took alchemy, astrology, and magic along with his Bacon and Locke, arguing that even if they could not be understood within natural philosophy, they might still be useful. "There have been many kinds of knowledge of no use of themselves," he wrote, "but which have led to result of great utility." The eclectic Comstock, like many of his peers, hedged his bets by noting that neither occult nor mechanical modalities alone were capable of answering every question in nature.[9]

Partaking to some degree in the quasi-mystical power of occult attraction, Adam Smith's "social" view of sympathy nevertheless tacked in a different direction, identifying the willful emotional identification between persons as a guardian against self-interested behavior and as a creator of social bonds. In this socially poetic theory, sympathy was a complex, constrained concordance between the sentiments of individuals stemming ultimately, paradoxically, from the intrinsic affective isolation characterizing humanity. It was "a mark," as Jean Christophe Agnew has observed, "of the immense distance that separated individual minds," rather than "a sign of their commonality." Rising to the challenge of Hobbes and Mandeville, Smith attempted to construct a truly social view of morality from the building blocks of ardent individualism. His was a high-risk effort to bridge the irreconcilable, to be at once atomistic and social, imaginary and incarnate—an effort that many of his contemporaries recognized fell short of the mark, even as they appropriated his concerns, his terminology, and his methods.[10]

Reflecting the diverse connotations of the concept, Smith's sympathy was both natural and inseparable from the bodies through which it was expressed, though never simply so. Both pleasure and pain, he suggested, were shared through sympathy, and to different degrees both were experienced corporeally. Under certain circumstances, sympathizing individuals shared physical pain, epitomized by Smith's striking example of "the mob," whose spontaneous sympathy when "gazing at a dancer on the slack rope" was expressed as they began "naturally [to] writhe and twist and balance their own bodies as they see him do, and as they feel that they themselves must do if in his situation."[11]

As natural and powerful as it was, however, sympathy had expressive limits: it was "habitual" (learned), and its experience was therefore predicated upon the tenor of the relationship of the individuals involved: a person sympathized most powerfully with those with whom he or she was most frequently in contact and much less powerfully with others. As a result, as Julie Ellison has suggested, the infrastructure of Smithian sympathy was supported by the practices of social proximity, bringing the differential social contact that emerged from inequities in practices of race, class, and gender directly into the theoretical constitution of society.[12]

Adding a further wrinkle, while the sympathetic response was like the originating sentiment, it was of nowhere near the "same degree of violence," particularly with respect to bodily pain, and it was of only limited duration. In a sense, sympathetic experience was as constrained by social relations as it was constitutive of them: the desire for self-command and the need for approbation were so powerful for Smith that they blunted the sympathetic sharing of pain. Smith believed that physical pain, as is "the case of all the passions which take their origin from the body," excites "either no sympathy at all, or such a degree of it, as is altogether disproportioned to the violence what is felt by the sufferer." Sympathy was experienced at the uncomfortable intersection between bodily indulgence and abnegation, between a desire for social contact and the reality of social isolation.[13]

In the same way that the capacity for sympathetic exchange was innate, so too was an "original desire to please, and an original aversion to offend," and these sentiments were so powerful, and the dread of social isolation so intense, that together they comprised a system that ensured not only that individuals would sympathize and restrain antisocial behaviors, they would need to sympathize. For sympathy to function in regulating moral behavior, Smith theorized that it required a conscious act to imagine the position of the other or, better, to imagine the position of an impartial spectator imaging both self and other. In this hall of mirrors act of self-reflection, Smith argued that a lack of "immediate experience" with what others felt forced one to imagine "what we ourselves should feel in the like situation," but imagining what others felt involved turning scrutiny on one's own behavior: one imagined the feelings of others within the social context of one's own behavior. The precise nature of Smith's impartial spectator in all this is notoriously difficult to fix, sliding ever further from fixity as the examination bores in. Seeming sometimes to be a projection emanating from within and sometimes an external entity unto itself, sometimes a natural property of the human condition and sometimes the hardwon product of mental effort, the impartial spectator might best be seen as a medium between internal and external, focusing upon the connections between, and a medium for exchange between the polarities of interpersonal isolation and affective connection.[14]

Smith's sympathy was therefore unlike Hutcheson's, that primitive fellow feeling productive of benevolent acts: it was a complex amalgam of individual desire and social need that affirmed the possibility of a stable society, perhaps a true community, even as it affirmed the bedrock of interpersonal isolation. As a moral system it trumped self-interest, operating even where there could be no hope of personal recompense for emotional expenditure. In his most conceptually revealing example, Smith argued that we sympathize with the dead, even though our efforts to provide them solace are necessarily unavailing, and even though the impotence of such a gesture might seem only to "exasperate our sense of their misery." Instead, we extend our sympathies out of "our own consciousness of that change [i.e., death], from our putting ourselves in their situation." Surpassing our sympathetic experience with physical pain in intensity, this "illusion of the imagination" was possible because it connected us with death, the ultimate in alienating and socially isolating experiences. Smith continued: "From thence arises one of the most important principles in human nature, the dread of death, the great poison to the happiness, but the great restraint upon the injustice of mankind, which, while it afflicts and mortifies the individual, guards and protects the society." More than the pleasure of mutual joy, more than the abatement of pain through emotional exchange, fear, dread, and death were the stuff of society. Adding paradox to paradox, the society of the living was therefore not the product of living sympathy but of sympathy with the dead.[15]

Adela Pinch has suggested that in the hands of Hume, not only was sympathy socially poetic, it was individually poetic. Skeptical about the content of the self and believing that the self "independent of the perception of every other object" was, in reality, nothing, Hume argued that when the passions were turned onto the self, they perform, in Pinch's words, "a kind of person-ification" that ties the complex "bundle of perceptions" within the individual into a package that can called the self. There is a further tendency in the literature on sympathy to see that the sets of relations and identifications established through sympathy provide definition and shape to the individual as he or she navigates the terrain of passions and affective associations.[16]

The high-water mark of Smithian sympathy was reached during the somnambular years of the 1790s through 1830s. Although Smith's theories were far from universally accepted, familiarity with them was widespread. Many writers parroted the grim belief that a true knowledge of others was possible "only through the labours and struggles of our own minds" and echoed Smith's contention that "we cannot develope our faculties, understand our nature, and enjoy our existence, without the relations, the wants, and the sympathies of society." Abraham Rees's *Cyclopaedia* of 1798, for example, defined sympathy with respect to the system of that "late ingenious writer," name not necessary, adding a less than favorable gloss upon how this system had been appropriated in utilitarian philosophy and physiological discourse.[17]

Lest the mantle of sympathy shift too far onto Smith's shoulders, however, it should be noted that as early as the *Wealth of Nations,* Smith's sympathy had begun to evolve, and when the term was co-opted, adopted, adapted, and often misapplied by later writers, it became freighted with a suite of alien connotations. The older occult perspective on sympathy was never far from the surface, retaining its quasi-mystical power to preserve morality and unite society. In the hands of less subtle philosophers, sympathy was stripped of its grimmest details and reduced to little more than "fellow feeling," as when John Abercrombie equated sympathy simply with the Golden Rule, "Do to others as we would that they should do to us." In this formulation the reciprocity and "uniformity of moral feeling and affection" shared between sympathizer and sufferer were thought in themselves to be sufficient to instill a sense of reward and punishment, and consequently to be able to restrain behavior, even for "those who have subdued the influence of these feelings in themselves." Like many sentimental writers of his day, however, Abercrombie stressed the self-disciplinary value of the effort of sympathy but sapped it of its power to experience the actual emotions of others.[18]

The phrenologist George Combe took a different route, stripping sympathy of its socially poetic power by subordinating it to the mental faculties and delimiting its sphere of operation to those individuals who shared similar levels of "development" in their mental faculties, a more extreme application of a tendency seen within Smith's *Theory.* In Combe's phrenology, featuring over thirty discrete mental faculties representing discrete traits of character, sympathies did not exist between individuals per se but between their decomposable faculties. Even when individuals shared a similarity of development in one faculty, a tendency to sympathize might be offset by dissimilarities in others. Further undercutting the social poesis of sympathy for Combe, certain faculties, such as self-love, inherently precluded any meaningful connection between individuals, while sympathies between faculties such as destructiveness could hardly be considered socially productive. Partitioned and constrained, potentially as productive of social ill as social good, Combe's phrenological sympathy made no pretensions to the grand unification of the *Theory of Moral Sentiments*.[19]

Combe's objections were parried by the claim that while sympathy with unworthies might be productive of antisocial behavior, it was nevertheless a fundamentally moral phenomenon. Whether its fruits were good or ill, it was still "social in its nature," according to a contributor to the *North American Review*, and was "still social and benevolent as far as its own objects are concerned." Even those who found "radical unsoundness" in Smith's theories or who considered them simply "erroneous" admitted to the power of sympathy in fostering social order, and even many phrenologists preferred to weight their arguments toward the socially productive aspects of sympathy. For most, the circulation of sympathetically inspired emotion, imaginative or real, continued to cement society.[20]

As the social vision of sympathy was elaborated by Scots philosophers, their colleagues in the dissecting hall added a distinctive physiological twist. In the wake of Robert Whytt, sympathy became the key principle coordinating the relationship of sensation, cognition, emotion, and bodily state. Like social sympathy, physiological sympathy was conceived as a relation between parts, as "an association of feelings communicated . . . by nerves," witnessed when "the affection of one organ is felt by one or more organs more or less remote."[21]

The influence of the sensationalist epistemology of Locke made study of the nervous system a medical priority throughout the eighteenth century, yet the mutualistic interaction of Scots philosophy and physiological sympathy was particularly productive. One need not look far for the connections between the physicians and philosophers: William Cullen was a confidant of Hume and Smith, for instance, while William Alison was related to both Gregory and Reid and was an acquaintance of Stewart. Like the philosophers, Edinburgh physicians shared a core set of ideas or propensities in approaching their subject: an antipathy to mechanism, a commitment to naturalistic language, an insistence upon the mediating role of mind in sensation and action, and more generally, a view of the body "in which sensibility, a property of the nervous system, predominated" and in which sympathy loomed as the overarching, integrating principle. Through their influence sympathy had assumed so central a role in physiological theory on both sides of the Atlantic by the 1820s that it was considered the "foundation of medical science." What it looked like, how it was constructed, and how it functioned were among the great questions of medical research.[22]

While mechanically inclined physiologists maintained that sympathetic relations between bodily parts could be explained by positing a nervous anastamosis (usually sought in the intercostal or "great sympathetic" nerve), others argued that explanations relying solely upon nervous anatomy were insufficient. In the absence of anatomical proof, the physician, later theologian, John Ranicar Park called such explanations a "mere subterfuge for ignorance." Prior to the consolidation of anatomical opinion around Marshall Hall's theory of the reflex arc in the 1830s, the structure and function of the nervous system remained open to debate, and Park could cite numerous examples that indicated that no direct nervous connection need obtain between sympathetically associated parts, as when a dimness of sight resulted from a disordered stomach. He preferred, therefore, to revive theories current almost a century before that identified the vascular system as the medium of sympathetic transmission and that explained the "affections of the mental powers" as "sympathetically occasioned by impressions on distant organs."[23]

From Whytt to William Alison (a "zealous disciple" of Reid and Stewart), it was more typical, however, to envision the nervous system as implicated in the sympathetic response but only with the participation of the brain, the seat of the mind. An irritation at the surface of the body or in the viscera was thought to excite a sensation in the brain, which then excited a response elsewhere in the body. Based firmly in a naturalistic mode of explanation, this approach charted an explicit reciprocity between body and mind, physical sensation and emotion, and tacitly asserted that the human body was more than merely the sum of physical relations between its parts.[24]

James Rodgers has argued that the ideological nexus of occult, social, and physiological conceptions of sympathy provided the means for the nervous system to become a discourse about social systems and vice versa, and even a cursory examination demonstrates how readily such connections were made and how slippery the argument could be. Several historians, for example, have argued that physiological discourse was an expression of class interest. Christopher Lawrence depicts the antimaterialist, antiskeptical, antireductive physiology of Whytt as a rearguard maneuver of an old elite to consolidate social power, while Ruth Leys argues that the materialist, skeptical, reductive mechanicism of Charles Bell was part of a similar rearguard maneuver. While the difference in time between Whytt and Bell makes such divergent claims possible, the juxtaposition raises the question whether class interest alone suffices to explain the shape of sympathy.[25]

Without wishing to dismiss class interests entirely, in America at least, I find that several other aspects of social identity seem to have played a prominent part in discussions of physiological sympathy. At its most basic physiological sympathy referred to the transmission of sensation through the nervous system, as well as to the "affection of the whole body, or any other part, consequent on injury, disorder, or disease of any other part." John Godman, later editor of the *Western Quarterly Reporter*, envisioned sympathy as uniting the body into a vastly interconnected network by which, for instance, "caries or extraction of the teeth" could result in the "inflammation of the eye" and in which both pleasurable and painful sensations were experienced throughout the body, forming a common experiential ground to integrate or reinforce a sense of the individual. The "nerves and ganglia are entire nervous systems," he argued, "to a great degree independent of each other individually, although the perfect chain of actions demands the consent of the whole." Similarly, Arthur May concluded that "the whole system, mind and body, is one mass of general sympathy: no sooner is any part affected, than the impression is communicated throughout the whole. Sympathy is the conductor of disease, and the same sympathy is the agent of cure."[26]

The interconnectedness of the sympathetic body and mind extended to the literal core of the individual, forging a close bond between biological and social identities. In defining sympathy, Thomas Dobson's *Encyclopae-dia* remarked upon the "connection between the affections and sensations of the female mind and uterus," setting sympathy as a distinctly, though not uniquely, feminine trait. The influential medical educator Charles Caldwell reached further in his assessment, transforming sympathy into an "habitual and universal" principle governing the interaction of mind with mind, body with body, and each with the other. Through "corporeal sympathy" sense impressions passed from the skin to the interior or, as in God-man's example, from organ to organ, but by "mental sympathy" minds influenced minds through "the contagion of the soul." In camp meetings or in recitals of poetry and music, through the innate human tendency to imitate "manners, looks, and modes of thinking," mental sympathy provided evidence of the integration of the individual and the prospect of the integration of society.[27]

Analogously, the state of mind affected the body, and body affected mind, and this recursion helped to define an individual's social identity through the complex of traits surrounding sex and gender. Caldwell concluded that the "tender glow of maternal affection" and the natural sympathies between mother and child were responsible for an "immediate and copious" lactation and for the "thrilling flow" of mother's milk as the infant approached the breast. Conversely, he argued that castration utterly robbed a man of physical, moral, intellectual, and social identity. To Caldwell a eunuch was not merely a beardless being deprived of the manly traits of perspicacity, bravery, benevolence, faithfulness, and warmth;, "his soul," he insisted, "is as completely emasculated as his body." Disrupting the flow of bodily and social sympathy fundamentally altered the basis of gendered identity. As Caldwell concluded, "The sympathies that originate in the genital organs of both sexes . . . *literally make the sexes what they are*—man and woman—not merely in relation to the propagation of the species, *but in their entire character.*" In a sense, gender was not a state but an affective, sympathetic relation between parts of the body and between body and mind.[28]

Taking the argument further still, such sympathies stretched beyond the confines of the individual body. The English natural historian John Mason Good believed that sympathy, like gravitation, electromagnetism, and chemical affinity, was part of a natural system of mutual "inclinations and antipathies" whose "influence, in perhaps every case, commences before such bodies are in a state of contact, and in many cases while they are at a considerable distance from each other." Based on experiments demonstrating the sympathy of organ systems, Good was led to anticipate "a similar influence or association of action between different parts of different frames, or, which is the same thing, between living body and living body," as well as living minds.[29]

As bodies and identities were united through the diverse discourses of sympathy, somnambulism became the centerpiece in an extended conversation over the issues of automatism and mechanism, will and habit, mind and desire, and a key means of assessing the limits of sympathetic action. The languages of sympathy suffused discussions of sleepwalking during the early Republic, revealing how these theories were embodied and experienced. For somnambulists and their observers, somnambulism addressed the limitations of sympathy by creating an embodied world in which those limitations did not exist, where sympathy, by its very nature, overcame atomism and individualism to create a renewed community bound in sensation and affect. Yet at the same time somnambular expression transformed community into an expression of the body and reflected the uncertainties of human behavior and the fear that human nature might be, after all, inaccessible or, worse, pathological. Sympathetic somnambulism became the unconscious, corporeal site of contestation between various theories of social order, a point at which medical, philosophical, and popular discourses converged to shape the experience of social relations, physically and emotionally.

THE SOMNAMBULAR BODY

In 1788 the English animal magnetist John Bell defined somnambulism as "that peculiar state when the senses are suspended between sleeping and waking; partaking of both," though "productive of many phoenomena, which each are strangers to." Although today the "phoenomena" seem benign, little more than walking and talking in sleep, during the half century that followed Bell's definition, physicians, writers, and moral theorists plumbed the depths of sleep and consciousness to reveal a far more complex set of behaviors and modes of being and a far more obscure moral terrain. While antebellum somnambulists arose from "natural" sleep to stroll as they had for years, they flourished as well in association with organic disease, ecstatic trance, and animal magnetism.[30]

In recent years the "artificial" forms of somnambulism—mesmerism and animal magnetism—have become a favored subject of historians interested, as Alison Winter is, in the power dynamic of operator and operand and in its implications for social theory and practice. "Natural" somnambulism, on the other hand, presents a less-traveled road, one that from the present vantage offers novel analytical ground, even as it shares a theoretical and ideological vocabulary with the other forms of somnambulism. Inevitably the discourses of all these forms intersect, and at the time they were considered as facets of a single phenomenon, but in natural, as opposed to "artificial," somnambulism, the absence of an external operator was a critical factor in shaping meaning, transforming its moral, mental, and social implications. In natural somnambulism the behaviors and phenomena exhibited by the sleepwalker were indisputably the product of the individual, and not of any external agent, providing clearer insight into the inner structure of the body, mind, and soul.[31]

In its most pedestrian guise, somnambulism encompassed behaviors that ranged from simple walking at night to more complex extensions of quotidian life during which the somnambulist "engaged in some occupation which he continues although sleep overtakes him." Sleepwalking farmers pitched hay or fed chickens, millers ground corn, students studied, and clergymen wrote and corrected sermons, saddlers worked leather, and servants performed domestic service. To the most mechanistically inclined observers like Benjamin Rush, this implied that the "habitual exercises or employments" of daily existence had imprinted themselves so firmly on the individual's being as to shape the sleeping self—we were what we worked—suggesting that human behavior might be little more than the product of the association of memory and habit expressed through neural and physiological channels. More cautious physicians preferred to avoid the mind-body question altogether, complaining with John Vaughan that "when a problem is traced to its connection between the mind and body, it has arrived to the *ultimatum* or *ne plus ultra* of physiological investigation."[32]

For others, however, these behaviors were little more than a bodily gloss on a deeper mental substrate. Although mechanicist interpretation was well entrenched in the medical community by the first third of the nineteenth century, I emphasize here a vigorous counternarrative—what might be called a naturalistic countermechanicism—in which naturalistic modes of analysis of the physiology and experience of the somnambular body were employed to assert the dominance of spirit and mind over body and, in some versions, to insinuate a stratum of "occult" phenomena beneath the rationalist veneer of physiology and anatomy.

"The Springfield Somnambulist," Jane C. Rider, was one sleepwalker who was unusually exacting in her habitual behaviors. Deprived of her mother at birth, Rider was raised as the only child of a "very ingenious and respectable mechanic" in Brattleboro, Vermont, until at age sixteen she was placed out as a "favored domestic" in the Springfield, Massachusetts, home of Festus Stebbins. Always a nervous child, Rider had occasionally walked in her sleep, and by the time of her remove to Springfield, she was showing signs of serious nervous derangement. On several occasions she experienced a "momentary interruption of consciousness" during which "her notions of time and place were exceedingly confused, and she had but an imperfect knowledge of what was transpiring around her."[33]

In June 1833 Rider's somnambular interludes began in earnest. Lemuel Belden, a local physician called in to treat her, witnessed an incident in which Rider set the table, skimmed milk, sliced bread, and arranged a complete breakfast—in short, performing all the tasks required of her position in the Stebbins home—all with her eyes shut, asleep. With precision and address Rider went about her work so well that even the vegetables, Belden reported, were "very well cooked." But to Belden, as for many commentators, the significant factor in these "paroxysms" was neither the excellent performance of her duties nor the particular nature of the actions, but the peculiar nature of Rider's physical senses. Always sensitive, the young girl's vision became so acute during her somnambular interludes that she could thread a needle in near darkness and so sensitive that when the light of a lamp fell on her eyelids, she recoiled as if shocked by an electric battery, exclaiming, "Why do you wish to shoot me in the eyes!" To lessen the pain Belden had her eyes heavily bandaged, but even in this state she was able to read in the dark and discern the dates of well-worn coins held at a distance. Although Rider was unable to see through truly opaque barriers, other somnambulists could, like the boy examined by the Physical Society of Lausanne or like Abigail Cass, the "Stanstead Somnambulist," who could "see" through insensate eyes. According to Belden, these examples signified that a "change in the brain itself" had occurred, with the physical body conforming to the mental state. Rider's sight and cerebral functioning had become so "exalted" that her brain could take the fragmentary and disorganized images passing through layers of cloth wrapped over her eyes and resolve them into a single coherent picture.[34]

Rider's case, however, was even more complex than these already unusual abilities implied, for like most somnambulists she exhibited a pastiche of perceptual abilities. For every instance in which her vision was "prodigiously penetrating," to use the physiologist John Bell's words, there were instances in which it appeared to have been "entirely lost or weakened," and still others in which her vision shifted unstably between exaltation and extinction. Moreover, all the senses were equally affected. The "sensibility" of the somnambulist's bodily surface might be "remarkably impaired" or "partially or entirely abolished," so much so that while some sleepwalkers "appear to hear the slightest noise," others were utterly "insensitive" to even the most violent sounds. Complicating the situation still further, Bell noted that a "privation" of sight or hearing in somnambulists was often "amply compensated by an incredible delicacy both of feeling and taste," analogous, as a later writer suggested, to the exquisitely refined sense of touch exhibited by the sightless marvel Laura Bridgman. In the most advanced stages of somnambulism, sensory compensation produced synesthetic forms of sensation. A young Italian woman suffering from "spontaneous catalepsy" reportedly could hear nothing through her ears but sensed even the faintest of whispers directed to her palm, the sole of her foot, the pit of her stomach, or to "the traject of the sympathetic nerve." Other women were able to "read" playing cards placed upon their "epigastrium" (belly) or to see through the surface of their skin; still others tasted at various points along their bodies or, like Abigail Cass and Nancy Hazard, "saw" through their fingertips.[35]

In an individual deprived of waking consciousness, such adventitious forms of sensation, such "magic sensibility," seemed to corroborate theories of the sympathetic integration of bodily and mental systems: somnambules, one physician reported, showed that sound impressions were "transferred to the great ganglionic system of the grand sympathetic" nerve, which then assumed the role of the quiescent brain in registering sensation. The physician Joseph Comstock hypothesized that the "metastasis of the peculiar sentient principle of the optic nerve with the nerve of touch" enabled Nancy Hazard to distinguish colors at a touch. The Irish physician Andrew Ellis attributed the ability of a cataleptic man to perceive sound through the pit of his stomach to "sympathetic imitation" of the parts and concluded that catalepsy (a phenomenon intimately related with somnambulism) might be transmitted from one person to another sympathetically, suggesting that physiological sympathy could, in certain cases, extend beyond the confines of the physical body. In the highest forms of somnambulism, such seemed clearly the case: a number of advanced somnambules exhibited true clairvoyance, where it appeared that the body no longer mediated the senses, leaving the somnambulist to see clearly at a great distance using nothing but the power of mind.[36]

The insights derived from the study of somnambular sensation were several. For many physicians sensory selectivity confirmed the phrenological theory of cerebral localization: the combination of exaltation and extinction of sensation reflected the underlying neuroanatomical fact that mental organs operated semiautonomously, with some remaining active while others became quiescent, or more generally, as one physician claimed, it confirmed that "the mind may be awake as to some of its functions, whilst utterly dormant in others." Yet even in the face of phrenological autonomy, sympathy reigned. Social proximity, as Adam Smith would suggest, played an important role in governing sensory selectivity: habitual contact enhanced its operation. John Bell argued that sympathy explained how a sleepwalking man could hear his whispering wife but not a shouting stranger, while Jane Rider's physician reported that she never recognized him at all when she was in her paroxysms, that is, "until she became a member of [his] family." Similarly, Joseph Comstock was convinced that the finger-seeing Nancy Hazard "preferred the hands of her father and other relatives" to those of all others.[37]

Such capabilities pointed the way for extending somnambular sensation from an individual trait into a social relation. The ability to see with closed eyes or blind eyes or through blindfolds and barriers or above all the ability to see clairvoyantly permitted somnambulists to "know everything which is going on inside their own persons," making the opaque, to their "eyes," transparent. Clairvoyant perception enabled the somnambulist to peer through the skin and describe "the healthy and diseased parts of her own person, and of other individuals," enabled them to prescribe treatments and to explain and share pain. An ebullient James Cowles Prichard believed that if such diagnostic abilities could be induced magnetically, they might one day lead to the introduction of "a magnetic nurse in each ward of an hospital, who could perform autopsy while the patients are alive."[38]

Whether clairvoyance could be confined to analysis of the physical body was another matter, for somnambulism unveiled more than just the physical interior: through clairvoyance, thoughts became as transparent as skins, making the mind as legible as the body. A distinctive and controversial property of somnambulism, clairvoyance was "a peculiar mode of sensation," according to Prichard, experienced across the entire body surface but especially "in the epigastrium and fingers' ends," and although it was "not exactly sight or hearing," Prichard believed it fulfilled "all the functions of both." One somnambulist, however, was more exacting in distinguishing her experience of clairvoyance from sight and drawing it deeply into the world of mind and affect. "I see nothing;" she said, "but I feel something that makes an impression on me, which I can not explain." In either case, as a contributor to *Gentleman's Magazine* insisted, clairvoyance was as natural and common as sight. In the Scottish Highlands, he wrote, "not only aged men and women have the Second Sight, but also children, horses and cows."[39]

At regular intervals both Jane Rider and Abigail Cass entered a clairvoyant state, gaining "absolute" knowledge, as was said of Cass, "of whatever was going on in the room," regardless of the impairment of their external senses. Through her ability to see at a distance, Rider became a clairvoyant resource for the steady stream who gathered about her, wishing to use her "vision" to locate lost objects.[40]

A more highly elaborated capacity to see at a distance enabled other somnambulists to engage a taste for mental travel. An Italian somnambulist with bandaged eyes enumerated every object not only in her room but in "*the next room,* or *in the street,* or *out of the town,* or *even at enormous distances,*" just as the magnetic Rhode Islander Loraina Brackett "traveled" to New York, describing the contents of her physician's house down to the pictures on the wall and even suffering seasickness during the imaginary steamboat ride across Long Island Sound. The more adventurous som-

nambulists traveled to the "the moon, several planets, and the sun," and
needless to say, time was no more a barrier than space. Such cases led Good
to argue that the soul could indeed separate from the body and maintain, at
least for a time, its own separate existence.[41]

Clairvoyance and sympathy also produced some remarkable mental capabilities under somnambulism. Rider, the daughter of a mechanic, became "distinguished" during her paroxysms "by a degree of brilliancy and
wit" she did not demonstrate in waking. She read poetry and prose with facility, sang ably, and displayed an "extraordinary power of imitation" of
which she was otherwise incapable, adopting the "manner as well as the
language and sentiments of those whom she personified" (a perfect sympathetic response). With a suddenly acquired skill, Rider repeatedly bested
her attending physician at backgammon, leaving the doctor "a little mortified at being beaten by a sleeping girl." Exalted intellect, strength, or musi-
cal ability were everywhere among sleepwalkers, ranging from Abigail
Cass's poetic prowess and her acquisition of new languages, to the knowledge of astronomy and geography that suddenly appeared in the Scottish
servant Maria C., to the mental dexterity of another young woman who
was suddenly able to extract roots of numbers up to 4,865 and to expose
"with much lucidity several philosophical systems." Sympathy opened
avenues for mental expansion ordinarily unavailable to such women or to
persons of such social status.[42]

In sympathetic terms clairvoyance offered more than just the expansion
of the mental world; it offered the literal means of becoming a spectator of
human relations, that most vital element of Adam Smith's philosophy. Di-
vorced from the body, a somnambulist could freely judge the content of
human interaction by direct apprehension of the parties' motives, desires,
and thoughts. In so doing, however, second sight evoked second thoughts.
When "every thought and desire which was passing through the mind"
were unveiled by the fictional somnambulist Eulalie, her physicians were
stunned, some turning away in anger and others in confusion. Nonplussed
that "the evil [had grown] to such a height" and that "so many secrets got
afloat," they dismissed her "before a complete schism was created among
the authorities of the hospital." This mental penetration of the self so disturbed Nathaniel Hawthorne that he pleaded with his fiancée, Sophia, to
avoid mesmerism, for the "sacredness of an individual is violated by it,"

and "there would be an intrusion into thy holy of holies." Worst of all, he wrote, "the intruder would not be thy husband!"[43]

The somnambular self was therefore a permeable, transparent self, with implications both good and ill. A somnambulist might leave the body in sleep to travel across space or time or might visually or mentally penetrate his or her own body or the bodies of others. Rejecting the soulless automaton, the somnambular body was animated by mind, porous, fluid, and partible, interconnected within itself and with others, and liberated of spatial and temporal restrictions. As sensate beings mutualistically engaged with the universe, somnambulists were primed to supervene the barriers of human limitation. Defying the affective inaccessibility at the core of Adam Smith's theory of sympathy, the practice of the somnambular body offered an avenue for the creation of a sympathetic society. Yet as should be clear, somnambulists also exposed a disquieting personal vulnerability. Like the double-edged theory of sympathy, somnambulists embodied not only the hopeful construal of bodily union but the implicit fear of the indeterminacy of internal states.

SOMNAMBULAR BEHAVIOR

When first entering the Stebbins home to treat Jane Rider, Lemuel Belden was struck by the girl's "false conception" of her surroundings: she believed fully that she was at home in Brattleboro, having "no recollection of ever having been in Springfield. . . . Even the name of the people with whom she lived seemed infamiliar and strange to her." Sensing the disturbance to Rider's senses, Belden had himself introduced to his patient as Rider's father, "whose absence she had been lamenting," and he then proceeded to converse with her and dose her with ipecac without any awareness on her part that he was anyone else. During her "paroxysms" the tangible external world made only selective impressions upon Rider. Indeed, Belden concluded that her ideas of her surroundings "generally corresponded with the idea of the place in which she conceived herself to be" and that she failed to recognize anyone present outside her "family"—her imagined sympathetic circle—paying no attention at all to women in the room and noting the arrival of males only by "mutter[ing] something about the indelicacy of being seen in that situation." In a sense Rider inhabited a world structured by her desires, a world in which external reality, like bodily activity, was subordinate to mind.[44]

By the 1830s physicians began increasingly to explore the ramifications of this world in which, as J. C. Badeley later suggested, the power of the mind seemed to shape sensory experience and seemed to reveal the essence of human nature and society. The most interesting feature of somnambulism, according to one writer, was that it revealed "a preternatural state of being, in which the body is seen moving about, executing a variety of complicated actions, in the condition, physically, of a living automaton"; acting solely under the influence of soul to prove, "incontestably, that the mind is independent of the body, and has an existence in a world peculiar to itself."[45]

Although the comic (or tragic) potential of living in a world apart was milked by novelists and playwrights, somnambulists seemed to harbor deeper insights into the basis of human behavior. However absurd it was that Negretti, the famed Italian sleepwalker, mistook a bottle for a candle, cabbage for salad, or took water for wine and coffee for snuff, there was an undeniable internal logic to his actions as far as they corresponded with his mental world. Badeley insisted that the somnambulist "*acts* under the influence of his conceptions" and his sensory impressions conform to his desires and expectations.[46] The mind of the somnambulist, according to another common interpretation, was fixed intently on a small number of ideas or desires, and by "concentrat[ing] its powers and energiz[ing] itself within," it worked within this delimited mental sphere in which "the sensibility of the body diminishes." Lemuel Belden differed slightly in arguing that although somnambulists were blind by waking standards, "the power of vision is not suspended as to those objects which the sleep-walker wishes to see." The barriers of flesh, blindfolds, and thick paper had no effect upon the somnambulist who wished not to see them, nor did darkness, sound, or distance.[47]

In a limited sense the mental world of somnambulists could be said to transform the external world. Both Jane Rider and Abigail Cass had their "own notions of time," which they insisted upon respecting, but which failed to correlate with time as measured by the clock. For them day was night and night, day; a moment might extend indefinitely, an hour elapse in an instant. Andrew Ellis concluded that ecstatics "lose all connexion with the physical world," though they established "associations of the most pleasing and enchanting nature" with "an ideal existence in an unknown region." For more ardent materialists these cases suggested that the human mind might have a dual structure. In 1845, suggesting that "the domain of science" now appeared to be "less bounded than that of the imagination," Arthur Wigan proposed that humans possessed two separate brains, not necessarily coincident with hemispheres, that "*always,* and under all possible circumstances, act independently, and that their concurrence is nothing more than *unison,* not *union.*"[48]

The peculiar nature of somnambular memory, however, threatened to devastate Wigan's notions of cerebral unison, and certainly unity, and seemed to suggest that the mental constructs of somnambulists might be indicative of a more fundamental shift in the perception of the self. Philosophers had long identified memory as a key element of personal identity, but somnambular memory seemed pregnant with disturbing implications; in somnambulists, the sleeping self was separated from the waking self not only by disparate mental traits and disparate abilities, they were cleaved by a stark amnesiac divide. For Jane Rider "none of the transactions" she experienced as a somnambulist "left the slightest impression on her mind" when awake, and none of the remarkable abilities or skills she acquired translated to waking life. Awake, Jane Rider knew nothing of what had gone on while she was asleep, yet in every instance when she reentered the somnambular state, she immediately recalled her previous paroxysms with perfect clarity. "The thread of this strange supplementary life," one writer asserted, would be "taken up where it was broken perhaps months before," resumed with such fidelity that the somnambulist might even complete a sentence cut off midstream. The ideal Brattleboro world of the sleeping Rider was cleaved from her waking existence in Springfield, each phase of her memory self-consistent, complete, and bound by its own rules of time.[49]

In extreme cases these "supplementary" lives diverged for extended periods, resulting in true "double consciousness" in which two distinct personalities were exhibited alternately, neither of which were necessarily tied exclusively to sleeping or waking. In 1815 Mary Reynolds entered into a long and profound sleep, awaking as a tabula rasa, unable to remember who she was or anything that she had learned in life to that point. After painstakingly relearning how to write, read, spell, and calculate over the course of several months, Reynolds relapsed into somnolency, reawakening as her old self, with her old memories intact, although periodically thereafter she switched back and forth. In her "new state" not only did she have no recollection of her "old" one, but "there existed as little resemblance between the two, as is found in the character of the most opposite persons." Years later the neurologist Silas Weir Mitchell determined that Reynolds's "ideas, sentiments, passions, forms of expression and gesticulations—even the temperaments, were those of two contrasted individuals. She was slow, indolent, and querulous when awake; quick, energetic, and vivaciously witty, when asleep."[50]

The presence of a secret, interior self—a self necessarily isolated from the operation of self-restraint and self-control—had disquieting implications, particularly in a society struggling toward a more rigorously circumscribed, rigorously protected private self, distinct from the public. The experience of somnambulists suggested that this "sort of double life" brought individuals repeatedly into situations of physical and moral peril. Incapable of reliable perception, deprived of consistent memory, and unconstrained by social norms, they entered situations that exposed them, both literally and figuratively, to the public eye. The sleepwalking son of G. Knock, for example, was found "quite naked" in a neighbor's pond, nearly drowned, and Mary, servant to Mr. Bell, was discovered walking down the street "with nothing on but her shift." The stereotypical somnambular activity, walking along dangerous rooftops (often semidressed), resulted from the sleepwalkers' inability to gauge the danger of their surroundings accurately. With the sense of fear suspended, sleepwalkers readily bounded over rooftops, parapets, and ridges, displaying, "an inexplicable association of the most perfect penetration, with the greatest stupidity," as John Bell wrote, who asked rhetorically "how a man, who had address enough to climb up the top of a decayed house, and run on a few weak beams, could not perceive the profound abyss which lay under?"[51]

That this abyss was moral as well as physical was equally apparent. Exposed to the entire town in only her shift, the fictional roof-walking Ernestine Dormeil was seen gamboling from the frying pan of a high gutter into the licking flames of a man's bedroom. More pointedly, the Scots somnambulist who learned astronomy, Maria C., was raped during a somnambular fit but was incapable of recalling the experience upon waking. Switching male and female roles, a sleepwalking plasterer was robbed in broad daylight by a woman. In sleepwalking, as one contributor to the British medical journal, the *Lancet*, surmised, the ordinary affective response is suspended, and occasionally even inverted. "We may see the most extraordinary object or event without surprise," he wrote; we may "perform the most ruthless crime without compunction, and, see what in our waking hours would cause us unmitigated grief, without the smallest feeling of sorrow."[52]

What sort of spectator, then, was this second self, a self with no knowledge of its other life or memory, a self that questioned the nature of personal identity? When Lord Kames remarked that "in a dead sleep, we have no consciousness of self," he intended something other than the duality of sleepwalkers, but he inadvertently pointed to the key question about somnambulists: was this sleeping consciousness a separate consciousness, or was it in fact a reflection of our true being? Was this what lay within the private self?[53]

In part, somnambular activity implied that the self was buoyed by waves of submerged desires and emotions, as simple as the desire of Miss H to view a cetacean corpse, as comic as the desires of Sylvester Sound, driven to roam by a love for peaches and his true love, Rosalie, or as poignant as Alan Pinkerton's guilt-ridden somnambular thief, bent compulsively on concealing his crimes. Such desires, however, were frequently discomforting, often painful, betraying the unresolved fear of affective isolation implicit in Adam Smith's theory of sympathy and in the modern, private self. In somnambulism, where "muscular functions, which though naturally in subordination to the will, [were] performed without a consciousness of mind," the naked soul could be as poetically brutal as it was poetically intellectual. The removal of the will exposed the savage within. Although somnambulism was believed to occur more frequently in females than males, the delicacy of their nervous systems being more prone to disorder, male somnambulists displayed particularly potent instantiations of subterranean desires. Aggression, that characteristically masculine passion, shaped the lives of many sleepwalkers, male and female. For women like the fictional Emma Grandson, self-violence and suicide might result when sleepwalking was surcharged with grief over the death of a father, and as other cases showed, somnambulism made a woman vulnerable to violence and crime.[54]

Male somnambulists, however, were notoriously prone to commit violence upon others. The story of the Carthusian monk Cyrillo Padovano was recounted frequently in the Anglo-American literature. Brillat-Savarin reported being awakened in bed one evening to find the sleeping monk walking toward him, and upon reaching the bed, Cyrillo "put down the lamp, and felt and patted it with his hand, to satisfy himself he was right, and then plunged the knife, as if through my body, violently through the bed-clothes, piercing even the mat which supplied, with us, the place of a mattress."[55] Upon waking, this melancholic monk confessed to having had a disturbing dream in which he killed his mother, though of course he remembered nothing of the physical act he had committed.

Another version of the same story held that the young monk was a pious man, but he was when asleep, his somnambulism "overturn[ed] the whole system of waking morality" and turned him into "a thief, a robber, and plunderer of the dead." After becoming a monk, he was observed variously stealing silver from the church and jewelry from a female corpse, mangling the body in the process; when awake, he professed an inability to recall anything of his sleeping exploits. In this version some observers felt that Cyrillo was accountable for his actions while asleep, that his behavior should not be viewed as an aberration but as evidence of his inner moral state. "When the control of the will was suspended," wrote an anonymous commentator, when Cyrillo "was left to the unrestrained exhibition of his true character, he appeared as he was, and thus destroyed in his sleep all the reputation for piety and holiness which he had earned by his waking hypocrisy."[56]

True character often bore traces of Adam Smith's fear of interpersonal opacity, often implied that beneath the habitual gloss of social role lie motives, emotions, and desires unknown that imply doubts, as well, about the coherence of social order in a privatized world where the self was guarded by an amnesiac wall. In the United States the antisocial implications of this state of being entered into the sphere of jurisprudence as the result of two men, Abraham Prescott and Albert John Tirrell, who allegedly murdered women while in somnambular paroxysm.[57]

On June 23, 1833, Abraham Prescott joined Sally Cochran, the wife of the man to whom he was apprenticed, as she went into the fields to pick strawberries. After they veered away from the best berrying localities, Prescott bludgeoned Cochran with a stake, killing her immediately, and after committing the act, he fell into a profound trancelike stupor. Although he immediately admitted to the crime and seemed genuinely remorseful, his likelihood of acquittal was not high; after all, six months previously he had attacked the Cochrans in their sleep with an ax. Prescott's attorney, therefore, sought to focus the defense upon the question of responsibility, using both the previous nocturnal attack and Prescott's odd postmurder behavior as evidence that he was unknowingly a somnambulist and arguing that because Prescott was devoid of the controlling power of reason, he could not legally be held liable for his actions.[58]

Prescott's lawyer built a strong case. First he established a family history of mental illness, calling upon respected members of the community to testify that several members of the family were altogether mad, including a hypochondriacal grandfather, a melancholic aunt, and an alcoholic cousin, and he gathered the testimony of relatives who verified that Abraham himself had shown signs of insanity in his youth. According to his mother and father, Abraham's head became frightfully swollen when he was an infant and broke out in sores, leading their doctor to suggest that the child would become insane later in life. In an attempt to cure him, the family took Abraham to the sea to dip him, but "the salt water did him no good."[59]

Several witnesses testified that they had known of Prescott's somnambulism before the murder. As a coup de grâce, the defense brought forth several expert witnesses, including Rufus Wyman, superintendent of the McLean Asylum, and George Parkman, later murdered by John White Webster, to expound upon the hereditary nature of insanity and the character of somnambulism. Wyman testified that somnambulism is a "different affection from that of insanity," though at the same time he suggested that Prescott suffered from a form of monomania. Both he and Parkman concurred that insanity might be present in an individual like Prescott without necessarily manifesting itself for many years, yet both undercut the defense by denying any inherent connection between somnambulism and violence. These authoritative opinions and the testimony of family and friends did little. Despite the best efforts of the defense attorneys, and despite encouraging instructions from the judge, Prescott was convicted of murder and sentenced to hang.[60]

Twelve years later somnambulism was once again called in by the defense when Albert John Tirrell was brought to trial in Boston for the murder of his mistress, the "beautiful prostitute" Maria Bickford. The black-sheep son of a well-to-do shoe manufacturer from New Bedford, Tirrell had left his wife to lead a life of debauchery in the city, meeting up with the similarly debauched Maria Bickford, a once-respectable young woman from Maine who had abandoned her own spouse. Tirrell spent lavishly on Bickford, acquiring fine dresses, jewelry, and luxury goods for her, and the two traveled together openly. They were known to quarrel frequently and publicly, but only, so Bickford was reported to have said, in order to make up. Unfortunately for the young roués, this flagrantly prosecuted affair attracted the notice of Tirrell's wife's family, who lodged charges against him for adultery. Before he could be put away, however, he fled back into Bickford's arms.[61]

Late in October 1845 Bickford was discovered in her blood-soaked bedroom, her throat slit six inches wide with a razor. After committing the deed, the murderer apparently had attempted to conceal the crime by setting fire to the body, and that evening eyewitnesses had spotted a man at a distance running from the house. When a letter and clothing belonging to Tirrell were discovered in the room, he immediately became the prime suspect and after a major manhunt was apprehended on a boat off New Orleans, attempting to flee the country.

From the outset Tirrell's case looked as grim as Prescott's, and his lawyer settled on the same strategy as Prescott's. Unlike Prescott's attorney, however, Tirrell's developed several different working hypotheses for what might have happened that night, hoping that one might be enough to exonerate him. First of all, he insisted that the evidence linking Tirrell to the murder scene was purely circumstantial and that the testimony of the eyewitnesses was inconsistent and insufficient for a conviction. To place further doubt in the minds of the jury, the attorney argued that it was impossible to rule out that Bickford had cut her own throat, since suicide was the natural end for prostitutes, and he added that if Tirrell had committed the crime, he must have done so in a state of somnambulism and therefore could not be held accountable for his actions.[62]

After establishing Albert's lifelong habit of sleepwalking through the testimony of his relatives, the defense called the eminent Boston physicians Samuel B. Woodward and Walter Channing to deliver their professional opinions on suicide and somnambulism. Citing Hume, John Elliottson, Johann Spurzheim, and Franz Josef Gall, both experts testified that it was "practicable for a female in a high state of excitement to commit suicide with a razor by one blow," even such a ghastly gash as that on Bickford, but what the defense most wanted to hear came in Channing's claim that "*in Somnambulism, a person may have the will to act, and yet the moral nature is entirely wanting. . . . For a person to rise in the night, in a sleep, and kill a person would be perfectly consistent.*" Furthermore, because somnambular senses were heightened, it was entirely plausible that a somnambular Tirrell could have seen well enough in the dark to use a razor in committing the murder and that he might then "set the house on fire, and run out in the street." "A person in a state of insanity is dreaming awake as a somnambulist is dreaming asleep," Woodward said. "They act on false premises, and have lost the regulating power of their minds. They have lost, in such cases, all power of moral distinction."[63]

Perhaps most significantly, Tirrell's attorney attempted to elicit the sympathy of the jury by having them see that we might all become somnambulists, that we might all be capable of such acts. "Many persons," he suggested, "indeed most persons, may be said to pass through a species of mental derangement, every time they pass from the natural sleeping state to that of waking. At first, how confused the sense of sight and hearing? How difficult it is, sometimes, for the mind to become conscious of its condition, or even the location or condition of the body?" Here, he went for the throat: "Now, suppose this state, which with some persons, is of so frequent occurrence, to be continuous for an hour! Or five minutes even— that is insanity for the time being; just as real, as thought it had lasted for an age."[64]

The great surprise in Tirrell's trial was that his defense was successful: he was acquitted of murder, although he was sentenced to three years' hard labor for his previous conviction for adultery. The court pointedly advised that Tirrell had been acquitted due to a lack of evidence, adding that "the question of somnambulism had not entered into the consideration of the jury." Not all of the popular press was so certain, and both the pro- and anti-Tirrell pamphlets that proliferated relished in the indeterminacies in masculine and feminine behavior that sprang from the sleepwalker's story. Tirrell was a modern man, suffering from the modern maladies of nervous exhaustion and hereditary mental instability, and prone to the eruption of the brutish inner man lying beneath even the most cultured exterior. In the most hostile pamphlets, those written for a working-class audience, his was said to be a story of the "fall" from respectability into debauchery and a lavish, corrupt lifestyle. Through his "insinuating plausibility" Tirrell the seducer lured Bickford, "one of the most virtuous of her sex," deep "into the whirlpool of vice."[65]

"Reckless and improvident," Tirrell rejected the counsel of friends and joined in a slumming life "seldom equalled by rake, libertine, or murderer." Tirrell's inner condition, the condition of the upper classes, was exposed only through the loss of self-control incident to somnambulism. "Faithful snapper-ups" like the *Eccentricities and Anecdotes of Albert J. Tirrell,* written largely in the first person, allowed the reader to participate in the life of this young urban flaneur, to experience his double world, his mastery of the dangerous urban landscape, and his command and conquests of the opposite sex. By infusing the narrative with a surficial morality and attributing the authorship of the pamphlet to "A Lady of Weymouth" (female and nonurban), the narrator enabled the reader both to participate in these experiences and to remain distanced from the potential moral implications; in other words, the narrative can be said to recapitulate the amnesiac divide of the somnambulist and the distancing effect of sympathetic relations.[66]

THE NEW AERA

The great whale lying inert, decomposing on a Long Island beach, would hardly seem an object of desire. Yet in the logic of somnambulism, it became desirable and became the object on which the identity of the sleepwalking Miss H ultimately hung. Observing case after case of bodily action in the absence of will, in the absence of mental control, the absence of consciousness, writers in the early national period faced the uncomfortable proposition that the emotional universe created by the sympathetic imagination was insufficient to overcome subversive desire. The sympathetic body that produced such wondrous effects, that promised to unite, seemed also to reveal the potent threat of affective isolation. The promise held by somnambulism for enabling a dying woman to share in the "prevalent sentiments" of her community decomposed before it ever was composed, compromised by the very fears that animated it from the start.

"It would appear," said one critic, "that we are entering upon the magnetic æra of the world. Cause and effect, physicians and patients,—we beg pardon—patients and physicians, are to be abolished, magnets of superlative pungency are to be substituted for smelling-bottles, and evil humours, moral as well as physical, will be dispersed by convenient tractors . . . and our belles and beaux will exert an elective attraction upon each other by means of magnetic fans and quizzing-glasses, to the dismay of the uninitiated papas and mamas." This magnetic aera was both promise and threat.[67]

Celestial Symptoms

SPREADING MADNESS with a kiss in the summer of 1801, the mother of John S. infected her son with the belief that he would become a "preacher of the everlasting gospel," and with kiss after kiss she passed the contagion to her other children and daughters-in-law, each of whom fell prey, one upon another, to the common delusion. By the time that William Simonson, a man of "unquestionable integrity," arrived at the Wilmington, Delaware, home two days later, the divinely inspired John had swayed the entire family to believe that they were "possessed with an evil spirit," preaching that after their real mother had died a week earlier, Satan had entered her body and spread through her kiss to fill their own. As Simonson struggled to comprehend the scene, the children burst into action, dragging their mother screaming from bed and beating her almost to death, and when thwarted in their aims, they lit the house on fire "to consume the tormenting demon in the image of their mother." Only the removal of the inspired John restored order to the home, although nothing alleviated the madness of the old woman, and neither doctor nor mesmerist could cure the ragged and raving preacher.[1]

The concept of mental and moral contagion had a peculiarly tangible feel at the turn of the nineteenth century, and for the attending physician in the case, John Vaughan, the violent and addled ministry of John S. provided solid evidence of the mode of operation of "that physical something, usually stiled sympathy." Within the maternal kiss and the habitual bonds of mother and child, Vaughan saw a bridge of intimacy over which madness and religious delusion flowed, revealing how sympathy could become "susceptible of morbid influence beyond satisfactory explanation."

When David Hume emphasized the transpersonal, vagrant nature of sympathy, the tendency of "all the affections" to "pass from one person to another, and beget correspondential movements in every human creature," he put his finger on the phenomenon so troubling to Vaughan: through sympathy, affections, all of them, good and ill, were highly contagious.[2]

As "a connection or relationship between the different parts of a system," rather than a fundamental law of "animal economy," Vaughan argued that sympathy varied with "the states of the system" in which it was expressed, the constitutional tendencies of the individual, their habits, and the vagaries of life history working in concert with sympathies to shape the course of disease, so that madness flowed from a madwoman as surely as love from a mother or inspiration from the divine. "Predispositions of the body, and sympathy of mind," he wrote, "probably deserve an equal rank in the formation of corporeal and mental diseases. The translation of diseases from the blood-vessels to the brain and nervous system, and the transformation of febrile action to mania, also evince that physical relationship so frequently mentioned by physiologists, as connecting mind and body, and subjecting each to a participation in the morbid affections of the other. Fanaticism appears to be as much a primary mental disorder, as febrile action is a vascular disease."[3]

The thread (or threat) of divine inspiration that Vaughan unraveled from the story of John S. suggested that this "physical something" might illuminate the material origins of the most disorderly forms of religious enthusiasm then shaking the revival tents of the western states. In reaping souls by the hundreds, the first great evangelical wave added a new impetus to the project of clarifying the origins of fanaticism and of divining the connection between material reality and religious inspiration. Relentlessly material observers like Felix Robertson, a physician from Tennessee, pathologized revivalistic phenomena in the same way that Vaughan pathologized the inspiration of John S., rejecting the contention that the gyrations and spasms of those stricken with the spirit were evidence of "favourable religious visitations from the Deity" in favor of interpreting them as an outbreak of "epidemic chorea." Charging sympathetically through the audience, the etiology of this chorea was both predictable and gender-specific, progressing through the bodily "jerks" and gestures common to men, to swooning, the "running exercise," and ultimately to total paroxysm, all spread through the sympathy of mind.[4]

Although his fellow physician William Young disputed Robertson's contention that the exercises were the product of an "idiopathic bodily disease" like chorea, he nevertheless saw the "convulsive operation of the moral faculty upon the system" as a product of a material sympathy. "Feelings," he wrote, played the greatest part in producing the exercises, feelings exacerbated by the mechanical effects of music upon the "passions," by the excitation of the revivalists, and by the "sympathy of association," recalling, perhaps, the swaying of Adam Smith's mob at a hanging. Taken as a whole, Young argued, the impact of the revival atmosphere "conspires to give a sudden impulse to the moral faculty, which it can neither resist nor confine within ordinary limits."[5]

The sympathetically based skepticism of Vaughan, Robertson, and Young encountered its mirror image in the argument that sympathy promised more than the bonding of mind and body. William Belcher was no less certain than his peers that sympathy was "some external power," something real and tangible and "naturally accounted for" that drew similar souls together, yet for him sympathy was a substance that opened the gates to the "grand mystic secret." Whether this substance was equated with electricity or oxygen (his favored suggestions) or was something altogether different, Belcher argued that it linked not only thought and sensation but soul and the divine. "Sympathetic affection" surely drew human to human, but it forged a link as well "between mankind and the spiritual world; and also between its probably different spirits," and he reasoned that "if the souls of men naturally tend to the surrounding world of spirits, all beings whatsoever may thereby finally concenter to the ONE SUPREME BEING."[6]

Alternative readings of the role of sympathy in mediating expressions of the divine and in sorting true religion from false found their fullest expression in discussions of a distinctive species of natural somnambulist, the "sleeping preacher." As prophets of false religion and fanaticism or sympathetic proof of the infusion of the divine into mortal life, as the victims of mental disease or as mental marvels, sleeping preachers were insinuated in the intense debates over the meaning of morality, reality, and truth and who had the right to judge. At a time of great revivals, they proliferated so rapidly that one popular periodical proclaimed that "a SLEEPING PREACHER is no longer considered a novelty."[7]

SLEEPING PREACHERS

From the 1760s onward, reports of sleeping preachers circulated widely in the popular and medical press. In somnambulism individuals of lower social status discovered a preternatural ability to discourse upon religious subjects, to deliver moving prayers and pious sermons that belied the limitations of education and class. Typical of the lot, the young weaver Job Cooper suddenly began to preach in his sleep in 1774. After going to bed, Cooper was wracked with bodily spasms, shivering, groaning, and gasping for breath, but once he began to preach, he settled into calm and quiet and continued to hold forth. His discourses inevitably began with a prayer, proceeding into an exhortation of the most pious nature, before concluding with another heartfelt prayer, but when awake, Cooper always denied awareness of his preaching, appearing "somewhat mortified, as he expressed it, at becoming an object of curiosity, from a circumstance neither within his own knowledge or control." Another sleeping preacher, the sixteen-year-old "country lad" Joseph Payne, was employed as a servant to a farmer in Lambourn, England, when he began to sermonize on the topic "They led him away to crucify him." Payne's only recorded sermon was said to be of irreproachable orthodoxy and was thought a competent, if not elegant, expression of deep-seated religious sentiments.[8]

But the apotheosis of the sleeping preacher was reached in 1814 and 1815 when a young woman held forth nightly from her bed in New York City, preaching and praying before audiences of skeptics and believers, men of science and men of the cloth, as many, it was reported, as three hundred a night. Rachel Baker was born into a devoutly Presbyterian family in Pelham, Massachusetts, on May 29, 1794, and her biography resembles nothing less than a précis of the life history of a typical Awakening convert. At nine she moved with her family to the marchlands of the Burned-Over District of New York, settling in Marcellus, a village on the eastern fringe of the Finger Lakes. Seemingly destined for the obscurity of an ordinary life, Baker was unremarkable as a child, blessed with banality and moderation. "Never inclined to superstition on the one part, nor to enthusiasm on the other," she possessed a "sober contemplative disposition" and a "fair and exemplary" moral character, and if she had any interest in improving a mind that was neither "sprightly nor vigorous" to begin with, it was well hidden. She had received only a few months of instruction in a common school, and "chiefly confined to religious subjects" at that, and her educational achievements could hardly be considered an adornment.[9]

However, in Marcellus, Baker began to acquire the things that set her apart, beginning with strong presentiments on God and things eternal. Acquiring thoughts that "would make her tremble," at the age of fourteen Baker was led to unite with the Presbyterian Church, and by the time she turned seventeen in 1811, her religious fervor was all aroil. Witnessing the baptism of a young woman while on a trip to Scipio, New York, she fell under an "increased conviction of her own sinfulness, and consequent endless misery" and "underwent a religious submersion" into the Baptist Church. Yet even this change of denomination did nothing to forestall salvationary despondency, and although she struggled to keep her concerns secret even from her mother, Baker's fears soon spilled out.[10]

After several days of little rest and less food, on the night of June 28, 1811, Baker entered a troubled sleep and somnambulated (or, more accurately, somniloquated) for the first time. With a sigh and crushing groan "as if in excessive pain," she announced that she had but little time to live, and in the months that followed, her sleeping hours were devoted to disordered and nearly incoherent cries of religious concern. These fits increased steadily until January, when she was seized with a particularly violent bout of trembling and awoke shrieking, "filled with terror and agitation. Horror and despondency came upon her with overwhelming power—with an agonizing sense of her own vileness, her imagination ran wild with the dread of a miserable eternity, and of her speedy and inevitable doom." This cathartic and searing self-examination, like catharses to come, gave way to penetrating calm. Thereafter "in her nightly devotions, which were now regular and coherent, she poured forth a spirit of meekness, gratitude and love."[11]

Although she felt no pain when awake, the physical and psychological toll of Baker's experience led her to move to New York City in October 1814 "to procure medical counsel, to try the effect of traveling, and to experience the influence of the maritime atmosphere." Under the scrutiny of a small faculty of surgeons and scientists, she held nightly performances before swelling throngs of the curious and faithful, who believed variously that they were in the presence of fraud, disease, or divine inspiration, or perhaps a more complex admixture of all three.[12]

Evenings at Baker's began when she retired into a "private" chamber (to permit greater "decorum on her own part," and "greater satisfaction to her hearers") and went to sleep. With body and soul immiscibly bound, a violent paroxysm "invaded" her body, sometimes lasting more than an hour, and the behaviors of the first disordered months of her ministry emerged full-fledged to transform her into a supine version of the convert slain by the spirit as she engaged in an ascetic and characteristically feminine bodily discipline. Accompanied by "anxiety in respiration, and hysteric choking," the young somnambule emitted groans so dreadfully distressed and prolonged that "she appeared to be dying."[13] Despite the distress, despite her "violently agitated" expressions and the "convulsive movements" of her head that "denoted extreme agony," the remarkable fact was that "the *rest of her body, from her shoulders to her feet, was tranquil as a statue.*" She became, in short, the stoic embodiment of pain disembodied.[14]

As Baker's agony passed from turmoil to tranquillity, she moved from the sublimated expressions of the body to religious expression and began to preach. In the posture of a holy corpse, she lay with eyes "turned upwards, and their muscles in a tremulous spasm," and like any good somnambulist, she became "insensible to all the stimuli which has been thought prudent to apply, for the purpose of rousing her." Like other somnambulists, too, her senses were fundamentally reordered: asleep she now saw all about her the "souls of men just made perfect," and she now heard a voice "that was not mortal, and administering to her consolation, in her agonizing distress." Tranquilly, Baker stated that she was unaware "whether she is in the body or out of the body . . . yet she declares that she feels high enjoyment, and benevolently wishes that others could have the exquisite sensations which she experiences." Pleasures of the body, it seems, paled before the spiritual pleasure of somnambulism, and freed from the body, Baker finally enjoyed a spiritual apperception undiluted by the material.[15]

A typical performance was comprised of the three parts of a standard religious service: an opening prayer ("similar to those of our reformed preachers"), a sermon or address to the audience, and a closing prayer. From the skeptical to the devout, Baker's audience praised these displays for being "strictly conformable to the general faith of the Calvinistic churches," even if she occasionally "strongly insist[ed] on the peculiar tenets of her own sect," and her unalloyed piety was taken as evidence against fraud, if not disease. For a young woman of limited education, Baker displayed an "extensive acquaintance with the doctrinal parts of the scriptures," citing with ease from the Evangelists, the historical, prophetic, and epistolary writings alike, and reciting "not only texts, but long passages, readily and accurately."[16]

Many sermons, like the one described by a female supporter, revolved around the need for self-reflection and repentance and "the duty of Christians searching themselves and seeing if they were not deceived in their hopes," and they were filled with lamentations for those who "thought they were at peace with God when their hearts were still in the fall of bitterness."[17] Baker "entreated all to become interested in Christ," this woman observed, and awakened so "many to a sense of their guilt & danger," that if only disbelievers simply listened, "their opinions I am confident would be changed." Through her sermons Baker established a conceptual parallel between her own disembodied self-examination and the self-examination that she demanded her audience carry into waking life.[18]

Baker's sermonic style further strengthened her credibility, coming across to one reviewer as "plain, but not vulgar . . . distinct and earnest, generally monotonous, but now and then marked by strong emphasis." Baker was no fiery evangelical enthusiast but a psychological wonder who poured "forth her words in a fluent and rapid stream." When interrupted by questions from the audience, as she often was, she responded fluently, though with a touch of reticence, employing words that were as "pious and discreet" as the sermons themselves.[19]

Even apparent defects in her preaching served to support her veracity, though not necessarily her communion with the divine. "When the current of her discourse" was broken by a question, one observer noted, "the original idea is abandoned, and she goes on with a new train of thought suggested by the question." For this observer associationist psychology militated against any allegation of fraudulence, for although "her ordinary discourses" greatly resembled one another, "the difference is such as to show that they are extemporaneous, and not the repetition of a set of words impressed on the memory." A stenographer who witnessed Baker's performances, Charles Mais, observed that most of the sermons resembled those she had been accustomed to hear, differing "about as much as glowing and connected dreams vary from waking thoughts." In contrast, Joseph Comstock, who had treated the sleepwalker Nancy Hazard, argued both that Baker was too uneducated to preach so well herself and that her "inventive powers" were too great for mere imitation, leaving the door open to the divine. Having witnessed Hazard's ability to tell colors by touch, Comstock was more impressed with the "oracular corpse" in New York, more convinced that occult or divine sympathies were involved.[20]

Under any interpretation the impact of such pious thoughts emanating from an unconscious, uneducated, and unprepossessing girl was profound. One witness claimed no religion could match "such sensations as those I experienced last night, while attending the devotional exercises of Miss Rachel Baker." For him, Baker, "this moral phenomenon," held the potential to "become the immortal founder of a new form of worship, which for human convenience, novelty and interest, has no parallel." Further confirming the purity of Baker's thought and actions, she, unlike the notorious Jemima Wilkinson or Joanna Southcott, never attempted to establish any "peculiar system of religious faith," nor did she attempt to turn her ministry to "private emolument."[21]

Fluid or mechanical, authentic or fraudulent, regardless of their perspectives, nearly all observers accepted that Baker's pious teachings were beneficial to humanity, and even the skeptical were moved by the sight of her preaching. An "intelligent gentleman of Cayuga," for example, described the mutual sentiments of the crowd overcoming his natural skepticism. "The deep attention of the auditors, the sighs of the women, the patterns of the hall, the howling of the tempest, united with the speaking corpse, as it appeared uttering its awful warnings to mortality, offered one of those moments of retirement to the soul, when we shudder and shiver in sublimity, like a culprit at Rome, with his heels to the precipice; indeed, I was ten times within an ace of coiling up my logic and uniting in the sympathies of the crowd."[22] When her audience entered into sympathetic congress with Baker, he implied, this unconscious girl led them commutatively into sympathetic congress with the divine.

The physicians and writers who left the most detailed accounts of Baker's preaching, Samuel Latham Mitchill, Charles Mais, and Ansel W.

Ives, nevertheless asserted the primacy of scientific explanation over the irrationality of personal revelation, and all three interpreted Baker's surprising behavior as a characteristically female disorder. Although somnambulism was not necessarily viewed as a female disorder itself, gender added an important layer to interpreting its etiology and cause. Despite his overall positive assessment of Baker's message and moral condition, Mitchill noted that there were whispers that "some cunning, or some concealment . . . may lurk under feminine disguise," particularly given that Baker's "sex precluded the freedom of inquiry necessary to complete elucidation of the occurrences." Following Mitchill, Mais traced Baker's somnambulism to the onset of puberty, "a period when the female frame acquires additional sensibilities, and undergoes a peculiar revolution." In this regard the physicians were in line with a near medical consensus that somnambular behavior and female disorders were sympathetically linked. Thomas Miner, who attended Jane C. Rider, attributed "all the principle derangement" to amenorrhea, arguing that her "stomach sympathized with the uterus, and the brain with the stomach." For the same reasons M. F. Colby carefully monitored the menstruation of Abigail Cass, and the Scots physician H. Dewar attributed somnambulism to uterine irritability.[23] In any event, Mais insisted, Baker's case was "capable of solution upon medical principles" alone, with no need to invoke either supernatural causes or natural fraud. Baker was simply an impressionable girl, raised in a religious household "frequently opened to travelling preachers," who stored up words and phrases that now spilled out in her sleep. This typically feminine, "docile and susceptible mind" was molded by habit and imitation in such a way that Baker, the female infirm, came to represent both a feminine denial of body and, in effect, a feminine denial of mind.[24]

The performance of infirmity was a critical element in interpreting Baker's case, and the almost literally "disembodied ideas" that poured forth recalled a long history of women (and male scientists) who wrested veracity and epistemological control through abstemiousness, corporeal discipline, and rejection of the body. Baker's infirmity was the site of an intense unconscious struggle over the interpretation of her preaching, a struggle recorded stenographically during a session in which physicians and clergymen queried the sleeping preacher on her views on religion and her physical condition, pressing her above all on the Pauline injunction against women preaching. At one level Baker's response to her interrogators was mediated through the amnesiac divide of somnambulism, in which the waking and sleeping selves lived separate lives and held separate views. Baker's waking and sleeping selves were starkly divergent, and even her voice, one woman averred, was "very different when speaking in her sleep from when she is awake." Awake, Baker maintained that "individuals of her sex are prohibited by apostolic mandate, from acting as public teachers," but asleep, she preached with conviction. One might surmise, as Ann Braude did in her discussion of Spiritualist trance lecturers, that Baker's somnambulism was a strategy enabling her to transgress social restrictions on women's religious expression by behaving transgressively only in a state in which the conscious will did not reign, while denying her intentions when it did.[25]

But Baker did not rely solely upon plausible deniability, and her behavior, including the way she responded to her interrogators, was mediated through a distinctively feminine body. Her reticence in responding to questions, Mais wrote, was not the mark of any "reluctance called in to resist our incivility," but rather a "female delicacy, busy in secreting a deformity." How could she reconcile her preaching with the Pauline injunction, and how could she do so, in particular, before an assembled body of the clergy, the erudite, and the wealthy? When asked directly, Baker adroitly deflected the criticism implicit in the question by denying that she assumed any authority over men or ministers at all. When asked by John Griscom why, in an enlightened age, it should be thought "the duty of an illiterate female to give instruction on religious subjects," Baker readily confessed her ignorance and lack of education but added that "it is easy with him to accomplish his will by the weakest instruments." She was, she insisted, merely a passive being fulfilling God's instructions. "I do not preach," she suggested; "I do not presume to preach; but the Lord hath given me a lesson to read to the children of men." When pressed still further, she complained, "I, even I, do speak unto the children of men because it is the will of God, my heavenly father; if it were possible to avoid the dealing of God I would do it; it is mortifying to my natural pride. . . . I am under the hand of the Lord, and I cannot help it." That God would choose such a frail instrument to deliver this important spiritual message was significant: metaphorically she was merely the mechanism for producing divine sounds—the instrument, and not the musician—and it would be wrong to expect women to be silent rather than follow the Lord's word, she said, and foolish to expect an "insane" person to act rationally. By choosing a weak and passive vessel, God only demonstrated his unfathomable power all the more.[26]

Yet Baker was far from passive in rising to the defense of her ministry and in carrying out the aggression of infirmity. When pressed repeatedly, she lashed out, defending her right to preach before men of whatever status: "Shall I—O, shall I, then, hold my peace? The apostle saith, let not a woman stand up in the church as a public teacher: But are you hard of believing? are you hard of understanding? I have told you that I cannot avoid doing these things: My God knoweth what they mean. I do not pretend to teach men; but I only tell them of their danger, and tell them that there is woe to them that are at ease in Zion. . . . Shall a woman hold her peace, because she is a woman? Methinks the apostle meant not so; but meant that they should let their light shine before men."[27]

Arguing on one level that she could not prevent herself from preaching because God had required it and, on another, implicitly, because her "disease" had impaired her good waking sense, Baker made partners of disease and revelation in the economy of her waking and sleeping selves. For the observer the issue was how to distinguish which was disease and which revelation, if they could be distinguished at all. For Mitchill and other observers Baker represented the knife's edge of reason and revelation. For all his investment in naturalistic explanation, Mitchill remained impressed by the moral value of Baker's religious expressions, as marvelous in their way as the marvelous and seemingly supernatural abilities of other somnambulists whose histories he compiled.

THE SLEEPING PREACHER AWAKES

Each of Baker's somnambular services ended as they began, with the preacher's body reinvaded by paroxysm, her fingers clenched, the muscles of her back and her arms and legs stiffening spasmodically as her throat became "affected with something like inflation, strangling, or choking." Once again Baker shuddered and groaned and entered into convulsions like those that initiated her sleep, though "visibly in greater pain"; she was like "the contortion of an incubus" in the "last conscious grasp of life to its fixture; she was as colourless as dead." The superior calm of her religious phase, then, was bounded by an intense and painful somaticity, as if a conflict between body and soul was resolved by allowing each to assume alternate control. Before and after the sermon, her body was the focus and her soul seemingly sublimated, but during the religious interlude the disciplined passivity of body, its rejection, left the soul freed for the influx of spirit for a brief time before the body regained the upper hand. "At last," one writer noted, "she has a few small spasms of the arms and throat, and is agitated by an emotion between sighing and groaning; after a few minutes of restlessness and moaning, without opening her eyes, she passes to a state of natural sleep."[28]

The ultimate denouement of Baker's ministry, however, was medical. During the winter of 1814–15, her malady showed no signs of abatement, but several physicians questioned whether a cure was called for at all. Although Baker was sometimes said not to feel pain—at least none that she remembered when awake—Mitchill believed that she had come to "lament her malady as a sore affliction; and consider it as a visitation upon her to punish her sins, or to try her constancy and virtue." Yet, as he wryly observed, if the patient "knew of no disease," then "it was rather off to prescribe regimen, remedies, and austerics." Certainly there were profound external pressures to leave Baker in the throes of her malady. Charles Mais reported that he had "heard a sentiment from worthy people, that it would be a pity to cure, what they term, such a divine disease," a disease marked by such "celestial symptoms." Baker's supporters cautioned Mais "not to disturb the workings of a distemper, caused and hallowed as it were, by a kind of propitious influence," and urged him to refrain from treating a "malady, so physically and morally edifying." Why would physicians not desist, they asked, in curing a "patient, whose voice in so peculiar a manner enforces the precepts of the scripture, bedews the cheeks of beauty with tears, and warns sinners to a speedy repentance?"[29]

As the debate raged, the physicians attending Baker resisted their inclinations to administer a cure. Although Baker went home to Cayuga during the winter, in February 1815 she was lured back to the city by a group of six philanthropically minded women who installed her in a boarding school to improve her education. All the while, Baker's preaching infirmity continued unabated, and within a few months infirmity gained the upper hand. After an incident in which she hemorrhaged from the lungs so severely that she was "not expected to live long," Baker was forced to withdraw from school. She was bled copiously by a physician to reduce the excitation of her system, but her health continued to deteriorate, and it was decided that she should return once again to Cayuga to recover.[30]

In June 1816 Dr. Rowland Sears entered the scene, and although he, too, remarked that "her bodily health appears to have had little or no influence in the origin, existence, or cure of her mental malady," he set out to cure what he believed to be the primary pathology: somnambulism. Sears deduced that Baker was in the grips of a profound reverie, "in which the energies of her mind became concentrated upon a single object, and were exercised with such vividness as to exclude, in a great measure, the stimulus of external bodies." Over the objections of Baker's supporters, who continued to insist that curing her "would be nothing less than resisting the special revelations of Heaven to the people of the present age," the doctor set to work. To alleviate Baker's melancholy, Sears sought to "invigorate her faculties by the cordial and exhilarating influences of hope," not to mention the liberal use of narcotics. Advising his charge to break the chain of her habits by going to bed earlier than usual, Sears dosed Baker with two grains of opium, and when it appeared that her nightly exercises were about to begin, he splashed her forcefully with cold water, "which dissevered the chain of catenated motions." The process was repeated several times that night, and for several evenings in succession he repeated the therapy, altered only by the application of camphor, castor oil, and "gum foetida" to prevent overstimulation and of cathartics to avoid costiveness and to prepare her better for the stimulants. Within a few days Baker was liberated of her ministry.[31]

SOMNAMBULISM, SELF, AND SOCIETY

Rachel Baker's moral and physical liminality made it possible to view her as either flawed or fraud and simultaneously as a "moral phenomenon." As the story circulated and recirculated during the first half of the nineteenth century, attempts to subordinate her experience to naturalistic explanation never flagged but never fully succeeded. Lifting an account in *Fraʒer's Magaʒine*, for instance, the Scots physician Robert Macnish denigrated Baker's sermons as nothing more than Hartleyan "connected discourses" that "consisted chiefly of texts of Scripture strung together." Describing her somewhat inaccurately as a Presbyterian and as "the daughter of respectable and even wealthy parents," Macnish inserted Baker into a particular cultural economy. "We know individuals who have heard her preach during the night in steam-boats," he wrote, "and it was customary, at tea parties in New York, (in the houses of medical practitioners,) to put the lady to bed in a room adjacent to the drawing-room, in order that the dilletanti might witness so extraordinary a phenomenon." Baker became little more than an object of display, a curiosity with no higher value.[32]

In contrast, the review of Mitchill's account, *Devotional Somnium*, that appeared in the conservative *Analectic Magazine* milked profundity from Baker's predicament, arguing that the facts of Baker's case supported "a system of medical metaphysics, which again send us back to doubt and uncertainty," but doubt of a very particular kind: doubt "whether those who live, and move around us—the politicians, the divines, the men of business, the wits, the belles, who rule, and instruct, and animate the world, are awake or asleep."[33]

Confessing his American predilection for practical knowledge over theory, the reviewer took on both the specter of "immaterial philosophy" that he associated with the high-toned pages of the *Edinburgh Review* and the equally threatening specter of materialism. Common sense and intersubjective experience had rescued Americans (if not Scots) from the epistemological morass of Humean skepticism, but the richness of Baker's case offered something that all disputants could see as uniquely important. Even the Edinburgh crowd, he noted, saw dreams and delirium as an *experimentum crucis* for the hypothesis that "a real external existence" was not necessary for perception or thought, and Baker's dreams offered rich empirical fare.

Surveying the writings of the ancients, the reviewer noted that dreams were once viewed as the product of a body at sleep yoked to an active mind, a view still widely held. Under such conditions, the ancients believed, the "soul, being purified from material grossness," could become "fitted to hold mysterious colloquy with superior and celestial intelligences," with prophecy and divine insight the result. Surely, he reasoned, the mass of facts accumulated by Mitchill demonstrated the "extraordinary state of the intellectual and corporeal powers" and their extraordinary potential. Yet unlike the ancients, modern moral philosophers sided with the thoroughgoing materialism of a Charles Mais. The evidence amassed by

Mitchill, the reviewer claimed, supported Dugald Stewart's contention that somnambulism was produced by a physical alteration of the body in sleep. Whether by the compression of the brain stem (as Joseph Priestley would have it) or something else, as the body slept, the will lost control over the "intellectual and physical powers; whilst the habitual trains of thoughts go on with their accustomed rapidity" in accordance with "the same general laws of association which influence the mind when awake." Thus, he believed, "we find the sleeping preachers engrossed with those religious ideas which occupied their waking minds; the mathematician employed in his equations, and the dream of the poet filled with new combinations of those commonplace poetical sentiments, images, and phrases, with which his memory is stored."[34]

Yet while the *Analectic* reviewer appeared to arrive at the same point as Charles Mais, at the last minute he stepped back from the precipice. For all his love of common sense and American love of facts, for all the value he placed on Mitchill's explanation of Baker's behavior, he could not accept the fact, as he put it, that "the doctrine of election is nothing more than a particular atom of the brain, or the idea of repentance is similar to that tremulous motion which may be seen in a custard, or jelly." The sympathetic body of Rachel Baker that fused the scientific and religious, the material and spiritual, in sympathetic embrace offered more to the reviewer's mind, and in this light he concluded that "the doctrine of the materialists, instead of bringing intellectual operations down to the level of our understanding, only serves to envelop them in tenfold obscurity." Staring down the Edinburgh skeptics who believed that nothing could be proved through human senses and the medical skeptics who believed that human senses were all there was, the reviewer took Baker in all her liminality as comforting reassurance of the value of the unknown.[35]

Somnambulists like Rachel Baker continued to raise questions about the division between material and spiritual realities and continued to affirm, in Emerson's words, the "unity and connection between remote points," which formed such "excellent criticism on the narrow and dead classification of what passed for science." John Bovee Dods, a man whose wanderings took him through the varied branches of materialism, Swedenborgianism, and Spiritualism, asked "who does not know, that the somnambulist is in communication with nature—with surrounding circumstances, and can feel and read by impress the thoughts of those whose nervous sympathies are congenial with his own." For Dods, somnambulists demonstrated that thought was an instinctive and involuntary property of the mind and that even in the absence of consciousness, the mind remained active. "If man is destitute of instinct," he asked, "how then can he, in the mesmeric state, or in somnambulism, or in catalepsy, or in any abnormal condition, intuitively perceive things that are beyond the grasp of his intellectual faculties—things that his reason never conceived?"[36]

As Baker demonstrated, the intuitive, sympathetically driven perception of things beyond the confines of the body opened the gates to new forms of knowledge, new abilities, and new insights, all revealed through liberation of the concealed selves within—the other Mary Reynolds unremembered in waking life, the other Rachel Baker, the other Jane C. Rider. According to Friedrich Fisher, writing in the 1830s, there was immense potential in this partible, amnesiac body. "The soul wanders in a region hitherto closed to consciousness," he wrote, "and in it begins a completely new course of life, one separated from the day-life, and possessing its own peculiar circle of ideas, its own closed memory and history. . . . In this somnambular region rules an unquestioned and accomplished plastic power, a creative fantasy and penetrating intelligence, such as the often very moderately endowed day-individual does not possess."[37]

Like George Lippard's literary madman, somnambulists might exclaim "all memory is a dead blank, only broken by dreams that might change heaven itself into hell. . . . My individuality was lost. I was a king, an emperor, a savage beast, a tree blasted in the midst of a blooming garden; I was my hag-wife, and Eva, any thing, every thing but myself." Unlike the madman, though, the somnambulist made the journey as part of a sympathetic community, emerging in the end into a hierarchically more inclusive identity.[38]

"It is a truth, we shall all sleep," Rachel Baker once said, "but it is a blessed truth, that we shall all rise again: and blessed are they that have a part in the first resurrection; for on such the second death shall have no power." In Spiritualism a new generation would take the persuasion of the sympathetic body beyond the limits of sleep and once again demonstrate its power over death.[39]

3

Transparent Spirits

To believe the soul formed merely for the present uncertain and unsatis-
fying mode of existence, to an enlightened mind was to believe it created
without a worthy purpose, in a universe everywhere displaying most
happy adaptation of means to ends. Possessed of desires that were never
fully gratified; aspirations never reaching their ideals; loves severed, but
not destroyed; hopes disappointed, but not obliterated—it seemed to exist
only as a splendid future and tantalization, unless it were regarded as sustaining spiritual affinities, yet to be realized, after its present organization
was dissolved.

—T. L. Nichols, *Supramundane Facts in the Life of Rev. Jesse B. Ferguson*

SPIRITUALISTS SPOKE OFTEN of the desires of mid-Victorian life: of
the desires sparked by developments in wire, steam, and rail that promised
the erasure of distance and social isolation; of those kindled by scientific
rationalism and its hopes for revealing the most intimate structures of cau-
sality and being; of the desires stoked by the marketplace and the polls and,
above all, by the pulpits and revival tents scattered across the nation. The
desire for a world of progress and social coherence encompassed all of life,
and death, as Spiritualists knew it, framing American society, illuminating
the barriers and limitations that seemed so copious at midcentury and that
seemed, one by one, to be melting away under the optimistic pressure of
the new.

Yet for Spiritualists, as for many Americans, optimism over the "splendid future and tantalization" was coupled Janus-like with the recognition
that the future too often failed to materialize—and failed not with the

abruptness of Millerism but with the slow, gnawing rasp of capitalism, democracy, and evangelicalism. Desire and its discontents were intertwined, the tantalization of erasure (of limitations, of boundaries, want, or distance) paired with the manufacture of new boundaries, conspiring in a cycle of desires spawning desires, of boundaries reconstituted in infinite regress into ever more distant boundaries, transforming the nation into a ghost of desire written on a familiar landscape, never fully visible, never attainable.

Turning their eyes to the dead of the nation, antebellum Spiritualists offered a solution to the ghost of desire and a means of identifying and healing its wounds. In linking a reified afterlife to the conceptual foundations and bodily practices of somnambulism, Spiritualists articulated a theory of community predicated upon the social practice of sympathetic communion, a transcendent nexus of emotion that connected and coordinated all of life and death. Spiritualism provided legibility to life, mapping the cosmos onto a distinctive topography of emotion in which the geographies of the body, heaven, and earth took part in suturing the individual physiologically and socially into the enduring structures that animated the cosmos.

Beginning with a discussion of the paths followed by Spiritualists toward belief, I explore the structure of the Spiritualist cosmos and its four cardinal points of reference—sympathy, transparency, boundlessness, and progress—before concluding with an analysis of the quintessential cosmic manifestation, heaven. What the subtle infusion of spirits into somnambular discourse attempted was the reconstruction of the ghost of desire as the desire for ghosts; what they accomplished was never so transparent.

BECOMING A SPIRITUALIST

In May 1850 Abby Sewall stayed home from church in Chesterfield, Maine, to write her sister, Serena Brown, "always glad of an excuse" to write rather than "hear such small stuff as we have to call preaching." For some time Sewall had suffered from "the horrors," and the opportunity to connect with kin provided a moment's respite from her despondency over the daily pains of life and death, over religious doubts and anxieties, and over the fraying state of the nation. Looking to the local churches for clarity and comfort, she found nothing to soften the sting of war in Mexico or the prospect of national disunion; the sects offered little to salve the lash she felt laid upon the slave or the "slavery nearer home" in the oppression of women.[1] When mired in the horrors, Sewall felt a peculiar sensitivity to the boundaries of life. The imaginary barriers that dissected nations, races, and individuals loomed in sharp relief for her, though nowhere near as sharp as the trickling dissolution of her own family to the ravages of distance and time. "O that family circle," she wrote, "all broken up,"

> the disolation of that old home, deprives the heart of the pleasure which would otherwise attend it, in refering to the scenes of early childhood. Still there is a sort of bitter pleasure sometimes in refering to those scenes. When one has the horrors and every thing around seems to wear a gloom, and the crushed heart fails to find a solace in friends who are near, then 'tis sweet to call to mind the loved of earth who have passed away, and think how soon we shall be like them, free from sorrow and care and a rest that remains for the sorrowing sons of earth, the thought of our final repose always brings joy to the heart, the thirst for immortality is not implanted in our hearts in vain, "hope on hope ever."[2]

Sewall's horrors welled from the depths of a world in which the bonds that tied society, the family, and the individual seemed altogether ready to dissolve. Only in the anticipation of death—the "etternal slap," the point of final social isolation—could she sense hope that once again "families will be united in an unbroken chain, where the longings of the immortal mind will be satisfied at the fountain of everlasting love." Within two years that fountain would overflow with spirits.[3]

Sewall's confrontation with the potent mix of frustrated religious desires and a sense of pervasive social dislocation may not have been unique to Spiritualists, but it was characteristic. As one of the last sparks to ignite the Burned-Over District of New York State, Spiritualism scorched a ground already torched by evangelical revival, already inflamed by a profound spiritual hunger that set the stage for the "sacralization" of the American landscape. Spiritualists were among the most ardent in proclaiming theirs a "generation seeking after signs," a generation who believed, like A. B. Child, that the very definition of religion was located within the *"longing* for something not possessed," within the congeries of "unsatisfied desires, by which we are influenced to actions which may answer the ends of these desires." But those who would become Spiritualists found that the traditional sources of authority failed to address their desires. "Where is the balm," one prominent Spiritualist asked, "where the physician? Can the church, the state, the society, the schools of medical science, minister to this disease of a starved heart? Nay. They would blister and blast with curses."[4]

Drawn into the maelstrom of revivals in the search for spiritual clarity, many passed from sect to sect before lighting upon the spirits: before becoming "crystallized and ossified" within any sect, the "Spiritual Pilgrim" James M. Peebles experienced the ways of Presbyterianism, Baptism, infidelity, and Universalism in succession, while Thomas Richmond voyaged from Congregationalism through Methodism, Adventism, Universalism, and Presbyterianism. Even those safely in the nonevangelical fold, like the Unitarian abolitionist Giles Stebbins, gadded about the sects and seculars, dallying with old-time Congregationalism, transcendentalism, and free thought before settling on the spirits.[5]

What most distinguished the Spiritualist path, however, was not simply the failure to settle into denominational conformity but that at each transition they experienced an increasing unease, disoriented by the competing claims to authority, truth, and salvation. "To join the Congregational Church," Richmond wrote, "was saying, I am one of the 'elect.' To join the Universalists, was saying, God will take care of his offspring. Joining either of the others, was saying, we will try." Like the young Joseph Smith, exhausted by the "war of words" waged by competing revivalists, future Spiritualists turned inward to ask "who of all these parties are right, or, are they all wrong together?"[6]

For many, the answer was as obvious as it was succinct: "These churches of the living God, so called, are shams every one." For such minds the sight of a myriad of churches sacralizing the landscape could never promise the unification of the Christian body but seemed rather a symptom of its utter and irreparable rupture. "Behold families, communities, and nations," lamented Jesse Ferguson, "severed in their aims, in devotion to false views of man's Spiritual interests; men aiming professedly, at the same ends, while industriously engaged in each others injury or destruction." The "animating principle" that Ferguson saw behind "such enormous and brutal wrongs" was hatred, he insisted, not spiritual advancement, and the end result was social division and moral decay. Under threat of dissolution in the mortal world, the individual found no solace in the spiritual. The spirit of John Quincy Adams complained with eminent bile of the impact of "the antagonistic faiths of the churches" and how "their continual war-ring against one another, only serves to augment, in the minds of many, the gloomy belief of the soul's total extinction." Evangelicalism, for those without its fold, rang the death knell of the individual.[7]

For the spirit Adams, for Ferguson, and for many of their peers, the sharpening of theological and doctrinal boundaries by which the sects dis-tinguished themselves in gleaning souls served only to replicate and mul-tiply the social boundaries, the divisions of life that seekers such as Abby Sewall felt so keenly. In making their "chief aim . . . to build up sectarian platforms," Adams asserted, the churches had discarded the fundamental principles of Christianity, "the Fatherhood of God, and the Brotherhood of Man!" Although evangelical religion shone a powerful light on social and divine order and instilled an intense sense of earthly community for many Americans, it did not answer the needs of all. For those who could not, or would not, settle into denominational conformity, the repeated re-vivals only exacerbated the friability of life. In a culture in which religion had become the primary discourse through which social contestation took place, the scythe that threshed souls reaped with a double-edged blade.[8]

For Sewall, raised a Baptist and educated well in the whys of Calvinist doctrine, the thumping revivals left her passing Sundays at whichever church seemed most promising on the day, complaining that she did "not often hear such preaching" as she liked, though still eager to attend when the sermon appealed. When the topic of "the final triumph of the Re-deemer's kingdom" was announced, for example, she attended despite being "afflicted" with a headache, for to her the topic was "all engrossing and interesting, and dear to the heart of every true Christian, and philan-thropist."[9]

Balm for the horrors, however, would await the arrival of an itinerant phrenologist in Chesterfield in January 1851, a man come to lecture "on the subject of love, marriage, and happy domestic [l]ife besides temperance and religion." Offering to instruct the young in how to make a proper mar-riage "and how [to] retain the honeymoon in after life," this phrenologist offered incisive readings of character and lectured on the moral, mental, and physiological meaning of the shape of skulls. When he "treated the moral organs located in the top of the head," Sewall wrote, he dem-onstrated "how they were in perfect accordance with religion, and they were pure and holy in their original character." In short, he confirmed the unity of religion and morality, demonstrating that both were writ upon the very body of the believer, a natural emanation of the divine.[10]

In these simple phrenological facts, Sewall discovered a clarity that she had sought in vain among the sects and a way to interrogate, if not dissolve, the divisions that fractured American society. Although the phrenological sympathy advocated by George Combe was anything but socially constructive, Sewall and her eldest daughter, Augusta, absorbed an altogether different message from this itinerant apostle, one more consilient with the cognate theories of somnambulism current in New England. Augusta lauded the new science for its ability to expose human nature, claiming that the ability to peer within the hearts of others "fortified" a person "against the deceit and calumny of this changing world," making it possible to "judge the pretended friends whether they be true or false" and enabling one to "seek the society of the noble, brave and talented, and also shun that of the vile."[11]

If practiced widely, phrenology would penetrate social distance and prepare the way for a true sympathetic community in which the participants would be bound by a level of intimacy and mutuality of knowledge reserved, in Victorian ideology, only to the romantically paired. For the individual this new science promised as well to dissolve all barriers to self-knowledge and to knowledge of the divine. When the phrenological lens was aimed within, Augusta wrote, "we shall hence know our own characters,—know what we possess of right and wrong, that we may cull the good from the bad, preserve and cultivate it, and trample the bad in the dust." Through knowledge of the true character of man "as just emanated from the hand of his Maker," she continued, "we shall know a pure system of religion and morality undefiled of erring man." In short, what Adam Smith had sought to accomplish with a willful mental leap—the overcoming of affective isolation and autonomous individualism and the forging of community—phrenology offered through a new scientific, religious, and corporeal discipline.[12]

Experience with phrenology or with the intimately related discourses of mesmerism and somnambulism was one of the most consistent waymarkers on the path to Spiritualism. One of the early non-Spiritualist historians of the movement, Frank Podmore, concluded that the interest in somnambular phenomena, so "recently excited and still actively spreading," contributed immensely to "the cause of nascent Spiritualism." It furnished a large number of clairvoyants ready to spread the word, he suggested, and furnished a ready-made philosophy in the form of theories about electric, magnetic, and odyllic forces. Even the critics of early Spiritualism accepted the validity of the basic somnambulistic and mesmeric phenomena. As it had for Sewall, phrenology supplied a framework for interpreting human behavior and social relations in bodily terms. The ur-Spiritualist Andrew Jackson Davis used the bodily basis of phrenology, for instance, to interpret the characters of religions: Judaism with its God of power and wrath was a religion of the "nether regions of the brain"; Catholicism, Episcopalianism, and Presbyterianism, of the cerebellum; Quakerism, of the frontal regions (but not "a whole harmonious brain"); and Universalists and Unitarians approached being religions of a whole, "well-balanced" brain.[13]

In commuting from mesmerism to Spiritualism, Davis blazed a trail that many followed in the 1850s, but more importantly, he provided a vital link between the triple sympathetic discourses of the Enlightenment and the developing discourse of spirit communion. Davis's mesmeric visions of the afterlife dovetailed so neatly into the early Spiritualism that most commentators saw only continuity. Many of the trance lecturers described by Ann Braude lectured only while mesmerized and were often referred to by the mesmeric term *somnambule,* while Emma Hardinge, Leah Underhill (the eldest of the rapping Fox sisters), and A. J. Davis all exhibited a penchant for sleepwalking when young.[14]

Allen Putnam was typical in considering mesmerism as little more than the "lowest form of Spiritualism," an early stage in a continuum of mental phenomena that progressed "by easy and gradual ascent, from the simplest forms of Mesmerism up to the highest phases of Spiritualism," passing through the stage of "minds impressed, and speaking by impression" to culminate in phenomena that connected all of the universe, animate and inanimate, to the animate mind of humanity. Conceptually, spirit communion was often seen as operating through mesmeric relations, with spirits controlling mediums mesmerically, or for skeptics, the alleged supernatural origins of Spiritualist phenomena could be dismissed because they could be adequately explained by reference to the well-known facts of mesmerism.[15]

During the long winter of 1852–53, Sewall continued her journey to the spirits. Devouring a book on the "Spiritual Manifestations," she quickly convinced herself that Spiritualism was no "humbug" but was rather a "glorious" new doctrine that amounted "to nothing less than the final holiness and happiness of all mankind." The book electrified her life, the phenomena it described requiring no further verification than that which came from laying her heart "open to receive the pure ideas it advances," the "pure and holy ideas" that took the physical and material potentialities of phrenology and translated them into cosmic principles with tangible form.[16]

What Sewall surmised of the doctrinal basis of Spiritualism was scant but far-reaching. When asked what the spirits taught, she responded, "in the words of a believer," that they taught "first The immortality of the soul, secondly, The power of spirits to revisit the earth[,] thirdly, Their ability to communicate with relations and friends, and fo[u]rthly, The identity of the spirit to all eternity." When asked where these teachings would lead, she answered that they were already advancing the good of society, tearing down the separations of modern life. Spiritualism, she wrote, "is convincing the infidel of the truth of the christian religion, it is comforting the saints, and it is doing away that soul horrorfying idea of an endless hell. It teaches the doctrine of progression, it teaches that we are all the children of one Father, that none are so base as to be forever excluded from his mercy, that there is correction or discipline for all, that all are to be 'washed and made white in the blood of the Lamb.'"[17]

According to Sewall, the facts of Spiritual phenomena proved "that there are noble essences in heaven, that bear a friendly regard unto their friendly natures on the earth," implying that no one was ever truly alone and none need rely solely upon their own strength or ever become a "poor, forlorn [wanderer], with no guide save the suggestions of our corrupt nature." The spirits taught that the divisions of social life, of distance, death, and pain, were illusory, while the structures of affect and sympathy were real, tangible, and eternal. "When we think of the anguish of parting with those we love," she wrote,

> of looking for the last time on the face which has smiled away our cares—how gladly do we cling to the idea of their returning to soothe our distress, and lend their invisible influence to bind the bruised heart! Such a belief softens the bit-

terness of separation, robs death of its sting, and causes "the desert to blossom as a rose." How painful the thought that the loves and friendships, and all other endearments which lend a charm to existance, must perish with the hearts last throb! But let us believe that the love once so found, faded not with lifes taper, but even now "softly trembles with a pulse as true as ours,"—that the friend once so warm and pure, is still sympathizing in our joys and woes,—let us cling to the hope, for in it the bitterness of death is past.[18]

It is noteworthy that Sewall's belief quickened well before she had gained personal experience with the spirits; hers was a belief founded solely upon the written word. Until an opportunity to attend a séance presented itself, she continued halfheartedly to attend Methodist, Baptist, and other services, though increasingly glad to bow out when an excuse was possible (a misplaced bonnet, a headache). More tellingly, she became increasingly hostile toward the "sects," envisioning a day when the new doctrine would do "great work towards overthrowing priestcraft and its abominations." In contrast to sectarians, who shunned the good-hearted "infidel," she argued that spirits sought out their infidel friends to convince them of the fact of immortality, as was perfectly natural, because spirits "retain the same affection for us" as when in the flesh "and want to do us good." While sectarians divided the world into sheep and goats, always careful to reserve "a hell for their neighbors," the spirits ministered across the flock, teaching, as Sewall insisted, "that all will be happy, [and] the most degraded and sinful, enter into a state, where they commence improvement."[19]

This insight encouraged her to confront other "errors" in her upbringing, errors "heard from the pulpit, and . . . drilled into me before I had wisdom enough to think for myself." Relentlessly, and to her sister's dismay, she cataloged the most egregious examples:

An angry God on a great white throne, dispensing laws, and for the least violation of them he would hurl them into an endless hell of fire and brimstone, there they would duffer forever and ever. . . .

Another error is that God Almighty was born of a woman four thousand years after he had made woman, and then died on the cross to appease his own wrath.

Another error is the burning up of the world, and the resurrection of the earthly body after death, and finally of the day of judgement at the end of the world. . . .

Another is in throwing our sins onto Christ, and so evade the just penalty of sin. There is no way to get rid of sin, but by repentance, and growing out of the condition in which we sin.

Predestination was wrong; original sin, and infant damnation, and the rest of the "rubbish of church creeds, and church forms" were wrong, leaving Sewall longing to clear away the baggage of creed, "to cultivate the spiritual [l]ife of God in the soul," and to experience the sort of faith exemplified by the spirits, a faith "found only by retiring into the secret chamber of the soul, and there finding all of heaven that will ever do us any good here or hereafter."[20]

The edge of Sewall's antisectarianism, however, should be tempered with the recognition that antisectarianism was not supported by all Spiritualists with the same degree of vituperation and, more importantly, was cited as only one of several sources of social friability. Spiritualists such as Herman Snow railed against the "destructive antagonism" of some of his peers and their "sweeping denunciation against all religions," warning that such attitudes (the hangover, he believed, of their former infidelity) made them "about as exclusive and bigoted in their Spiritualism as are the most narrow of the sects in their adherence to their creeds." Snow's attention was centered instead on other forms of "narrowness" and social division, including political partisanship, race hatred, and aristocracy. In other words, "Demon Sectarism" could find abundant assistance in dissecting the social body.[21]

The story of the struggling, working-class Scots immigrant Kirk Cunningham suggests some of the ways in which the vagaries of social experience lent shape to Spiritualist views. A religious seeker like Sewall, though inclined more toward occultism than anything akin to orthodoxy, Cunningham faced the 1850s with sinking finances and a raft of tensions between his brothers and a domineering wife. After failing as a farmer in Massachusetts (having chosen, he said, the wrong sort of cattle for a seaside farm), Cunningham hoped to escape ill fortune by removing to Alabama. But after drifting from job to job as a saw filer or lock repairman, when he worked at all, and finding nothing to better his condition, Cunningham was led to a desperate attempt to change his fortune: parting from his wife to take a chance in the goldfields of California.

It was thus alone in San Francisco that Cunningham had a fateful encounter in 1855 with Andrew Jackson Davis's *Great Harmonia,* an experience that threw "the vail of superstition by Mythology & Theology, all aside," teaching "Spiritualism on the most sublime & phylosifical Systome." Despite his dire circumstances he wrote that the book "cheers the soul" and made him "thankfull for the existance of our being as a glorious gift from the hand of Almighty God." "Milton was a sublime poet," he wrote, "but Davise is a sublime *teacher.*"[22]

What Cunningham found was not relief from his financial woes but a new perspective on them. Having hoped that the golden West would open its financial doors, he found himself instead thrust headlong into the fringes of an industrial economy as scarcely legible as Sewall found the world before phrenology. Davis sharpened Cunningham's critical eye, now privileged with a view of society in which all social ties had been extinguished by a radical competitive individualism. "Self stands nearest to each & every one here," he wrote to his wife, "indeed so much so that the social & generous feelings are scarcely *readable* so small & dim. Go a head & legal thieving is the order of the day; Educated savageism marks the genaral feature of this advanced age—In small communities & rural life there may be some what of the grasp of friendship, but scarcely otherways. Artificial good nature (politeness) is the substitute." Politically, too, the consequences of disunity were dire. In 1852 a spiritual delegation of Jews had informed Davis that the "miracle" of the Jewish Diaspora was the product of their internal divisions. "A house divided against itself," he was told, "must fall; even so with the Jews as a nation. They separated, as every nation must, when the Law of Internal Unity is violated or disregarded."[23]

For Cunningham, as for Davis, capitalism, individualism, sectarianism, the cities, and "go a head & legal thieving" were the main agents in dissecting the social body, though other Spiritualists complained equally, at turns, of Socialism, the practice of marriage, labor relations, "aristocracy," chattel slavery, capital punishment, political parties, alcohol use, or the oppression of women and Indians. Spiritualists espoused a stunning range of social views, united by opposition to neither sect nor aristocrat per se but rather to the manner in which these were conceived as contributing to the dissolution of social bonds. In various combinations the church, the economy, race, and gender became means of conceptualizing the boundaries separating persons. In Spiritualist cosmology these boundaries were experienced in a particularly visceral fashion as tearing away of the organic integrity of the social body until, as S. B. Brittan insisted, that "body is rent in pieces and the fragments are scattered and quivering in the pangs of expiring life."[24] Significantly, death—the ultimate socially isolating experience—could be experienced as social disintegration. Anna Parsons, a friend of the Unitarian-cum-Spiritualist James Freeman Clark, described her sensation upon lingering near death in peculiarly resonant terms. "She felt the soul making an effort to break away from the body," Clarke reported, "& the spirit watching patiently from above, for the result.—Death, she said, she had got a distinct idea of, as *disintegration*, the loss of unity—the unifying principle.—She felt every particle in her body struggling to fly apart from the rest, & that was dying—if this had succeeded she had been dead."[25]

Parsons's and Brittan's words penetrate to the core of Spiritualist experience: social boundaries of all sorts were conceived of and experienced with reference to the body and physical and emotional sensation, reflexive responses in what might be called a Spiritualist social physiology. While physiologists conceived of sympathetic responses as the products of physical sensations transmitted between a body's organs and systems by electrical impulse, Spiritualists imagined them as extending beyond the confines of the physical body, connecting the organs and systems of all of society, all of creation. Unconstrained by material considerations, sympathy broke down the barriers within and beyond by establishing a comprehensive community of sensation. Sympathetic exchange resulted in a tight, organically integrated social body in which threats to the unity of the system were felt and responded to throughout, and in which all members of society exerted an influence mutually upon all others. "If Spiritualism teaches anything," William Stainton Moses wrote, "it teaches us surely, to work & not to dream: to look with revered gaze & rational mind into the truths revealed, but not to rest in dreamy curiosity & leave plain work undone."[26]

This is precisely the logic that spurred the Spiritualist editor Alonzo E. Newton to implore his readers to "grapple with and remove the gigantic and oppressive wrongs and evils which burden our present society," as a necessary step in preserving the health of the social organism. Only by action, he reasoned, could humanity "put an end to poverty and fear of starvation, to unfriendly competition in trade and labor, to temptations to the commission of crime, to antagonistic interests and the oppressions of wars which grow out of them." Until these plans were put into comprehensive effect, Spiritualism would no better be able to satisfy the "the yearnings of Humanity's great heart" than the church had been, and it would do little more than "feed the people on husks of *theory,* and not the true Bread of *practical life.*" Until these Spiritualist plans were enacted, the barriers within society could never be dissolved but would merely be replaced with others. What was needed, Newton insisted, was a "thorough re-construction of society on a new basis—on the basis of unselfish Fraternity, instead of unmitigated selfishness. And this is to be done, not by supinely waiting for 'spirits' or 'God' or 'Nature's Law of Progression' *to do it for us;* but by actively and earnestly taking hold of the work ourselves. It is *through us,* as coacting, intelligent agents, that superior Powers accomplish the elevation of our race."[27]

The cure for the centrifugal tendencies of modern life, Spiritualists insisted, was for the disparate members of the social body to unite, to "become one body—harmoniously constituted, and then the whole will be animated by the spirit of God." As nations, as individuals, sympathy promised coherence. A. J. Davis believed that the faded nations of the world were actively seeking union among themselves and when they "perfected" their "spiritual sympathy," their "*unity*" would "exert its energizing, its silent influence upon the corresponding nations still remaining on earth" and "the *same most excellent consummation will be possible* among all the nations, kindreds, and tongues that are now every where disunited and inharmoniously diversifying the globe." Such prospects led Josiah Brigham to urge his readers to "draw no line of demarcation to your sympathies; but let them range all immensity, blessing and ennobling all upon whom they descend!"[28]

From its rich instantiations in somnambular and mesmeric practice, sympathetic theory made such hopes possible. Sympathy offered a means of interpreting the changing shape of the political body and a ready way both for somaticizing those feelings and reifying conceptions of the unified physical and social body. The spirits insisted that sympathy was not mere sentiment; "this is not true of what we mean by 'sympathy,'" as one told A. J. Davis. Sympathy entailed a complete consonance of emotional and bodily states between persons; "it is like the sun's influence on vegetation," the spirit said, "or as the action of the brain upon the members of the body." Religion, politics, race, science, and the "body" were no longer separate discourses but discourses each of complex structure, that intertwined, informed, and competed with one another in dynamic fashion. The curious admixture of the languages of physiology, reform, romantic love, science, and religion that characterizes Spiritualist writing results from this fusion, creating a ground in which the telegraph might have as much effect on emotion as a shift from a Calvinist to a Universalist eschatology or the creation of a republic or the extension of suffrage or the abolition of slavery. And at the bottom is a particular battle over how the self is constituted, how it is to be configured, and how it relates with other selves in society.[29]

Yet for Americans struggling to cope with the modern sense of privacy, with the anonymity of urban and industrial spaces, and with the "burdens of [autonomous] individualism," this perspective posed a potential threat to the identity and integrity of the individual that required a response. It promised, in effect, to elide individuality in favor of unity, effacing the individual more effectively than any factory or faith could. It is little coincidence, then, that the final stage in the conversion of many antebellum Spiritualists came through one of its central rituals, the divulgence of a spirit's true identity by the exposure of information shared only with living intimates.[30]

Abby Sewall's epiphany, for instance, came when she attended her first séance in March 1855, more than two years after her introduction to Spiritualism. In the aptly named town of Temple, Maine, she and her brother-in-law William spent an evening with the Sampsons, husband and wife mediums who specialized in tilting tables. William took the lead in questioning their "spirit friends," according to Abby. "Have you had a child enter the spirit world lately," he asked. The spirit answered yes. "'How long since' then there came six raps, he then said 'Do you mean these raps for years.' 'no.' 'for months,' 'no.' 'for days,' 'yes.' It was just six days since sister died. The mediums looked up and said 'is that right' not knowing that he had so lately lost a sister."[31]

This revelatory detail, this affirmation of continuing personal identity, steeled Sewall's faith. Some inquirers, she suspected, might be swayed by mere words, but like many converts possessed of a skeptical mind, she confessed that she could never fully believe until she had experienced for herself "the evidence of the existance of the departed," confirmed by the spirit's willingness to "come back and identify themselves to me." Such evidence was often contained in the most trivial details, as in a séance described by James Freeman Clarke, in which the spirit of Harriet Mudge appeared to a Mr. Brackett and identified herself by recalling an obscure lesson Brackett had taught her years before in Sunday school. In contrast, when Clarke's own son appeared the next morning, identifying himself by little more than name, Clarke commented that the experience was "pleasant & sweet" but "it did not impress me with the conviction which I had in the evening."[32]

More dramatic episodes often seemed counterfactual. When contacted by a spirit claiming to be his brother Natty, the brotherless Allen Putnam grasped for surer proofs than personal memory. "How do you know I am your brother?" asked Putnam. "'By love,' he answered. 'By love?' said the questioner. 'But don't you love others as well as relatives?' Ans. 'We like others, and love relatives.' 'What,' it was then asked,—'what is the difference between love and like?' The word 'LOVE' was immediately written in large letters, two or three inches long, and 'like' was traced under it in very small letter." Heartened by these words, Putnam confirmed the affective proof when he discovered that unbeknownst to him, a brother had indeed died in infancy. Material reality, in this instance, conformed to spiritual truth. What might appear to critics as witless credulity was, at least in some cases, a reliance upon a different logical and epistemological standard. While critics sought "independent" verification of spiritual veracity, looking to the concordance of spirit messages with material experience, Spiritualists sought out the sympathetic dependencies, looking to the implicit relationships between the material and spiritual worlds.[33]

Natty's lesson was confirmed repeatedly. A spirit chastening the medium M. T. Shelhamer, for instance, bemoaned the fact that when "expressing their love and sympathy," too many spirits had their efforts at communication "repulsed with distrust and suspicion" due to their inability to meet proofs based on "material affairs." "Were I upon earth," Shelhamer wrote,

> understanding this matter as I now do, I would accept a loving, kindly communication, purporting to come from a spirit friend, not with over credulity, but with the thought it may come from my friend who is not yet able to give me all I wish to know; but I will not reject this token of love, lest in doing so I spurn

and wound my loving spirit friend. In this way I would throw out a ladder of reciprocal love, upon which my dear one could descend and bear me tidings of immortal life, thereby strengthening conditions, until that spirit gained power to give me all my soul required.[34]

In séance the moment at which the sympathetic bonds of spirit and communicant were revealed became the heart of Spiritualist practice, linking both the emotional and intellectual facets of Spiritualist discourse. In case after case the exposure of a spirit's obscure personal quirk or the utterance of a distinctive term of endearment confirmed the personal and often private basis of sympathy with the living participant, unleashing a flood of emotions. Overwhelmed at confirming the spiritual identity of his nephew, his instance, one man effused, "O! think of the joy—the thrilling Joy at this unexpected event. Mourn no more for the loss a dear soul—he lives! he lives! in a Glorious world of light & love." The revelatory gesture was never simply the means of confirming spiritual identity: it stood proxy for something greater, the immortality of affect and identity and the existence of a "ladder of reciprocal love" uniting even the most dissociated of worlds. This revelatory ritual demonstrated the endurance of individual identity, and like the sharing of secrets between lovers, it validated the intimacy that bound spirit to mortal, the next world to this. It was the final element in galvanizing a belief in the spirits.[35]

Even when the spirits appeared as disembodied raps or as the tilt of a table, their emotional impact was profound, and the feeling they established, real and persistent. "Sometimes when I have been conversing with them," Sewall wrote, "I have gazed at the table as though I would penetrate the veil that covers them from my view, and have said mentally, 'mother dear mother is it you.'" In moments of reflection, she often felt "as though the loved ones are with me," watching, communing, extending their sympathies. "O how sweet and pure the influence from those dear friends," she continued, describing the sensation, "a hallo of purity seems to surround, and a sweet voice seems to call me away to my spirit home. In such moments I am a firm believer in immortality."[36]

The critical lesson to be learned was that mortals, like the spirits, must seek to expand their circle of "benevolent feelings," to spark, in James Freeman Clarke's words, "an interest in the sufferings of others who are at a distance from us" and make an effort "to extend our sympathies beyond 'the little limits of our own State and neighborhood.'" When faced with the temptation to withdraw from the troubles of mortal life into the serenity of spirits, Sewall reminded herself to "wait a little while and let me do a little more for my family."[37]

Sewall's experiences convinced her that the affective relations established in life survived death to create a framework of love and emotion through which spirits operated and through which society became community. In the mortal world these divine principles demanded social investment, demanded that the influence of the spirits spill out of the parlor into daily life. "Now I have a surety that I, even poor I," Sewall wrote to her sister, "will, in the better world find full range for the exercise of my benevolent feelings, cramped, and pen[n]ed up as I have always been, and confined to do good only to a few, but in that better world my spirit will expand, and united with the loved of earth we shall find time to do that good to our race which we have been deprived of doing on earth. We shall come to you if you are here dear sister and strengthen and encourage you and bid you hope till you will join us in the same blessed work."[38]

Thus in struggling with the experiences of life and death at midcentury, Spiritualists imagined and felt divisions anastamosing throughout the body of the nation, and they responded sympathetically. Spiritualism offered tangible evidence that the most refractory barrier on earth, the barrier of death, could be transcended by the power of sympathy operating within a profoundly integrated social body. To examine the operation of this social physiology, I now turn to its most distinctive elements: sympathy, transparency, unboundedness, and progress, the therapeutic quartet that brokered the Spiritualist vision of national healing.

SOCIAL PHYSIOLOGY: SYMPATHY AND TRANSPARENCY

"I am now of this world as much as you are," said Red Jacket, an Indian spirit controlling the medium C. T. Buffum. "I see through the organs of this brain only, and hear through these ears, and that is the reason why, as you perceive, I have so much difficulty in hearing what other spirits tell me, as I have to depend upon them for all your spirit-friends say. I can see your spirit-friends—one, or sometimes more, at a time, but not steadily, and then they appear as if a veil were between them and me, so that my seeing and hearing them are difficult, and sometimes I cannot see or hear them at all. But the moment I relinquish control then I resume my natural spiritual condition."[39]

In describing communion with mortals, spirits like Red Jacket spoke of entering into a "community of sensation," a holistic sharing of body, mind, and soul that established a unique experience of the self. Persons (and spirits) in sympathetic rapport described sharing organs, thoughts, and sensations, physical and emotional. In such a state, according to the Christian Spiritualist Eugene Crowell, "the mind of the controlling spirit and that of the medium become blended," enabling the spirit to use "the entire organism of the medium, precisely as the spirit proper to the body uses it." In effect, they became a single, extended being, a reciprocal self.[40]

In casting about for an explanation of this unique state of being, Spiritualists latched onto the latest developments in medical physiology and particularly onto the function of electricity in the nervous system, though they steadfastly distinguished their views from the archmaterialism of neurophysiologists. From Charles Bell's discovery of the differentiation of the nervous system in the first decade of the century through Marshall Hall's discovery of the reflex function in the 1830s, physiologists had laid an increasingly elaborate foundation for understanding the relation between psychology and physiology. As somnambulism had before it, the presence in the reflex function of motor response with neither volition nor consciousness on the part of the organism challenged the divide between body and mind, suggesting a greater intimacy between psychology and physiology than had previously been assumed. In the extreme, neurologists like William Hammond reduced mind to little more than "a force, the result of nervous action," and concluded that the "spinal cord and sympathetic ganglia are not devoid of mental power." While neurophysiologists of the 1850s explored this intimacy, coining the term *psychophysiology* to describe their field, Spiritualists began to imbue it with more transcendent potential.[41]

Antebellum Spiritualists held an ambiguous relationship with contemporary scientific practice, combining an exuberant embrace of its methods and products with a resistance to the extremes of both supernaturalism and hypermaterialism. R. Laurence Moore, in particular, has emphasized the Spiritualists' adamantine rejection of supernaturalism in their discussions of (and with) the dead, claiming instead that they adhered strictly to natural law and observable, verifiable fact. According to Moore, Spiritualists regularly egged on their audience with the empiricist call to "try the spirits." Like Swedenborg before them, they saw no conflict between religion and science but rather attempted to co-opt the cultural authority of science, incorporating its products more integrally than epistemological concerns alone would suggest.[42]

Proclaiming theirs a "rational religion"—or, like Napoleon Wolfe, that theirs was "greater" than religion, "it is science"—Spiritualists eschewed the mystical in favor of the empirical and invested the spiritual world with a range of material, technological marvels. As Benjamin Franklin appeared at séances enrapt over his new electrical devices and Michael Faraday discussed spiritual chemistry, a host of anonymous spirits contrived to improve the lives of mortals through the mechanical mastery gained by spiritual insight. Spirits and Spiritualists seemed to strive for a means at once to naturalize and spiritualize science, mimetically reproducing its structures within the spirit world to incorporate the epistemologically foreign and threatening, to embody it, enact and consume it, and render it part of their quotidian lives.[43]

Yet Spiritualist attention to technological and scientific productions was highly selective, lavished primarily upon a select number of innovations in communications technology and travel. Canals, steam power, and rail in particular were lauded for enabling a person "to convey his thoughts and his person much more widely, speedily, and definitely to people and places on the earth," for drawing the distant in life within daily view. With the invention of steam power, A. J. Davis argued, Christianity could now take a "seat in the cars" and fly "speedily from state to state," or by ocean liner from port to port, to pay "morning calls to the heathen and the oppressed." Thanks to science and its new technologies, "theology" could now spread its healing balms across "a continent or a hemisphere." As if to emphasize this point, when the Fox sisters first left Hydesville for Rochester, their journey along the Erie Canal was accompanied by the symbolic sounds of spirits whistling and hooting in imitation of trains.[44]

More than anything, telegraphy became the hub of the antebellum Spiritualist cosmos, those arcane clicks that, as Uriah Clark was informed, "have a significance which anon rocks the continent with thrilling intelligence." Paired with electricity and magnetism—the phenomena that "steadily approximate the rank of demi-gods"—telegraphy served not only as a description of communication between mortal and spirit but as a harbinger of things to come. It heralded an unfettered age in which a person might "sit on Aladdin's tapestry," as Sarah Grimké wrote, and "pass off into electricity & go through the telegraphic wires" to join a friend, a loved one, or a political ally wherever they might be. An "electric telegraph trip-train," as Uriah Clark wrote, was an opportunity to visit "the other world, and have a message now and then from those dear ones we have loved and lost."[45]

In Spiritualist thought telegraphy began with the nervous impulses of the physical body and expanded outward. The Tennesseean Samuel Watson, for one, understood "our natural body" as telegraphing throughout "its members," with the electrical impulses riding nerves between organs and mind, transmitting and translating thought and sensation in such a manner that all were surrounded by "a mental atmosphere by which mind impresses mind." Epes Sargeant analogized the sensation of hearing the "inner voice" of spirits with "the sensation which would be caused by a telegraphic apparatus being hooked on to one of the nerve ganglia."[46]

But telegraphy rapidly passed from this physical basis into the sort of all-encompassing reciprocity of selves experienced by Red Jacket and Eugene Crowell. In connecting spirits, freed of the physical body, it promoted an intense fusion. Hudson Tuttle explained that when "a sympathetic cord is established" between two spirits "in such a manner that thoughts flow on it, from mind to mind, as electric fluid on the telegraphic wire," minds become united "and their thoughts become in unison."[47]

The extent of this fusion should not be underestimated: as one of the earliest spirit mediums declared, the fusion was so thoroughgoing that "space was nearly annihilated" and time had little meaning. The spirit of Deborah Franklin explained that for spirits, any distance was "traversed with the speed of thought," enabling instantaneous communion with "embodied" friends and disembodied, however distant they may be. "We mingle together," she wrote; "we have no walls of separation that confine us." Such "literally instantaneous" communication led Cora Daniels to deduce that "a place can be away and near at the same moment" and that there could "be no separation of space where there is no separation of time," such that every event on earth, present and future, would be known immediately in heaven. "There is constant telegraphy" between the two, she wrote, and ideas, like sensations, fired "without the loss of the millionth part of a second," as rapidly as nervous impulses fired from finger to brain. Physiologically and psychologically, spirits were boundless, a fact that William Denton built into the very definition of Spiritualism. "Spiritualism," he wrote, "is first a belief that man possesses a spirit (the unseen man) that is not bound by the limitation of the senses, but can see without using the bodily eye, hear when no sound is conveyed to the outward ear, and can travel without the body's organs of locomotion."[48]

The boundlessness of sympathy that promised to liberate the "unseen man," the true self, was a concept that resonated in both physiological and psychological registers. Spiritualist sympathy was "omnipresent," an architectonic element that pervaded "the whole ethereal ocean, in which suns and stars and planets and comets swim." It lay "around them all, and in them all; it reached everywhere, from point to point, throughout the limitless universe." Sympathy opened whole new realms of sensation that blossomed into the same "psychological" phenomena that had been seen among somnambulists, including "seeing without the use of the bodily eyes," clairvoyance, thought transference, adventitious sensation, and extracorporeal travel.[49]

This unveiling of new senses lent an occult cast to some Spiritualist interpretations of sympathy, even when it was analogized with the natural phenomenon of electricity: Spiritualists asserted that there was more to sympathy than met the nervous system. It was a "divinity of nature," wrote Charles Hammond; "it controls even animals. It will control enemies. It is a divinity that no enemy can resist. It will conquer." Shared between mortals, it could well up as a primitive force; between mortals and spirit it would spread inexorably, drawing kindred minds and spirits together "until all nature smiles with the love of God," until "all minds are linked together forming a chain of affinity co-extensive with the whole world, in heaven and on earth, and united by an immortal tie which no change will dissolve, but strengthen, forever and ever" (fig. 2). It was a cosmological constant that Sarah Grimké witnessed in operation, even at the molecular level. Nowhere was it more clearly seen, she wrote, than in the "phenomenon of crystallization. When several salts that have little analogy of constitution are dissolved in the same body of water, they are separated by crystallization: their respective units move towards each other & segregate into crystals of their respective kinds." Scientific rationality might shed light on the operation of sympathy, but sympathy might shed light on science as well.[50]

Through similar extensions sympathy created a universe of the body and a body of the universe, establishing a true social physiology. Although generally possessed of a Platonic disdain for the physical body, Spiritualists such as Kirk Cunningham traveled between body and spirit with ease. Having consumed his portion of Davis and grazed on the works of others, Cunningham gleaned that because the world was populated by a host of sympathetic "spiritual existancies" who influenced mortals for divine ends, the human spirit must then be a "real substance as shure as light, magnitism & electricity are substances," and thus "the sole of man (ie Male & female) is a real being, which actuates every motion of our narvise & muscular systome." Mental activity was a product of the influence of an "inbred Spirit," so tightly correlated with the bodily systems that health, happiness, and pain were all subject to mental influence.[51]

For Cunningham such observations established a corporeal consonance between mind and sensation, meaning that every thought would "vibrate every narve in fear, grief, love, or joy," every action of the mind would operate on the physical conditions of food or drink, clothing or habitation, to influence the body's overall health. The details of daily life—diet, dress, decorum—thus assumed a significance for the way in which they were integrated within the health of the entire being and the manner with which the being was integrated within society. But parting company with materialist conceptions of the unity of body and mind, Cunningham asserted the primacy of mind over William Hammond's dead body. Recognizing that the "mind or thinking principle tyranized over my boddy," Cunningham theorized that the cooperation of "psychology, Sympathy, & the temperaments" poised the body at the interface between the interior and exterior worlds. From without, the body was operated on through the "meadium of the sences," but at the same time it was "psychologised intarnaly, or mentaly from the internal action of the or working of the mind." This, he concluded, was clearly "the instrumentality by which the mind exerts its will."[52]

FIG. 2. Psychic force liberated from a spirit circle led by the medium John Beattie, in Bristol, England, 1872. *Left to right:* Beattie, Butland, Daniel Josty (photographer), unidentified man. (Eugène Rochas Papers, American Philosophical Society)

So coextensive with the cosmos was the body that S. B. Brittan conceived of the universe itself as an "infinite Sensorium," from the heart of which "the vital currents flow out through all the arteries of Being." The "vital currents"—sympathy—were the life force behind social physiology, like the nervous force that transforms the parts of a physical body into a single, sensing whole, tying the physiology of the individual into the more comprehensive physiology of society as a whole. To be in sympathy was to exist in a state in which mind and body, self and other, matter and spirit, sacred and profane, dissolved as distinct entities. Although the limitations of the flesh impeded the perceptions of the spirit, once freed the spirit saw nothing but continuity from body and sensation through spirit and the divinity. "All life is the action of Mind on Matter," Brittan maintained; "it is the revelation of a spiritual presence—of God's presence!" For the spirit, it made possible the claim, "I *feel* your minds."[53]

Seemingly paradoxically, this unbounded force was constrained to flow through predictable channels. Where the telegraph required the wire, and the reflex, the nerve, sympathy required the immaterial lines of "affinity." With few exceptions spirits were drawn only to persons with whom they shared strong affective ties in life, whether of spirit, mind, or blood. Sympathy drew spirits to earth, but communication across the grave was inherently difficult, requiring persons of "peculiar organism and culture" to act as mediums, and a strong affinity between spirit and mortal was required to complete the circuit. Where no "*natural* tie" existed, few spirits could go, but within the family, where the strongest and most natural ties accrued, neither consciousness nor mature deliberation was required to set sympathy in motion. Emma Hardinge was certain that spirit children were drawn irresistibly to the loved and living, "and sometimes even embryotic births" came calling. Fully two-thirds of the spirits she had brought into contact with mortals, she claimed, were under the age of twenty.[54]

Spouses were among the most frequent spiritual visitors, and marriage was one of the most frequent metaphors by which Spiritualists understood and experienced sympathetic union. In charting the path of marital love at midcentury and its implications for the experience of personal identity, Karen Lystra has traced the increasing bifurcation of a sense of privacy and publicity to an experiential split between the "real self" that was experienced (in the words of the cognitive anthropologist Roy D'Andrade) as an "internal place, where what happens is natural, unique, and the center of human agency," and the social self that "consists of the roles and masks one has to wear in the 'real world.'" The new ethic of romantic love and its epitome, marriage, were the ground on which the real self and social self met *mano a mano*.[55]

The desperate search for real selves among the social masks became a characteristic enterprise of antebellum American culture, whether expressed in concerns about confidence men or humbugs, until by the later decades of the century, writers began openly to confront the possibility that the "real" self had failed to survive the unmoorings and drift of modern life. With Lockean echoes chiming, a contributor to *Atlantic Monthly* lamented "when we once cut loose from geography, make friends and break with friends, become the very opposite of 'Bourbons' in that we are always even poor I, 'learning' and always 'forgetting,' then how far backward over our days can the uninterrupted 'I' be said to extend? . . . In truth, this whole matter of the individual identity—the I-ness of the I—is thick with difficult questions."[56]

In severing social and affective ties and the memories they entailed, the swift pace of modern life, its ruptures and departures, threatened the soul of personal identity. Lystra suggests, however, that a new ethic of romantic love in marriage helped preserve an "I-ness," a "true" and enduring identity in the midst of this fray, by creating a domain in which the real self was freely expressed. This ethic, she argues, was part of a complex negotiation that bridged the dichotomy of public and private, driving "an emotional and intellectual shift in world view toward the individual self." Through courtship and marriage lovers shared their secret, interior thoughts, revealing aspects of their "true" selves beneath the social gloss to construct "unique, emotional bonds" that simultaneously "emphasized their individuality, their distinctiveness, and their separateness." Whether in the form of billets-doux or sweet spoken words, "intimate communication between individuals" disclosed the real self, compartmentalized within the marital bond but intact.[57]

Thus freighted, modern marriage was a primary interest of Spiritualists, who extolled the virtues of sympathetic exchange for overcoming the "inharmonies, disorders and miseries" that were propagating within the affective heart of Victorian America. Modern marriages, as the editor A. E.

Newton argued, were too often struck for "convenience, love of ease or personal comfort, desire for show or pecuniary advantage, wishes of parents or friends, and, perhaps, oftener than all, mere animal passion," all of which were "dangerous to the welfare of the mind." Teaching "deception" to the loveless wife and promoting social disharmony by binding "discordant minds together, to fight and wrangle with each other," the spirits considered "conventional marriage" to be "the root of all evil."[58]

But, as Uriah Clark claimed, the spirits were gradually revealing "the laws of conjugal love, of true marriage, of sexual purity, of home harmony, and of the relations between parents and children," and these would "reveal the falsities and infernal discords of the past." The ideal sympathetic marriage, as described by James Freeman Clarke, was "a union or blending of soul—a melting of two willing hearts in one—an intertwining of the inner natures in a wedlock, which no human law can make or put asunder." In his own marriage he and his wife were "coming nearer and nearer" as they aged, "and I think we are to come nearer yet," he wrote, "to inter-penetrate each others' lives more and more, and to belong to each other more intimately and entirely." In such marriages, the feminist Caroline Dall wrote, "the stream of life would flow for both in one—there could be no concealment—of thought act or feeling, for the heart throbs of one—would be felt by both." In such marriages the reciprocal selfhood of mortal husband and wife would approximate the union of spirits.[59]

Such sympathetic marriages were contagious, according to A. J. Davis, promising to spread their benefits throughout society. When "agreeably united in the conjugal sympathies," he wrote, two "finally grow into analogous manners and habits of life," resulting in a condition in which "human interests are not intrinsically conflicting, but one, *and only one!*" Such harmonious tendencies produced a condition in which "all members must suffer when one suffers" and, by the same token, in which "the happiness of one is the happiness of all! The solidarity of the race is immovably predicated upon this mental law of interpenetration!" Dividing the "world of mind," whether living or dead, "into opposite parties and factions, or even to have the mental tendency to do a thing so prejudicially to human happiness and universal Brotherhood," simply reiterated the old sectarian tendencies to division, sacrificing "Reason" in its wake."[60]

A. B. Child adopted the term *soul affinity* to refer to the concept that "every man has a spirit bride, and every woman has a spirit bridegroom." Evoking the Aristophanic fable of the sexes, with bright tinges of Swedenborg, he asserted that "to perfect human existence, the male and the female, blended, are essential," and he claimed that every person born into the physical world has a counterpart in the spirit world with whom they are united and "inseparably blended" forever. "Pure affinity," he concluded, "makes all the love and all the ties of the spiritual world, and all these affections and ties are eternal. Pure affinity between a male and female soul is all the marriage that a spirit can know." It was the power of pure affinity that John Murray Spear hoped to harness in creating a perpetual-motion machine powered by nothing more than the bodily union of sympathetically paired men and women.[61]

The fallibility of the mortal world, as Spiritualists knew, ensured that true affinity might never be attained until the spirit had departed the body and come "under the control of the law of spiritual attractions." Then the "rightly mated" would converge, forever to "remain as one." If separated, they would never be truly apart, for they were "*united* in the truest sense, the sensations of both being still impressed upon a common brain-center." Both spiritual bride and groom shared an extended physiology, experiencing "mental and spiritual ecstasies somewhat like those resulting from a harmony of sounds or colors in the earthly life, only *intensified* and to a degree wholly inconceivable by those still in the mortal body." With synesthesia and the exchange of sentiment binding them, they hastened the day that "earth and the spirit conditions would be brought so nearly together, that there would be an almost constant blending of the personal experiences of those in each."[62]

Within these hopes lay the idea that sympathy and the liberation of bodily constraints would lead to a universal transparency, a concatenation of "real" selves that would propagate the spiritual intimacy of marriage throughout society. Spirits "manifest a power to read the thoughts, feelings and emotions which are concealed deep in the recesses of the soul," Joel Tiffany wrote, even those "which have taken upon themselves no exterior form of expression." Spirits recall long-forgotten facts, see distant events, answer "difficult questions in philosophy" or mathematics, and they communicate in foreign languages. Asked "mental" questions, they respond "with equal facility with those which are put in audible words"; sent a written missive in a sealed envelope, they answer without the need for eyes, for to spirits, the world of thought and sensation was transparent and unified. When spirits and mortals became mutually transparent, a perfect intimacy of knowledge and blending of memories, experiences, and sensations would usher in a new society.[63]

Such promises might hold even in friendship. A recently departed spirit informed Cora Daniels that in life, "I was not aware that I literally sent my body out of my body to you, and used a mutual friend to express some of my feelings and sentiments toward you. But it seems that I did actually do so. I can hardly believe the fact that when still I was a living man, pursuing my vocations in a distant city, that this spirit, this actual I, used to leave that body and converse with you by animating the thoughts of our mutual friend, influencing him to go to you and using him as a medium through whom I could have the pleasure of grasping your hand."[64]

In sympathetic congress mortals, like spirits, interacted according to intuitive principles and, through "spontaneous, unique, free actions without social constraints," exchanged thoughts and sensations as if bound sympathetically into a single organism. The path marked out by Spiritualists for negotiating the fragmentation of self thus entailed centering the "I-ness of I," "this actual I," not within the autonomous private realm but within the social. Although they zealously guarded the integrity of individual identity in the afterlife, Spiritualists proposed an intimate order of cosmic affect, where thoughts, sentiments, and feelings were ultimately shared by all. Privacy, as such, was restricted to the limited vision of the mortal world, but through spiritual transparency romantic love was transformed into a principle that bound all of creation.[65]

The transparency and concatenation of social and physical bodies became the basis for a medical and social therapeutics. United within "one body," Charles Hammond wrote, spirits existed in a state of such intimate relation with one another that they must all "unite in one harmonious work, or disease will prostrate the system," for "whatever disturbs the health of one member, disturbs the enjoyment of the whole body." For Hammond "the harmony of each member is essential to the health of the body," and the duty for each was clear: each member must actively engage in maintaining the health of the whole. "When men shall act in harmony with nature," he added, "in harmony as the body is harmonious in all its members, the day of salvation will dawn with brighter effulgence on the world of mind."[66]

The various strains in Spiritualist sympathy thus sit side by side, contributing to the construction of a uniquely integrated community of sensation and being, differing from the more limited operation of sympathy in the writings of Adam Smith in several regards, though on the surface these differences are not always readily apparent. Many Spiritualists greeted Smith's socially poetic economy eagerly, and many adopted his political economy as well. While men like Kirk Cunningham were experienced in the paradoxical and sundering effects of capitalism—the prospect of uniting persons and communities through the market, joined to the prospect of competition and atomization—writers like James Peebles lauded the market, despite recognizing the "antagonisms between stolen capital and daily toil." Looking to a future when a truly progressive society would be established through the propagation of Spiritualist values, Peebles predicted that "commerce would be a means of supply, or, rather, a transfer of commodities, upon the basis of equivalents." He confessed that there might still be a division of labor, with some members of society producing agricultural goods and others manufacturing, but commerce would unite them all, as "a chain of sympathy and common interest, looking to the good of all, would . . . grow up between these homes, whether located in this or foreign countries."[67]

More significant fissures cleaved Spiritualist and Smithian sympathy. Smith's vision of a nation united by exchange (of goods, of emotion) was predicated on a belief in the innate human capacity for sympathy and, equally importantly, on the desire to win sympathy from others: self-seeking behavior was constrained by the experience of sympathetic exchange, the promise of recompense, and the need for approbation. But the peculiar character of Smithian sympathy arose from Smith's belief that humanity suffered from a radical opacity of self. One could never truly know what another thinks or feels, and as a consequence one could never fully experience another's pain or joy but only a weaker, imaginative substitute. To escape this affective dilemma and to make sympathy work at all as a moral regulatory system, Smith looked to death, arguing that the fear of this most extreme of all forms of social isolation was so deeply rooted as to compel the imagination to compensate for interpersonal illegibility. For a spirit like George Washington, speaking through the medium Isaac Post, death played a different role:

> When man comes to fully realize that his bodily death is only an introduction to his eternal life—that as he leaves the body his real life commences—would he under such circumstances use his brother or sister cruelly? Would he enslave his fellow heir to the same inheritance? not an inheritance at some great distance, but one here, at this very place, this very room. . . . These truths being known, could man go to war and kill his brother? Could he bear the idea; did he know that he would soon have to face his murdered brother in the spirit life? Or could he tempt his weaker brother to take into his lips that liquid poison which would ruin himself and render his family miserable? I verily believe, that when men come to fully realize these things, a good time will have commenced indeed.[68]

If the "the horror of one's own isolation" and particularly the "dread of death" were the keys that "protected, regulated, and advanced society" for Smith, they were not for Spiritualists. When reifying sympathetic exchange and establishing it as their basis for social and moral order, Spiritualists crowed that they had expunged humanity of the fear of death, liberating them from the "dark uncertainty," the "dreaded gloom" cast by "the grim monster, the king of terrors." Instead, death provided the ultimate proof that sympathy was a socially cohesive force: through sympathy even this ultimate barrier no longer withheld; it became "the grand accoucheur of the soul," ushering persons "into light and life eternal." In this way Spiritualists reclaimed the dead for society, as crucial elements of both the moral and the metaphysical structure of daily life.[69]

It was not a Smithian opacity that compelled social sympathetic exchange for Spiritualists but a radical transparency of persons, their inner thoughts and emotions laid bare to all through spiritual (over-)sight. A cohesive society sprang from an intuitive apprehension of the implications of one's own actions gleaned from a radical, spiritually attained legibility. In practice, sympathy became the medium of exchange in a Spiritualist political economy in which sentiment was specie and its unfettered exchange the principle on which a stable moral order was established. If anything, the spirits suggested, persons were so thoroughly legible as to pose a problem. A "good and just" nature, Charles Hammond was informed, had provided sympathetic relations so that mind "shall see its relationship to mind," and once this occurred, he added, "it will not invade the rights of others; because each invasion would induce its own misery—a thing the mind must naturally dread."[70] Abraham Pierce learned that the deity had implanted mortals with a "spontaneous moral sense" which, when augmented by "moral and intellectual culture," served to guide them "in making as well as in obeying laws." Thus, although they drew upon the mechanism of Smithian exchange in some sense, Spiritualists resurrected the innate moral sense of Hutcheson to forge an internalized ethic of self-control.[71]

By linking a sympathetic system to the affective structures of death, family, and individual identity, by inflating it to a cosmic scale through the merger of physiological, social, and occult visions, Spiritualists created a framework in which to envision and enact a world that would bring "into one vast communion" even "those who have hitherto entertained the most discordant theological opinions." In doing so, they offered what denominationalism, commerce, or science could not: a transcendent community that annihilated the boundaries of belief, party, and sect, and even of time and space, a community that would exist in the next world but that could be constructed in this, a community founded on the basis of "real" selves.[72]

HEAVENLY PROGRESS

In heaven (the afterlife, the Summerland), the last of the cardinal principles of Spiritualist cosmology took center stage, and shorn of the impediments of the flesh, progress—"God's right hand angel"—reigned. At some level, as Colleen McDannell and Bernhard Lang remind us, there is nothing unique in the Spiritualist view of heaven. The "thick descriptions" of humanized spirits harmonized with Swedenborg, and their domestic arrangements and fealty to progress would strike a chord with an even wider audience among Victorian Protestants. But McDannell and Lang make a bolder claim, that "with a few exceptions" the Spiritualist heaven was not only consistent with but derivative of mainstream Protestantism, and oddly, despite the lengths to which Spiritualists went to distance themselves from the "sects," many Spiritualists would have agreed. Herman Snow saw only continuity between the spirits' understanding of heaven and the Protestant view, attributing this to a "natural outgrowth of the gradual unfolding of past religions, especially as taught by Jesus himself, the great Spiritualist and reformer of his own day."[73]

Most strikingly, Spiritualists and liberal Protestants (though not conservative) shared a heavenly geography, an activity of spirit, and a faith in gradualism and progress, and most importantly they shared in the attempt "to make sacred those aspects of existence which seemed ultimately relevant in the lives of everyday people," from love and marriage to family, friends, and social relations and the entire domestic economy. The domestic ideals of the American middle class and the thorough mundanities of mortal life were inscribed in their heaven, and heaven, recursively, was inscribed them. Yet the antebellum Spiritualist heaven was distinctively Spiritualist, expressing a distinctively Spiritualist topography of emotion that changed markedly, as I suggest in the final chapter, in the years following the Civil War.[74]

For antebellum Spiritualists heaven was synonymous with the afterlife, there being no distinct hell, no purgatory, and no theory of the extinction of the soul. It possessed, however, a distinctive geography, despite the annihilation of space and time. With faint overtones of Dante (though without the gloom) and even more of Swedenborg, heaven was usually mapped as a series of concentric "spheres" of variable and often indeterminate number, arranged from the lowest and most interior to the highest and most distant, with each sphere subdivided into a series of more or less discrete "circles." The career of the spirit began upon death when it entered the first sphere, where it transformed in Lyellian fashion under the metamorphic action of progress, "developing" spiritually as it absorbed knowledge of the moral and spiritual structure of the cosmos, rising successively, one sphere at a time, as it was perfected.[75]

Among the first important events for the newly liberated spirit was the arrival of "congenial spirits" drawn forth by affinities. Theodore Parker said he awoke in death to discover himself in the company of his mother, and shortly thereafter he was whisked away to a reunion with William Ellery Channing and others of his old literary companions. Spiritual or familial, the heavenly reunion of spouses with their spiritual mates, parents with children, and like minds with like minds demonstrated that a "similarity of thoughts and affection," as one writer put it, "makes proximity and presence in the other life." Spirits rapidly reconstituted the framework of family and community, "specially drawn to each other by secret ties and attractions," replicating, as McDannell suggests, a complete "heavenly culture" replete with the "social institutions, work patterns, artistic expressions, and value systems" of the Victorian middle class. The spheres were in effect a macrocosm of the affective world of life, with spirits joining those of similar levels of development to pursue their peculiar interests and engage in the exchange of sympathy and social healing.[76]

To a considerable degree the concentric arrangement of the spheres and the shape of emotional bonds gave form to heavenly relations and determined which spirits would visit earth. The assumption in Scottish Common Sense philosophy that proximity and the power of sympathy covaried suggested to Spiritualists that the spirits most likely to commune with mortals would be those from the closest, lowest spheres, those inhabited by the most recently departed and least "developed." Conversely, although only subtle gradations distinguished contiguous spheres, the cumulative distance between the lowest and highest, combined with differences in the spiritual and mental makeup between the residents, made long-distance communication unlikely except where the strongest ties prevailed or where intermediaries intervened. The residents of the highest spheres were barely even visible to the less developed. During his psychic tour of the spheres, the visionary Abraham Pierce ascended as high as the seventh sphere—lofty heights for a mortal—where he was barely able to glimpse "Jesus, the Great Medium" in the far distance, and even then "only for an instant—when the vision is closed." On another occasion Pierce found that in order to converse with the solar being Gamaliel, his words had to be translated through a chain of interpreters into Hebrew, Egyptian, and Hindi, before being rendered into the language of the sun. Whenever mediums spoke with the highest spirits, A. J. Davis insisted, they did so "by attorney," through a "long chain of 'mediums'" that connected the "exalted mind" of the next sphere, one after another in sequence until they reached the "person on the footstool" (fig. 3). Always, Davis wrote, "the spirit in closest sympathy with the earthly mind, is its own congenial protector."[77]

In whichever sphere they were found, all spirits enjoyed the same upward trajectory. Progress was immanent in the universe, one of the "established, invariable laws" that applied equally to all, from the inanimate earth

FIG. 3. A. J. Davis's "perfect representation of the philosophy of spiritual intercourse through clairvoyance, and also by impression." A clairvoyant in one city "sees" her son in another city by direct, "penetrative," and "all-pervading" magnetism. In contrast, the impressional medium communicates with her son by virtue of a "circle of sympathy" that includes both their spirit guardians, so that "the actual condition of the son is daguerreotyped upon the mother's brain—telegraphed, so to speak, or *impressed*." From A. J. Davis, *Present Age and Inner Life* (Hartford: Charles Partridge, 1853), 193, 194.

to the animate souls of its inhabitants. An early medium, R. P. Ambler, contended that the same gradualistic, unilinear rules of progress that resulted in the physiographic evolution of earth from primary elements to life applied to the evolution of spirit from life to death. *Natura non facit saltum,* indeed, but James Peebles assured his readers that the changes wrought in spirits were subtle, scarcely noticeable from day to day, for "true growth is a stranger to abrupt leaps."[78]

Not surprisingly, given the insistence upon the union of body and mind, spirits experienced continuity as they exchanged their material bodies for spiritual ones. The deceased Emanuel Swedenborg wrote, "I looked for my hands, and there they were, I looked for my feet, and they too were there; and so of every part of my body, nothing was lacking." So subtle were the gradations between life and death that many writers concluded that heaven was "not a place, but a condition of the mind," nothing more than "a continuation of mundane-life" where "the mind or spirit is the same." In more ways than one, as Caroline and Levi Smith announced on their tombstone, death was "merely a change of conditions."[79]

In the face of transparent union, gradualism ensured the continuity of personal identity, tastes, and prejudices and the preservation of earthly memories, and it thus ensured social diversity in the life after death. All the "*effects* of life upon the globe" were written on the faces of spirits, A. J. Davis claimed, "as well as in the secret chambers of their affections," so that a gathering of the dead was as diverse of mind and opinion as any gathering of the living. The experiences and memories written into the emotions in life, the affective structures and memories that made the individual distinct, endured. "Death effects no alteration in the form, or organization of the mind," Hudson Tuttle claimed, "but leaves the spirit the same individual, with exactly similar thoughts and ideas"; the individual, dead though he or she may be, was "as much an *individual* as before the change."[80]

Indeed, individuality itself was an intrinsic element of progressive design, operating upon the distinct personalities of the dead to reinforce them and make "each and every one a separate individuality." The circles that subdivided the spheres were a direct result. Horace Wood learned from Thomas Paine that the lower spheres were a paradise of the relativist's imagination, appearing "differently to its different societies." Spirits lived in heavens of their own imagining, convinced that what they saw and experienced was real: the poet congregated with other poets in a circle of spacious fields, bird-filled and verdant, "a perfect daguerreotype of his imagination"; the sailor met sailors on the circle of the open seas; and the Indian who enjoyed the hunt in life pursued the same in death and in "his imaginary world feels and acts as under a reality." Every circle was suited to the individual tastes of its inhabitants, and regardless of their experiences on earth, every spirit enjoyed a new life in the company of the like-minded.[81]

Rejecting the concepts of devil, hell, and eternal torment, antebellum Spiritualist writers acknowledged that "if there are evil-minded men, living and dying such, there must necessarily be evil-minded spirits." Horatio Wood discovered that misers, for example, congregated with other misers in a suitably imaginary miserly world, "congregat[ing] in separate societies from affinity" to apply themselves to their lucre, "counting over and stowing away their imaginary treasures." There were even circles of killers, gathered in a "congregated brotherhood of crime" to fight with "imaginary weapons, and commit imaginary murders." None of these suffered, as Wood was informed, and even the worst miscreants believed themselves happy in the moral poverty of their imagination. Many spirits, a later medium explained, remained so tightly "bound to physical life because of the grossness of their under-natures" that they felt "no desire to rise above to conditions of matter." Yet all these individuals eventually yielded to progress, the fruit of the cooperative labor of all spirits and the primary focus of spirit life and activity. Not only was it a force of nature, as the medium S. E. Park asserted, "*progression* is the duty of every spirit."[82]

All progress began internally, emerging from frustrated desires and a "feeling of dissatisfaction with the present" that opened the spirit to the possibility of improvement, and these sensibilities were soon reinforced by the ministrations of more enlightened spirits who helped supplant earthly desires with higher ones. Uriah Clark advised that the "wisest and best spirits" asked only to engage in sympathy, not to control, and sought only to awaken the "divine energies of our being" and "quicken the monitor within, and call on us to stand up on our own accountability." While some spirits admitted to experiencing a Smithian schadenfreude at witnessing "the spectacle of a great man struggling with misfortune," their main purpose always was "to do whatsoever good thing we find to do, With One Accord, for so shall at last Eternal Justice be done on earth as it is in Heaven."[83]

For the souls most damaged in life, spiritual nurture was quite literally therapeutic, and the heavens provided moral sanitariums for "undevelop'd" spirits and the "mentally diseased." Higher spirits were joined in these "big hospitals" by a multitude of others, including even mortals. While some media, as Ann Braude has suggested, were imagined as weak, passive, and perhaps sickly, exhibiting, in the words of John Worth Edmonds, the "very unnatural, very difficult and very dangerous" trait of a total exclusion of "selfhood—a suspension of his own will and spirit control," others were the opposite, taking an active role in restoring the well-being of spirits. Francis Smith, for example, intervened with the recently departed alcoholic William E. to make him own up to his moral failures in life and thus begin on the road to progress. Herman Snow virtually specialized in assisting spirits in their first steps in the afterlife, aiding a victim of a railroad accident who for eleven years had been "lingering upon the borders of the spirit-world," thinking he was still trapped in the wreck. "Gradually," Snow wrote, "through the combined efforts of those in and out of the material form," including himself, "this spirit was made to understand that he is already in the spirit world, and entirely free from the calamity that had befallen him." Sympathy was exchange, not unidirectional flow, implying that all participants in sympathetic networks had a role to play in the abatement of pain and suffering.[84]

Labor in the heavens also furthered social harmony, drawing spirits into labor collectives in a reformed industrial order. Sympathetically led, spirits flocked together not in the pursuit of profit but to indulge their natural talents in creative and intellectual pursuits, forming institutions and associations to advance commerce, manufactures, education, the arts, or politics. George Washington worked with a committee of patriots in an institute of advanced study of politics, for example, while Benjamin Franklin was prominent among those developing new inventions for the nation. Discovering that "dynamic electricity" facilitated communication, Franklin and friends devised a new battery to benefit mortals, by which the positive energy of humans could charge objects such as tables "by the free electricity which pervades its nerves," and this and other ideas were transmitted to earth through a sympathetic spirit crew "united together . . . by a small, subtle chain, as thin and delicate almost as air." Working through a variety of other spiritual organizations, Franklin promised that he was now "investigating laws more hidden and abstruse than those I rudimentally determined. My mind soars onward, *onward*, ONWARD, to grasp the most concealed laws of our own organic, spiritual natures, of man and the universe, and to discover the relation the ethereal fluid bears to them." So impressed was Isaac Post by the degree to which spirits assisted humanity that he exclaimed, "Let no man claim that he has made great improvements in the arts and sciences, unassisted by spirit friends."[85]

The major activity of spirit life, and the greatest contributor to spiritual progress, was applied education. Each day in the afterlife revolved around education, with spirits dedicating themselves to "learning new truths each hour of our existence," as one of them reported, "and perfecting ourselves as rapidly as possible." In some cases tutelage became a formal affair. When Thomas Paine reached heaven, he was "apprenticed" out to learn the meaning of justice, wisdom, progression, order, and harmony, the concepts that epitomized the need to assist other spirits (and mortals) in their pursuit of spiritual progress. Justice, he learned, was "doing what benevolence requires"; wisdom entailed relieving want, doing good, loving, and cooperating. Progress, he learned, "is the expansion of thy mind in the wisdom thou mayest receive from instructed minds around thee," while order implied obedience to law, "immutable and universal." The end result of internalizing these principles was harmony, "what we mean by social sympathy," a state "congenial with order. It is union of minds. It is wisdom in unity of minds. It is sympathy of thoughts and works." In the highest circles, according to Horatio Wood, "almost perfect harmony exists. . . . There is a mingling of thought and sympathy . . . a sort of mutual affinity and desire to assist each other in progressive advancement."[86]

Privileged with a visit to each of the seven spheres during his three-week trance in 1856, Abraham Pierce saw education wherever he looked in the afterlife. In the second sphere spirits studied the fundamentals of telegraphy, advancing in the next sphere to learn how to telegraph one another and earth. From there they entered into the study of natural science and by the fifth sphere learned to labor in workshops building roads, steamboats, and railways. In the sixth sphere spirits devised new inventions to benefit humanity, until finally they had gained enough spiritual insight to progress to the seventh and final sphere below the celestial heavens. Even there, though, education continued: they studied anatomy and carried out spiritual and material dissections, removing "the outer surface" and "showing the porous system, and also showing the glandular system and action, as well as the nervous and arterial systems" in a form of psychic transparency. In the highest reaches of spirit life, the material body and material science prevailed. In unconscious reflection, William Henry Holcombe suggested, "heaven is organized like the human body. Every atom works, not for itself, but for all others."[87]

What the unfulfilled desires of life wrought, death fulfilled by reconstituting life's affective networks and perfecting them in the absence of the material body. In this new society emotion (sympathy, love) brought all individuals, and all of creation, into a comprehensive organic unity, boundless and timeless. As much an extension of earth as earth was of heaven, heaven was simultaneously a thaumaturgical prospect for the future and a rationalistic exhortation for productive social action in this life. Like the poet B. T. Young, many Spiritualists imagined that through sympathy this "kingdom of heaven, in spheres above," would one day include "all nationalities and creeds" within its settlement, leaving nothing, and no one, outside.

4

Angels' Language

Oh, for that land of spiritual Daguerreotype, where thoughts and affections write themselves spontaneously in the angels' language of types & symbols! Yet to most, if not all of us, such spiritual Daguerreotype were one the of the fearfullest things! . . . Is not the *idea* of this present age written in the fact that any man can have his likeness taken in a minute, by machinery?

—LYDIA MARIA CHILD to Convers Francis, Oct. 20, 1840

TO MANY AMERICANS daguerreotypes were the "angels' language of types & symbols." With an ineffable ability to replicate nature in minute detail and to portray even the most elusive nuances of character, the daguerreotype resounded with a spiritual and moral authority, idolized as the potent spawn of art mated with science and revered for the mechanical ease with which it discerned the hidden essence of its subjects. For Lydia Maria Child, in a moment of Swedenborgian rapture, the daguerreotype imaginatively bared the mind and heart, transcribing thoughts and affections with spontaneous ease that rivaled phrenology as a diagnostic for psychology and morality. For Spiritualists this technology of the transparent emerged as a key site for sympathetic practice. For over twenty years spirit photographs—images of spirits of the dead—enjoyed an unusual currency among Spiritualists, circulating widely within the emotional economy, salving the wounds of "materialism," of spiritual and social isolation, and the divisions of race, class, gender, and "sect" that tore through American society.[1]

For its most ardent admirers, the daguerreotype emerged as a recording angel, maintaining a cosmic ledger of all acts, good and evil, and providing a guide to behavior and a guard against the errors of modern life. In 1859 a recently departed spirit of a Methodist clergyman claimed through the medium James V. Mansfield that when he saw his past life "daguerreotyped on the broad canopy of the eternal spheres," he felt compelled to return to earth and, in his words, "undeceive where I had deceived many" with his orthodox sermons. Although the clergyman's errors were unintentional, even unconscious, the daguerreian image demanded restitution. The spirit of arctic explorer Elisha Kent Kane magnified the power of the photograph, informing Francis H. Smith that "every thing which exists in the smallest form on earth is faithfully daguerreotyped in the spirit-land," adding that in the afterlife there are "separate departments for all the planets, and for all articles used therein," even "minute copies of the planets themselves." Photography was a spiritual medium, an aspect of the spiritual nervous system, according J. O. Barrett. "Wherever a nerve is," he wrote, "is spirit. . . . Rays of light are the undulating carriers of the image of an object to the optic nerve, and then, by a beautiful chemistry, analogous with photographing, it is impressed where the mind catches it up into living consciousness."[2]

The geologist and Spiritualist William Denton cast his net still further, expanding the photograph to the scale of the cosmos itself. In a studio, he noted, a daguerreotype is produced when light from the subject's body is cast onto a cleanly polished silver plate, creating an image where none had previously existed, but to become visible, this image requires proper development. Because the great authority on light Sir David Brewster had demonstrated that all objects in nature "throw off emanations in greater or less size and with greater or less velocities" and had suggested that these emanations "enter more or less into the pores of solid and fluid bodies, sometimes resting upon their surface, and *sometimes permeating them altogether*," Denton theorized that if properly developed through the use of psychometry—mental science—all surfaces would display photographic images, catalogs of their entire histories and of all acts to which they were mute witness.[3] The implications were vast: the world is an all-recording camera, a moral apparatus with divine overtones:

In the world around us radiant forces are passing from all objects to all objects in their vicinity, and during every moment of the day and night are daguerreotyping the appearances of each upon the other; the images thus made, not merely resting upon the surface, but sinking into the interior of them; there held with astonishing tenacity, and only waiting for a suitable application to reveal themselves to the inquiring gaze. . . . Not a leaf waves, not an insect crawls, not a ripple moves, but each motion is recorded by a thousand faithful scribes in infallible and indelible scripture.[4]

The natural world in this model assumes the role of monitoring and perhaps mediating the fates of all beings, observing not only every sparrow that falls but every insect that crawls and transcribing every action into divine word. This natural, all-encompassing camera enabled Denton to indulge his geological fantasies by psychometrizing sandstone to unlock the secrets of the Triassic grabens of the Connecticut Valley, connecting mind with a scrap of fossil to view the teeming coal swamps and even paying psychometric visits to the cities of Venus and Mars.[5]

Passing through at least eight ever-expanding editions, Denton's treatise *The Soul of Things* cast a long shadow over Spiritualist moral theory, spilling out even into a novel written by the Swedenborgian William Henry Holcombe who employed a version of Denton's theory to solve the murder and mysterious disappearance of a young couple and their daughter twenty-five years after the crime. Bearing the psychic traces of their unique histories, the victim's last letter and a lock of the little girl's hair provided ample psychometric fodder for viewing and emending a hidden crime.[6]

Implicit in these Spiritualist visions of photography is the notion that technology—in the form of the photograph—creates a basis for a stable and consistent moral order. The self-described anticlerical rationalists who formed a prominent segment of the Spiritualist movement sought a "natural" grounding for moral systems shorn of reliance upon the increasingly shaky foundations of Scripture and faith. In photography they discovered a safeguard for morality as pervasive, modern, and effective as Jeremy Bentham's panopticon, promising individual reform and the policing of morality. It is no wonder, then, that in 1874 the spirit of Daguerre was invited to join the select Spiritualist circle headed by James V. Mansfield, one of the nation's first and most successful writing mediums. Daguerre graciously accepted.[7]

THE IDEA OF THE PRESENT AGE

Dead or alive, Daguerre presented a paradox. Although the daguerreian image was saturated with a spiritual presence, in practice it remained relentlessly material. Despite the best efforts of antebellum evangelical Protestants to "disembody death," as Gary Laderman argues, to remove the body from the center of eschatological and theological concern, the corpse retained a powerful fascination for many Americans. Mourners, especially women, displayed an intense interest in the physical state of the corpse, and many Americans closely monitored the bodily decomposition of loved ones, exhibiting, as one observer commented, a "morbid desire . . . to descend into the damp and dreary tomb—to lift the lid—to look upon the changing, softening, corrupting features of a parent or child—to gaze upon the mouldering bones." Death fascinated and consumed the living along with the dead, providing an important site for the exchange of sentiment and consolidation of social bonds.[8]

In such a milieu the authority that the daguerreotype commanded as a form of scrupulously exact representation and its beauty, singularity, and expense made it an ideal medium for memorializing the dead. Almost from the time of its introduction in 1839, the daguerreotype was adopted for depicting the corpse, preserving it in a state resembling, if not quite identical to, its state in life. Even its physical presentation reflected the exalted status of the deceased (and survivor alike). The delicate, mirrorlike plate was enclosed within a protective package consisting of more or less ornate framing devices (velvet or satin pad, glass, mat, and preserver), and the whole was placed for further protection within a rigid, tightly fitting case. This housing demarcated a strongly privileged space—already ideologically and morally charged—in which the act of viewing became a ritualized encounter akin to opening the lid of a casket or the door of a tomb. The daguerreotype reinforced a sense of intimacy and personal contact with the deceased by requiring the viewer to unlatch the clasps while cradling the image in both hands, the emotional potency of the moment enhanced by the uniqueness and expense of the image, and particularly by the sight of one's own face reflected on the silvered surface, superimposed on the image of the dead. By shifting focus slightly, the viewer could alternate between an image of the self and an image of the deceased in the same space, the daguerreotype thus becoming a reification of the emotional correspondence of living and dead. In the fetishized trappings of their presentation and their jewel-like surface that collapsed the self and the sympathetic community, visually and conceptually, postmortem daguerreotypes became common fixtures in households from the working class through the elite.[9]

Whether vestigially or more, the fixation on the material body of the deceased continued even after the daguerreian process was supplanted by the glass-plate negative, and for Spiritualists, at least, the potency of photography as a moral force and representational authority seems hardly to have abated. Postmortem photography remained a viable practice through the end of the century and, as Jay Ruby has shown, remains so today. Yet the glass-plate process, involving a single negative from which innumerable positive copies can be produced, fundamentally altered the emotional context for the interpretation of photography, with one of the unexpected fruits of this technological transition being the advent of spirit photography. It is no coincidence that although the modern Spiritualist movement began in 1848 and enjoyed its greatest period of growth during the height of the daguerreian era, there are no known daguerreotypes of spirits and very few tintypes. For spirits, the negative is almost essential.[10]

In 1862 when William H. Mumler first dabbled in photography at the Boston studio of A. M. Stuart (usually referred to as Mrs. H. F. Stuart), the results were anything but promising. A self-described "honest and trustworthy" engraver for a jewelry firm, his attempted self-portrait was marred by the unexpected appearance of the shadowy face of a young girl, although he insisted that during exposure there was "no visible person present but myself." Looking back on this episode fifteen years later, Mumler recalled having chalked up the failure to produce a suitable image to his inexperience as a photographer and to the use of a previously exposed plate, and he claimed that he set the image aside until one day the chance visit of a known Spiritualist presented an opportunity for fun. "Without telling an untruth," he insisted, and without adding any of P. T. Barnum's "drapery," Mumler put on "as mysterious an air as possible" and brandished the photograph in front of his mark, probably Dr. H. F. Gardner, informing him that he had been alone during the session and allowing Gardner to reach his own conclusions.[11]

The consequences of this joke were unforeseen, according to Mumler, and entirely undesired. Having allowed Gardner to keep the image, Mumler was drawn out of the domestic tranquillity of Mrs. Stuart's parlor into the glaring light of publicity: the next he heard of it, the image was being bruited about in the New York Spiritualist newspaper *Herald of Progress* and, still worse, the news was soon snapped up by the hometown *Banner of Light.* "Considerably mortified" at seeing his jest recoil, Mumler confessed that the whole had been only an embarrassing misunderstanding; after all, he had never claimed that the image was supernatural in origin, and his conscience was clear of evil intent. But this confession, as Mumler recalled, did little to quell the public interest, and when "a scientist from Cambridge" asserted that the appearance of an unseen figure in a photographic image "might be possible, and even probable, in daguerreotyping, it was an impossibility in photographing on glass," Mumler was left grasping for explanations. With the authority of science nagging and Spiritualists beating a path to his door to have their portraits taken, Mumler relented and gave photography another try, soon discovering that he possessed a unique, natural ability to record spirits with the camera.[12]

Even in these earliest sessions the features that characterized Mumler's practice were sharply defined: clients arrived at the studio as agnostics or skeptics, some bearing secrets with which they tried to outwit Mumler or others. In the end, however, with the product in hand and their secrets exposed, the sitters acknowledged the identity of the spirit and on this basis acknowledged the authenticity of the photograph. In the great majority of cases, the spirits that appeared in photographs bore a close, personal relationship with the sitter: friend, spouse, or relative, or less often, guide. Alvin Adams, founder of Adams Express Co., visited Mumler's studio late in 1862 accompanied by an undercover Spiritualist medium. On learning that the negative of his portrait included a spirit, Adams announced, "If you have a form on that plate beside my own, I know who it is." He had already been doubly informed of the spirit's identity, first by the medium but more importantly by a "private signal" from the spirit himself, Daniel Webster, his personal spirit guide and constant companion. Mumler therefore passed a "treble test": the image of the spirit was recognizably Webster's, down to the balding pate and upswept hair, his sunken cheeks and statesman's clothes. Always, proof of the spirit's identity verified that sitter and spirit were connected in an affective or genealogical plexus.[13]

At various points in his practice, Mumler established strong professional affiliations with working women who materially abetted his career. Mumler discovered spirit photography while under the eye of Mrs. H. F. Stuart, a manufacturer of hair jewelry (often used for memorial purposes), and the earliest reports of the discovery of spirit photography credit her with supplying the "studio" at 258 Washington Street. Both remained at the address until at least 1865, pursuing their respective professions, but with some overlap. In fact, as early as January 1863, Stuart produced spirit photographs that carried a backmark advertising her hair jewelry, suggesting that she may have been more deeply implicated in the "discovery" of spirit photography than previously suspected and was certainly keenly interested in its commercial potential. From early in the game, spirit photographs became popular commercial objects, entering commercial and affective patterns of circulation simultaneously.[14]

At the height of his career, Mumler also worked closely with his wife, a "natural clairvoyant for diagnosing and treating disease" and "a perfect battery in herself." Like Stuart, it appears that Mrs. Mumler assumed a direct role in the studio, although there is no evidence that she took images. Nevertheless, her role was vital. Moses A. Dow, editor of the *Waverly Magazine,* reported that after William had twice failed to secure an image of a spirit, Mrs. Mumler entered the room looking "as if she was under spiritual influence" and, in response to Dow's inquiry, announced that she saw "a beautiful spirit," Mabel, hovering nearby. In short order Mabel, Dow's spirit guide, controlled Mrs. Mumler and, exerting all of the spiritual magnetism she could muster, permitted her photo to be taken wearing a striped dress and a wreath of lilies about her head (fig. 4).

This dramatic, entranced entrance was not unique. When one day a "Mrs. Lindall" called to retrieve her portrait but hesitated in identifying the spirit, Mrs. Mumler came to the rescue. "Almost instantly entranced," she approached Mrs. Lindall and demanded, "Mother, if you cannot recognize father, show the picture to Robert; he will recognize it." Controlled by Tad Lincoln, Mrs. Mumler and Mrs. Lindall—now exposed as Mary Todd Lincoln—engaged in a lengthy, tear-filled conversation, interrupted later by Abraham himself. In the end Mrs. Lincoln readily acknowledged that the spirit clasping a hand on her shoulder was her assassinated spouse.[15]

By 1872 Mrs. Mumler was listed in Boston city directories as a clairvoy-

FIG. 4. William Mumler's photograph of Moses Dow, editor of *Waverly Magazine*, accompanied by the spirit of Mabel Warren, ca. 1871. A protégé of Dow, Warren died in July 1870 after a painful illness. When Dow was introduced to Spiritualism shortly thereafter, Warren became his most frequent spiritual visitor. Dow testified for the defense at Mumler's trial on charges of fraud (Mumler, *The Personal Experiences of William H. Mumler in Spirit-Photography* [Boston: Colby & Rich, 1875]). (Darcy-Haven Collection: Private Collection)

ant physician, was seeing patients, and presumably was earning income at her profession. According to her husband the simple touch of her hand left patients feeling "the subtile current . . . distinctly coursing through every tissue of the body," so powerful that it caused men to faint "under the peculiar reaction" to this "wonderful, life-giving principle of *animal magnetism*." Mumler insisted that his wife's magnetic talents were "directly connected with spirit-photography" and acknowledged that he was "largely indebted" to her for his ability to visualize spirits at all.[16]

Belying his "athletic" appearance, Mumler's "artistic experiences" were said to sap his strength, leaving him capable of performing only three or four photographic sessions a day. In most accounts he acknowledged that the spiritual favors sometimes came through his wife's magnetic gifts, but more often they were the free gifts of his spirit guides. "The whole process with the exception of coating and developing," he wrote, "is conducted by my guides entirely by raps that are audible in any part of the room." Without the active assistance of spirits, he was incapable of plying his trade.[17]

Searching for a metaphor to express this dependence, Mumler turned to high technology. "Mediums," he claimed, "stand in the same relation to spirits as vacuum tubes do to electricity: they supply the necessary elements by which spirits are enabled to be seen." He was convinced that however powerful a medium he became, he was truly a medium, one who could not control the spirits, and he took great pains to illustrate this belief. His portrait session with the test medium Charles H. Foster, for example, floundered when neither man could stop the camera from dancing a jig. No matter how pitifully Mumler pleaded, the camera danced on in time to a shower of spiritual raps, stopping only when Mumler was reduced to crying that his collodion was drying and would ruin the picture, and only then Foster chimed in that he would prefer to leave, rather than be "fooled" by his "spirit-friends." Less dramatically but no less significantly, after failing repeatedly to obtain an image of his wife's spirit guide, Benjamin Rush, Mumler came to the recognition that he must surrender his will to the spirits and "await their own good time." Only when he had aligned his sentiments fully with Rush's and achieved true sympathetic rapport, only at a time specifically selected by Rush, was Mumler able to secure the good doctor's portrait. The remarkable image that resulted displayed brilliant rays of light passing from Rush's hand to Mrs. Mumler's, the same magnetic rays by which healing "was imparted to the patients."[18]

To call Mumler's mediumship passive, however, is to oversimplify. Although Spiritualists were adamant that almost anyone, with suitable preparation, could become a medium, Mumler's mediumship was an unusual gift of high order. Visualizing the unseen was an extraordinary talent that put Mumler in complicity with the spirits, not as their servant, as he implied, but like the vacuum tube, as a "necessary element" for their manifestation. Although he might be forced to plead with them or wait upon them, his relationship with spirits was one of mutual, sympathetic interdependence, not dependence.

Passivity and control, dependence and interdependence, were part of the performance in studio, darkroom, and in print that established credibility, and credibility was a major concern that extended well beyond simply ensuring the flow of clients. Although it was common in the 1860s and 1870s to consider photographs as direct, unmediated reflections of nature, Americans were becoming increasingly concerned over the possibility that they might be open to manipulation and to the concealment of reality; they might become instruments in gulling or controlling a credulous public. Concurrent with the development of spirit photography, photographs entered into circulation in police stations, asylums, and hospitals, serving not only as forms of documentation but as a means of surveillance, prognostication, and categorization. Beginning in the 1850s, photographs became an increasingly important medium for illustrating books discussing the proper ordering of American society, reflecting their status as surrogate impartial spectators of the American scene. From capsule histories of the nation like *The Homes of American Statesmen* (Boston, 1854) to E. B. Hillard's *The Last Men of the Revolution* (Hartford, 1864) and more programmatic works such as Isaac Newton Kerlin's *The Mind Unveiled* (Philadelphia, 1858), Thomas Byrnes's *Professional Criminals of America* (New York, 1886), and Alphonse Bertillon's *Signaletic Instructions Including the Theory and Practice of Anthropometrical Identification* (Chicago, 1898), actual photographs tipped into a book's pages represented intellectual authority and authenticity. A startling number of the more than five hundred American books illustrated with photographs between 1854 and 1888 surveyed the landscape, the dead (in memorial volumes), or public and private enterprises such as parks, canals, railroads, or factories. With photography assuming such a major role in reflecting the interests of the state, claims of authenticity advanced by Spiritualists—and claims of inauthenticity by skeptics—necessarily carried broader implications about social power, the authority of representation, and the power to interpret or be interpreted.[19]

Indeed, authenticity became virtually the only issue seriously entertained in the non-Spiritualist press with regard to spirit photographs, and to this day authenticity comprises a constant theme in Spiritualist publications, as well. Spirit photographs, of course, were not intended by their purveyors to be read as fantasies or photomanipulations. At the most obvious level they made clear and specific claims about the ontological status of the particular spirit in the image and furthermore advanced claims about the spirits class. In other words, the photographs were read, and possibly produced, under the belief that the specific spirit represented in the photograph actually existed and, more generally, that spirits as a class exist. As such, spirit photographs were welcomed by Spiritualists as support for their theories of the afterlife.[20]

As they are wont to do, skeptics remained skeptical, demanding "scientific control" of the conditions in studio and darkroom, and it was during photographic sessions with skeptics that the self-creative performances of spirit photographers emerged in their sharpest and most distinctive relief. While working under the gaze of a skeptic, as Bill Jay notes, Mumler assumed a nonchalant, even careless attitude and spoke of the uncertainty of obtaining any image at all. For his supporters these displays reeked of veracity: how could a man afford to be so careless if he had something to hide? How could he lack confidence if he controlled the outcome? By the same logic Mumler's description of the "chance" discovery of spirit photography, his insistence that he never sought public recognition, and his open but limited admission that he had told half-truths about the first spirit image (though eschewing the "drapery" that distinguished the joker from the Barnumesque merchant of fraud) were all entered into evidence of Mumler's fundamental veracity.

Other spirit photographers adopted a very different approach to hostile scrutiny. W. M. Keeler was more aggressive in 1886 when he stymied the debunking efforts of the Seybert Commission for Investigating Modern Spiritualism, demanding not only the exorbitant fee of $300 for three sessions but the right to use his own darkroom and equipment and to bring along as many sympathetic people as he felt necessary "to harmonize the antagonistic element." Although his rejection of passivity did nothing to convince skeptics, he was so successful at discouraging close scrutiny that he left the acting chair of the commission, Henry H. Furness, gasping that Keeler's demands "were such as to render any investigation simply silly."[21]

The problems between spirit photography and the institutions of the state vested in the meanings of photography, however, were not quite so easily shucked. When Mumler relocated to New York in 1869, the mayor ordered his marshal, Joseph H. Tooker, to investigate. Posing as a client, Tooker was rewarded with a negative displaying a "dim, indistinct outline of a ghostly face," and although he had not directly witnessed any hanky-panky, he arrested Mumler forthwith for fraud. At the trial Tooker explained that fraud must have been involved because he "failed to recognize the worthy old gentleman [spirit], and emphatically declared that the picture neither represented his father-in-law, nor any of his relations, nor yet any person whom he had ever seen or known." The trial was brief, according to an account in *Harper's Weekly*, for "with this evidence, the prosecution rested."[22]

Mumler's defense revolved around a clever appeal to authority, calling in not only a professional photographer to testify but Judge John Worth Edmonds, who combined the authority of social and professional respectability with the ardor of a true Spiritualist believer. Edmonds testified that he believed "that the camera can take a photograph of a spirit, and . . . also that spirits have materiality—not that gross materiality that mortals possess, but still they are material enough to be visible to the human eye, for I have seen them." Although this eyewitness testimony resulted in a quick acquittal, the opponents of spirit photography remained dubious. The editors of *Scientific American*, a magazine committed to the authority and power of science, rued the fact that the decision was "rather favorable than otherwise to the spirits, as the impostors were not punished."[23]

The intensity of the struggle over the authenticity of spirit photographs and the pervasiveness of the debate make it easy to assume that the epistemological implications of spirit photographs were a central concern of Spiritualists. They were not. Although non-Spiritualists were obsessed with veracity, few Spiritualists mentioned spirit images as contributing to their faith, and there is abundant evidence that allegations, or even admissions, of fraud had little direct impact. Frank Podmore's exasperated cry that Dr. Gardner "and most other Spiritualists" continued to believe in "some of the photographs" even after discovering conclusive evidence of fraud in others reflects the attitudes of both skeptics and believers: believers rejoiced while skeptics rejected. When the French photographer Edouard Isidore Buguet admitted at trial to practicing deception, providing precise details on how he had contrived his spirits, his clients vigorously insisted that their pictures were genuine, even if others were not (fig. 5). One man claimed that the fuzzy likeness of his deceased wife must be genuine, crying: "My children, like myself, thought the likeness perfect. When I showed them the picture, they cried, 'It's mamma.'"[24]

Similarly, British Spiritualist William Stainton Moses commented to an American colleague that as far as he was concerned, Buguet's admission of fraud had changed nothing. "I have never changed my opinion as to the value of Photography. I have always believed that I proved my case up to the hilt: and I have much regretted that the subject shd have fallen into abeyance under the discredit brought upon it by Buguet. I always regard that business as a kind of Popish Plot, and I am as sure as I am of anything that very many of Buguet's pictures were quite genuine."[25]

Despite the prevalence of authenticity in "public" discussions of spirit photography, the central issue for Spiritualists was therefore not the indexical nature of the image. Spiritualists routinely rejected the valuations of skeptics, and even the admissions of "their own," privileging their own assessments based upon a personal attachment to the photographic subject. While the determination of civil and scientific authorities to discredit spirit photography speaks loudly to some perceived threat to the epistemic order, the equal determination of Spiritualists in claiming these images as authentic speaks just as loudly to their resilient emotional power.

It is the titration of authority and emotion in Mumler's trial that provides the key to unlocking the cultural valence of spirit photography. Both believer and skeptic saw the emotional connection between the living and dead as a key for interpreting authenticity. Joseph Tooker's abbreviated testimony, represented in *Harper's* as constituting the bulk of the prosecution's case, suggests that he had concluded that Mumler was a fraud not because anything untoward had been observed but because fraud could be deduced from the fact that "the worthy old gentleman" was neither "father-in-law, nor any of his relations, nor yet any person whom he had ever seen or known." If the spirit were genuine, Tooker implied, they would have known and loved one another personally. Furthermore, later skeptics like Frank Podmore implied that it was aberrant emotion that (mis-)led people into interpreting the fuzzy blebs that appeared in photos as relatives. Although there surely was a social struggle over who could

FIG. 5. Image of Dr. Puch and the spirit of Mme Puch, ca. 1870, by Edouard Isidore Buguet. (Eugène Rochas Papers, American Philosophical Society)

claim the right to interpret photography as a representation of reality, this struggle took place within a common ground that assumed a particular, affective relation between the dead and living, a correspondence of emotions—sympathy. In case after case, the first step in reckoning with the spirit image was for the sitter to recognize an intimate, usually familial, relationship with the spirit, and it was this connection that provided the only certain verification of authenticity.[26]

Spirits in photographs caressed their living relatives, threw their arms around them, gazed affectionately upon them, or prayed over them, reinforcing the bonds that united living and dead and providing proof of identity. Indeed, in a variant of the story of Mumler's first self-portrait, he claimed immediately to have recognized the spirit that appeared, "equally unexpected and startling to the artist," as a cousin who had died twelve years before. Even Mrs. Mumler's portrait with Benjamin Rush, which might be excused for lacking such intimacy, involved a strong, though unexpected, personal connection. The spirit's identity was actually doubly corroborated, first through comparison with a portrait of Rush hanging in Independence Hall and second, and more importantly, by the testimony of an elderly woman who had known the physician in her youth and could tenderly recall "his dear, good, pleasant face" as if it were yesterday. Finally, even the few images that did not include an intimate, personal relationship between sitter and spirit underscored the importance of the sympathetic connection between mortal and spirit. Mumler described how he came upon a photographic studio while walking through the Bowery and, locating the proprietor, inquired whether it might be available for lease. The man replied that if his portrait were taken, it would probably include the devil or his cloven hoof. "Not being acquainted with his antecedents," as he said, Mumler went ahead with the session, producing a negative featuring "as perfect a cloven hoof as could be imagined." Evidently the man knew his relatives.[27]

Predictably, sympathy was a key ideological element underlying the meaning of spirit photography, an element intimately bound up with the public struggles over authenticity. In interpreting their own portraits along with the spirits beside them, the living engaged in a self-creative process, asserting their authority to define themselves in relation to categories of social reality. Spirit photographs became sites for an insistent desire to re-

construct the memory of the dead on the sometimes fuzzy and obscure images identified as spirits and the memory of the living on the equally fuzzy
views of cultural institutions and practices, with sympathy and family
forging the links. Just as importantly, the albumen spirit photograph, available in limitless quantity, was able to enter as specie into the exchanges that
marked the sympathetic community. In this sense spirit photography consisted of a recursive process of self-construction on the parts of photographer, skeptic, and subject. Imbued with a spiritualized power, the photograph provided a space in which the observer was defined with respect to a
genealogical/affective nexus and to an ideological or moral system, forging a community of cobelievers.

MACHINERY OF THE PRESENT AGE: THE CIRCULATION OF SPIRIT PHOTOGRAPHS

In October 1862 Dr. H. F. Gardner received an image of himself, taken in
Mumler's Boston studio, surrounded by his deceased children. Within
weeks he was all the talk from coast to coast. Whether it was Gardner's
prominence in Spiritualist circles or his authority as an educated man that
made his case stand out, or whether the photos alone were enough, the
news that spirits had been visualized flashed across the continent, retracing
the expanding lines of the Spiritualist community. By December news of
Gardner's image reached the remote shores of California and the eager
eyes of the "Spirit Postmaster," James V. Mansfield.[28]

In the eight months since the spirits had urged him to come to San Francisco and spread the "beautiful doctrine," Mansfield had established himself as the most respectable "test" medium in the city, though certainly not
the most profitable. Struggling from week to week to make a comfortable
living, he had an extra incentive to welcome the photographs, hoping that
they would quell the critics and convince a few new investigators of the validity of Spiritualism. "That Spiritual photography beats all thus far," he
wrote to his wife; "hope it will last and thus the fact of the dear departed be
recognized by there Earth ones—thus settling the fact of Spirit communication beyond doubt." The people of California badly needed the philosophy of Spirit communication, he felt, especially the "Loafers, and thick
skulls" who thrived there, and Mansfield was aware that such startling fare
as a spirit photograph would fill his slate.[29]

San Franciscans certainly seemed primed to embrace the news. In late December the first news reports of Gardner's images created a splash in the papers, carrying just enough whiff of scandal to arouse the curious and promise enough of truth to entice and intrigue the respectable. The local papers buzzed, "full of the news," and the people debated their authenticity. According to Mansfield, "Some think it a trick of the operator—some fancy it is real. Some think that the spirit figure is the figure of some person who had once been taken on the same plate and not fully *erased*. Various are the conjectures concerning it—but you may depend upon it the affair has produced a great stir here—I hope it will result in the awakening of many who have doubts of the souls immortality."[30]

Even before seeing his first spirit image, however, Mansfield began to show caution. With eight years of experience as a public medium, he had insight into every facet of the enterprise, the honest and dishonest alike, and he was keenly aware of the veering dangers of public opinion. In 1857 he had taken part in one of the most widely discussed tests of Spiritualism in the antebellum period, the "Cambridge investigations," in which the Boston *Courier* assembled a group of Harvard professors (Benjamin Peirce, Eben Horsford, Louis Agassiz, and B. A. Gould) to examine phenomena produced by a handful of the most prominent mediums, including Mansfield, Leah Fox Brown and her sister Catherine Fox, and the Davenport brothers. While the professors—all avatars of modern scientific thought—remained unimpressed, this episode forged an important link between Mansfield and Gardner, who had organized the Spiritualist response to the *Courier*. Gardner was connected to Mansfield in a second way as one of the few stalwarts of eastern Spiritualism to visit California before 1862, having followed the behest of the spirits there in 1849. Thus the first news of spirit photographs reinvigorated a deep and multifaceted chain of connections binding men across the distance of a continent.[31]

However confident Mansfield may have been in Gardner's honesty and sincerity and however strongly he felt about the existence of spirits, in the absence of a personal acquaintance with Mumler, he could not shake the fear that fraud might somehow be involved. Mansfield had only to consult the catalog of wrongs committed by persons "cloaked under the garbs of Christianity or religion and spiritualism" to realize the peril presented by the stranger, by the figure who stood outside of the bonds of love and sympathy circulating among family, friends, and community. Yet in the face of such peril, Mansfield chose to remain optimistic that the moral order of the universe would set things right, and he drew a typically Spiritualist moral about behavior in this world and the next. "Methinks when their doings are exposed by the light of Eternity, separate the selfishness from the good deeds, they will be found wanting. Then how careful ought we to live—who have been blessed above the majority of our fellows, we who have heard the angel voices, and whispers, we who have there dear presence from day to day—and while we are in the amidst of evil doers let us have all the charity we can possibly have for them—let us ask ourselves what we should do better th[a]n they do with the same light they have."[32]

Mansfield's fears mounted when an article was reprinted from the eastern papers asserting that the spirit photographs were all "a fizzle." While interest climbed in the city, Mansfield drew upon his network of family and friends in the East to supply him with the actual goods, both to see for himself and to sate the curiosity of his clients. "Many run to me," he complained to his wife, "expecting I would have such a picture if any there was in Existence," but like a merchant short of stock, the best he could manage was to tell them shipment was expected soon. Yet reports from Boston were not encouraging. From reports received from his Spiritualist friends, Mansfield grew ever more dubious about the "Mumbler affair," for he felt that if the photographs were genuine, "it would seem ere this the Public, or at least the Boston Community, would have been all alive to it." But the community demurred, and in Mansfield's eyes it must have been because Mumler stood outside of Spiritualism, having "no sympathy with such an undertaking." Thinking, perhaps, of counterfeiting, the archetypal covert peril of the antebellum period, Mansfield insinuated that after all Mumler was "an engraver, not a photographer and the whole thing was given him while other people was attending to religious rites on Sunday." The appearance of a second spirit photographer, Mrs. Stuart, was even more alarming, for she, too, stood outside of the Boston Spiritualist community. "Who is Mrs. Stuart?" he asked his wife, "and how came her to photograph Dr. Gardner & family?" Despondent, he concluded, "If the whole thing is a 'Hoax, a Fizzle,' then the Quicker it dies out, the Better."[33]

Early in January, Mary Mansfield finally delivered. The image she obtained created exactly the stir that Mansfield had both anticipated and feared, and one after another the members of the Spiritualist community in San Francisco traveled to Mansfield's rooms for a viewing. Whatever doubts Mansfield might have entertained, San Franciscans reacted with enthusiasm, powerfully and emotionally. Mansfield's description of the reception of the image is worth quoting at length as an indication both of his ideas about the photograph and the manner in which others responded.

> Well my friend Colburn came in this Evening and after we had chatted awhile I held up to his gaze the Gardner photograph, and his eyes filled with tears in a moment. Says the Judge My *God* if that is so, then he was satisfied to die at once. He wept as a child would, and that to after I had told him the Stories that were in circulation about it, but the Judge says they may Humbug it but he believes that one is as true as the one of the doctor. Colburn has it at his house this Evening but will not let it go beyond his wife. We will keep it close until we hear more about it. Dear me dont I hope it is a *success.*
>
> But the Gold & Silver coin of all countries [has] been counterfeited. In fact it is an argument in favor of the real coin for was there no real, there would be no need of counterfeiting. But send me some that the friends can recognize positively is there no one but Doctor Gardner that has made trials of this kind? You *must have* a nice old time in defending spiritualism with such odium heaped upon it as would most naturally be from such Exposition & too from the Spiritual organs too—well we have waded deep through trouble, made by pretenders, and we may find such in our pathway while we tabernacle below, but with the wheat, tares ever was found and ever will be found, and why marvel at this report of imposture on the part of the photographer, even if it be true—. . . .
>
> But if they get a Story going through the papers here about those "photographs," I am fearful it will dampen the good feeling, so much in favour of spirit intercourse, or so prevalent in this City at the present time.[34]

Colburn's reduction to tears, recalling Mary Lincoln's, and his hyperbolic claim of preparedness for death are an indication of the remarkable emotional power subtended by the spirit image, but they are all the more remarkable when one considers that Colburn was responding to an image of a man he probably had never met. In Spiritualist terms Colburn's response was based upon a deeply felt sympathy established with Gardner and Gardner's spirit child through the medium of the photograph. Sympathy and its derivative, harmony, were the foundational emotions of Spiritualism, uniting spirit with spirit, spirit with mortal, and mortal with mortal. Sympathy and harmony were the nuclear forces that bound the atomic

Spiritualist community. "The spirit kingdoms," according to a popular work on spirit life, "may be said to consist of one grand co-operative society, the various members of which are so united in sympathy and purpose that all work together as one person for the amelioration of human sorrow and suffering." Even William Mumler recognized the centrality of these emotions in arguing that "harmony is one of the first principles of all spiritual manifestations. It is the conducting wire through which our spirit-friends are enabled to transmit their messages of love." Linked to a man in Boston he had never met through the medium of a photograph, Colburn established a sympathetic bond that, like mourning, enabled him to share vicariously in the man's emotions and abate his "sorrow and suffering" even at a distance.[35]

Predictably, the crucial piece of evidence required to validate this highly charged image was the positive recognition of the close relationship of spirit and mortal, a corroboration that the sympathetic bond unites living and dead as well. Mansfield implored his wife to ask Gardner for "particulars" of the sitting and, more importantly, to clarify how it was that he recognized his deceased children. "If Doctor G. says they are his departed children," he surmised, "then that will go far towards establishing the fact spirits can present themselves as claimed by Mumbler. But if Doctor Gardner has no recollection of his children or friends, no resemblance in the photographs then we may conclude the whole thing is bogus."[36]

By March 24 the evidence relayed by Mary and Spiritualist friends confirmed Mansfield in the belief that Mumler's images were produced "by some hook or crook of the opperation," though he was not prepared to jettison his belief in the possibility that spirit images might be taken. One instance of fraud, he believed, could not kill the larger truth. "Truth may have to struggle hard," he argued, "as it ever has to cut its way through error, but it is sure to carry all before it, though it may not travel half as rapidly, as a *lie*."[37]

In a particularly revealing response to the pressures he felt as his doubts swelled, Mansfield attempted to withdraw the image from circulation, to isolate it from the chain of sympathetic exchanges that linked the community and remove it from introducing inharmonious influences. In doing so, he feared that he might "extinguish a spark of fire which may be fanned into a blaze," might stultify the extension of his community, but he felt the removal was essential, given the potential response if the image proved false. At the least, Mansfield hoped to hold onto the image until receiving more definitive reports from Spiritualist colleagues who were investigating Mumler, but his efforts to latch the barn door were foiled by the bolting horse. Despite his desire not to "let it out generally," the news spread "like wild fire." Ironically, the effort to suppress its currency was confounded by the very phenomena it had produced: the network of communications established among Spiritualists on both coasts. Mansfield's friend General Rowe had pursued a direct connection with Mumler and obtained pictures independently, while Mumler followed his own family connections into California, sending "likenesses taken of himself" to his sisters who lived there, possibly copies of the very first spirit photograph. At the same time spirit images also turned up from an unknown source in Marysville, 125 miles northeast of San Francisco, where they were put on display before a small but lively Spiritualist community.[38]

As the curious, credulous, and faithful streamed into Mansfield's rooms, he informed them of the rumors but allowed each individual to "make what they please from the picture"—not unlike what Mumler later claimed to have done with Gardner—and the majority accepted the truthfulness of the image wholesale. As the intense excitement over the images wore down in the heat of summer, Mansfield returned to his business as "post master," making little further mention of what he concluded was an unfortunate episode.[39]

Three major conclusions can be drawn from the reception of spirit photographs in San Francisco. First, the interpretation of the images by Spiritualists was founded in a complex understanding of the position of the subject, photographer, and image relative to an extended network (community) of people and spirits. Mansfield, an ardent Spiritualist, became a thorough skeptic about Mumler, believing that the critical issues lay not so much in Mumler per se or in the technology of photography, but in a pair of sympathetic relations: Mumler with the Boston community and the spirits with Dr. Gardner.

Second, information for assessing the veracity of images was evaluated largely with reference to a system of personal relationships, and particularly through people connected by a perceived emotional mutuality (sympathy) rather than by the impersonal or abstract relations of authority or "rationality." The system of emotional exchanges and resulting indebtedness that bound the community thus became the criterion by which moral judgments were made: distinguishing truth from fraud, social peril from spiritual purity.

Finally, spirit images are remarkable for the ease with which they slipped into promiscuous circulation, where they reinforced, connected, or even created communities of relatives, friends, and believers bound to one another by sympathetic ties. Gardner's *cartes de visite* set off a chain reaction that propagated from coast to coast; as the images circulated, they strengthened, renewed, and formed cycles and epicycles of relationships. Mansfield, for example, communicated through his wife and friends to other friends and colleagues, who interrogated yet other colleagues about other persons who stood apart from the community. As a result of the arrival of spirit photographs in California, Mansfield, Colburn, Rowe, and others were yoked with Gardner, Stuart, and Mumler in Boston to comprise a great anastamosed network spanning the continent. Like minds descended upon Mansfield or others in the network or visited inland centers like Marysville to view the images and share emotions.

Metaphorically (and functionally) spirit photographs functioned within these communities as specie, the physical objects of an exchange that represent a deeper system of exchange and indebtedness at the emotional level that serves as a socially binding force. Here the center of circulation is the corpse, love, and faith, with sympathy as the factor governing the transaction. Spirit photographs struck deeply into the heart of the moral structure of Victorian society because through these images individuals were able creatively to reconstruct themselves within the moral heart of Victorian culture and to engage in contesting its most corrosive effects—the sundering of family, friends, and church and the riving of society into Hobbesian atomism.

THOUGHTS AND AFFECTIONS: THE MORAL ECONOMY OF SPIRITS

In 1865 the veteran daguerreian Thomas Easterly implored Americans, "Save your old daguerreotypes, for you will never see their like again."[40] His longing for the images on which he had cut his photographic teeth was more than mere nostalgia. The direct-positive process that resulted in the daguerreotype—each image unique—had already been replaced by the wet-plate negative process from which a limitless number of positive prints could be generated, and Easterly recognized that glass plates were reordering the very meaning of photography. Beginning in the mid-1850s, glass-plate technology rapidly supplanted daguerreotypy, and by 1862 paper photographs pervaded the nation. The temporary and permanent separations imposed by the Civil War, combined with the relatively low cost with which paper images could be produced, spawned a revolution in photographic currency. Small, cheap, and durable, *cartes de visite*—the most popular format—flew through the mail by the hundreds of thousands, forming a vital link between soldiers and their families and friends at home.

Through sheer reproducibility negative technology permitted the photographic image to enter into much broader circulation than was possible for daguerreotypes. From a single session dozens of photographs might affordably be produced for distribution, and unlike daguerreotypes, these were a tractable technology for publishers. The transition to glass therefore generated a radical increase in the cultural presence of photography, bringing it into contact with ever-expanding audiences, replicating on a national scale the cycles of circulation that drew James V. Mansfield into circles upon circles of Spiritualist communities. Marcus Aurelius Root put his finger on the nation's pulse in anticipating how this increased circulation affected its citizens.

> In the order of nature, families are dispersed, by death or other causes; friends are severed; and the "old familiar faces" are no longer seen in our daily haunts. By heliography [photography], our loved ones, dead or distant, our friends and acquaintances, however far removed, are retained within daily and hourly vision. To what extent domestic and social affections and sentiments are conserved and perpetuated by these "shadows" of the loved and valued originals, every one may judge. The cheapness of these pictures brings them within reach, substantially, of all. In this competitious and selfish world of ours, whatever tends to vivify and strengthen the social feelings should be hailed as a benediction.[41]

The response of many Americans was intensified still further by the popular notion that photographs were more than mere representations of individuals, they were a synecdoche of the self. Under a daguerreian regime the identity between image and referent was taken for granted by most observers, and in the popular imagination, at least, such ideas were translated directly onto the glass plate, turning the *carte de visite* into a deeply personal object, tightly bound up with the identity of the individual, serving as a virtual surrogate for the dead or absent original.

The conjunction of Mumler's and Mrs. Stuart's spirit photography with Stuart's other occupation as a manufacturer of hair jewelry—two seemingly disparate enterprises—provided another avenue by which the photograph and individual identity were linked. The practice of removing locks of hair from the deceased to weave into bracelets, rings, or necklaces reached its apex in the mid-nineteenth-century culture of death. As an important product in the mourning kits of middle-class Victorians, hair jewelry was rooted in popular notions of spiritual respect for the body and affection for the person, but like handwriting, hair was something more: it carried a "palimpsest" of the individual. For psychometers and clairvoyants, hair could stand as a surrogate for the individual and could be assayed for the intricacies of character and selfhood. Spiritualist physicians like Frederick L. H. Willis or Mrs. A. B. Severance advertised that from a lock of hair or an autograph sent to them, they could delineate a person's "leading traits of character and peculiarities of disposition; marked changes in past and future life; physical disease," and they claimed that from these palimpsests they could advise their clients on business ventures and marriages, harmonious or inharmonious.[42]

Photographs, too, contained palimpsests of the individual. The most evocative evidence of this is found in a spirit image of Mumler's in which three full-length spirits are seen gathered about the photograph of a young woman (figs. 6, 7). In fact, Mumler not infrequently employed photographs to stand in for living sitters, obtaining excellent results, and in similar fashion he and other spirit photographers developed the ability to photograph handwriting from those spirits who were unable, for whatever reason, to materialize in form, the autograph standing in for the spirit. He was particularly proud of an image he had taken that featured a spirit's name written out in full next to her face. He insisted that "there can be no 'mistaken identity' in her correct name," even if the physical appearance of the spirit might be confounded.[43]

In essence, spirit images fulfilled two distinct functions. On the one hand, the image depicted the individual within a sympathetic framework, the living yoked to an extended community of living and dead, distant and

FIG. 6. Three spirits gathered about a photograph, by William Mumler, ca. 1870.
(Darcy-Haven Collection: Private Collection)

FIG. 7. Edouard Isidore Buguet's image of an unidentified female spirit attracted to a photograph, ca. 1870. (Eugène Rochas Papers, American Philosophical Society)

near, by the power of affect. On the other hand, the photograph was itself a commercial object, often bearing the photographer's backmark advertising his services or, like Mrs. Stuart, advertising services other than photography. Although little is known about the marketing of spirit photographs other than Mumler's claim that he had no need of advertising, given the efficacy of word of mouth, spirit photographers like Benson C. Hazleton and (as it turns out) Mumler are known to have advertised regularly in Spiritualist journals.[44]

Particularly in the years after the Civil War, spirit images themselves became objects of widespread commercial exchange, circulating not just within the community of friends and family but in the broader community, in much the same way that images of actresses, singers, and political figures were exchanged, serving simultaneously to draw the viewer into the affective nexus of the persons represented and as advertisement for the mediums' services. Mumler's image of Abraham and Mary Todd Lincoln, for example, sold well in the postwar period, as did Fanny Conant's image of her spirit guide, the Indian girl Vashti; and when controversy began to swirl around the materializations involving "Katie King," images of the materialized spirit were widely advertised and consumed.[45]

Each of these cases points out an important distinction between spirit photographic mediumship and other forms of mediumship: while rapping, table tilting, and clairvoyance could be performed publicly for a fee or privately for free, there were virtually no noncommercial instances of spirit photography. A surrogate, more than simply an image of the sitter, the spirit photograph thus became the means by which the sitter literally inserted himself or herself into the parallel economies dominating American society: into the moral economy of sympathetic exchange centered upon the dead body and into the market economy of financial exchange. As Esther Schor concludes, "The circulation of sympathies maps in a moral realm the dynamic process of exchange, negotiation, circulation—that is, the mechanisms by which both valued things *and values themselves* are distributed within a culture."[46]

The values distributed, however, require close inspection, and in the following chapters I explore, in different ways, the implications of the slippage between these (and other) parallel economies, as well as the boundaries of exchange. Ideally, circulation of either sort provided both the carrot of promoting social coherence and the stick of the fear of severance from these relations, guaranteeing the discipline of manners and morality while alive. Ideally, the spirit and its material manifestation, the body, formed the key element in evoking the imaginary power of death. Without claiming to have read *The Theory of Moral Sentiments*, Spirit Violet did her best to summarize its argument as it applied to the world of living and dead. "Oh, the power of sympathy!" she cried. "Mortals, you understand it not! When truly expressed, it flows toward the soul of its recipient in waves of light, which become tangible to the suffering one, and form a bridge over which he may pass to a condition of happiness and peace." In theory, and at times in practice, spirit photographs stitched Spiritualist communities together with affective bonds, providing a dynamic system by which the living subject could engage in the creative act of self-construction and self-definition within a tightly circumscribed, spiritualized space, spiritualizing the market, sanctifying exchange. Yet at the same time the spirit photograph commodified the spirit and the self.[47]

Spirit photography was an assertion of the centripetal force of familial and affective ties over and above the centrifugal forces of social disruption, including the forces of the market. But what sort of challenge to the market could spirit photos muster when they were participating in its extension? Alfred Russel Wallace, the socialist and Spiritualist, was among those who recognized the conundrum, and he distanced himself from the implications by claiming that he would "not depend on paid photographers for evidence as to the vali[di]ty of Spirit Photography." But images from the 1870s and after suggest that the slippage between the spiritual and commercial registers was nearly complete: the spirit image gradually evolved from an icon of affect into a commercial article. The early emphasis upon the affective nexus of family and friends and the assertion that sympathy could endure distance and death to "vivify and strengthen the social feelings" were supplanted by images that said little about the subject and less about community.

By the turn of the century, the images offered by spirit photographers depicted obscure spirits constrained to haunt a single locale, or amorphous ectoplasm oozing from the orifices of a medium, or Indian or "Oriental" spirit guides—isolated, furtive beings, when in the body at all. What sympathies they experienced never developed out in the darkroom.[48]

5

Vox Populi

ON A SUMMER'S NIGHT in 1851, a "bright and beautiful" spirit appeared
to Judge John Worth Edmonds, cloaked in a gossamer robe "as if it was an
atmosphere of a pale-blue . . . , transparent and ever moving like living
flame." This noble, gray-haired spirit shone forth with a "great firmness,
as if he could stand unmoved amid a conflict of worlds," radiating the purity and intellect seen only in the highest spheres of spiritual attainment.
Edmonds was moved. At last, he had met the great George Washington.[1]

During the 1850s Washington seldom called casually from the depths of
the grave, and his visit to Edmonds was far from casual. Still "deeply interested in the welfare of [his] country," Washington had returned to deliver a jeremiad to his nation, rebuking it for descending from the high
principles of the founding generation. "Bound up as my heart even yet is
in the continuance of its freedom," he wailed, "looking on its institutions
as the great fountain of freedom that was yet to flow over the whole earth,
I ask myself, 'Where now is the spirit that made us free?' and from dark
and dismal depths alone a voice answers, 'Here, buried beneath the load of
oppression and selfishness which has grown up and overwhelmed us.'"[2]

Although visits from the dead were common fare in the 1850s, there was
something unusual in the return of a Washington, Franklin, Jefferson, or
Paine, or any of a host of other historical figures who inserted themselves
in spirit circles from Bacon and Swedenborg to Osceola, Tecumseh, and
Jesus. Unlike the missives delivered by little-known spirits to their obscure
mortal relatives, the words of the late and great came truly from the land
of the unknown. Drawn by the attractive force of affective and familial
bonds, the typical spirit was a departed relative or friend come to provide

private words of solace, encouragement, or admonition. Familiarity—in its fullest sense—was a key element in the dynamic engagement of spirit messenger and mortal recipient.[3]

But with Washington, where was the familiarity? Among antebellum Spiritualists, who could claim a personal connection to the first president? Who bore kinship to Osceola? The Washingtons of the spirit world stood apart from the great expectation of spirit communication, no affective community of family and friend shepherded him to earth, and yet visits from Washington, Franklin, and Paine occupied a peculiar prominence in Spiritualist circles. On those occasions when these figures appeared, their words assumed a distinctly public cast, addressing the state of the entire nation, not just the state of the individual soul.

In this chapter I examine Washington's postmortem career as it played out on the landscape of antebellum reform, religion, and social tendentiousness. I suggest that the spirit Washington played a vital role in extending the affective ties of kin and kind to the extended nation, laying the emotional structures of interpersonal affinity over the corporate structures of life at midcentury. He was, as it were, a way to think and feel the nation, to create a constellation of love that consolidated family and state in mutually cognizable dependency and that offered a reformist map of the structures of the sundered body politic. For the Spiritualists who read these works, sympathy was the guiding star that led them not simply to enact a political idea but to create in their social and political lives an analog to the most deeply felt emotional relations.

And yet Washington also revealed an alternative vision, as well, one in which he unapologetically embraced the divisions of modern life and endorsed the social and racial inequality that wracked his nation. In his strange postmortem career, Washington delivered strident antisectarian messages that mingled anti-Christian or antireligious sentiments with the language of the revival tent. He spoke of immediate abolition and leveling equality, but also of social hierarchy and racial subordination. Through him the full workings of mnemonic poesis—memory as a creative act—were exposed: reified and vivified in the form of spirits and confirmed by the logic of sympathetic practice, memory assumed a wild, unkempt present. Washington's words exposed the deep roots of present life and brought the experiences of the past to bear on the issues of the present, but they exposed as well the incomplete, fragmented nature of memory, in which the fragments became resources for a reconstituted present. As memory made tangible and malleable, Washington was the wellspring of sentiments supporting radically opposed political and social visions.

GEORGE WASHINGTON, DECEASED

The evanescent George Washington and his "atmosphere of pale blue" presented a conundrum: here Judge Edmonds recognized the unmistakable figure of the ex-president, and at the same time here was a figure with whom he bore no obvious relation. With no one under the illusion that traversing the grave was easy, the prediction, as I have suggested, was that only where the ties of sympathy were strongest, where emotional exchange flowed most freely, could the distance of death be bridged, and although sympathy was not bound strictly by blood, it was habitual and most strongly developed within the family or within a circle of close friends where intimate contact occurred most often.

And yet in the 1850s how many Americans could claim intimacy with Washington? How many knew him at all? To a degree Washington's appearances were indeed structured and authenticated by sympathetic ties and by the revelatory moment at which a distinctive trait of character proved his identity. He was almost invariably described as being in the company of his old friend Lafayette or as standing near Mary, Augustine, and Martha, but where the living medium and living communicant fit into the equation was often more obscure. Washington's spiritual appearances therefore demanded additional explanation, as well as additional verification.[4]

Unlike the host of spiritual mothers, brothers, and aunts who populated antebellum séances, Washington was a public utility, a mnemonic resource constructed around the works of Parson Weems, Jared Sparks, Benson Lossing, and dozens of lesser-known histories of the nation's founding. When he came to greet Spiritualists, Washington came not as a part of the memory or affective experience of the individual but as part of the ambient memory, as a common affective resource for the nation, freighted with expectations about who he was and how he must behave.

With his spirit removed from the realm of the individual and particular into the collective, one of the primary factors influencing the response of witnesses to the appearance of Washington (or Franklin or Paine) was therefore how the shade met expectations of the living man. Not surprisingly, the spirits Washington were minor epitomes of popular images of the president, and on those instances in which they were not, doubt crept in. John Bovee Dods, who argued that spirit communication was the product of natural electrical phenomena, criticized the signature of one spirit Washington for failing to match the living man's well-known penmanship, and more damningly, he insisted that the spirit's style of writing was far inferior, simultaneously belying both what one would expect from the Father of Our Country and claims to postmortem progress. "Do Webster and Clay go backward in eternity?" he asked rhetorically. "Their communications show, that they have lost their eloquence and good sense by which they moved men's souls on earth. Clay has lost his knowledge of English grammar and composition, and become only about half-witted! and Webster, Franklin, and Washington are not much better off!"[5]

During her dalliance with Spiritualism, Lydia Maria Child similarly protested that in one book the spirits of "J. Q. Adams, Gen. Washington, Napoleon, &c. all write in the same florid style, like the very ambitious composition of a smart school girl," though she demurred from attributing this to fraud on the part of the medium. Already skeptical of such messages because they fell outside the expected sympathetic nexus, these critics made many Spiritualists doubly wary of messages purporting to come from the illustrious dead. At the turn of the twentieth century, a noted skeptic concluded that the "common sense" of the majority of antebellum Spiritualists soon led them to reject all such communications, particularly when coming through mediums seeking "to win recognition for themselves and their utterances by the use of great names."[6]

And yet Washington came to visit. In the absence of an affective link with the living, Washington's appearance at séances was best explained by positing a sympathetic affinity with all Americans. Although not a father by blood, he was, as he assured many listeners, the Father of His Country, and he remained deeply concerned "that nothing should disturb the harmony of the United States," their common nation, their extended affective community. Adam Smith had drawn the limits of sympathetic action at the boundaries of the nation, a point that Spiritualists would debate, but with Washington it was clear that in place of familial love, the dead president offered the love of country, suggesting that his mortal auditors were bound into a national web of sympathy as tangible and embracing as the family. As patriot or patriarch, he therefore became a point of articulation between the private world of interpersonal love and the public world of explicit politics and nationhood, mapping the affect of family relations onto the relations of state and nation. Werner Sollors has suggested that Benjamin Franklin, the great American scientist, served to help negotiate the conjoint excitement and tension over the impact of modern technology, but as the small, scattered rump of superannuated Revolutionary veterans were called forth to reflect upon the current state of their nation, who better to call than the revered Washington?[7]

The process of writing this spiritual history, however, required a severe editor. To begin with, Spiritualists needed to account for those aspects of Washington's public persona that conflicted with sympathetic expectations. The president's archmasculinity, for example, ran counter to the Spiritualist norm, and his military mien was troublesome to those who advocated a golden rule that verged on, or subsumed, pacifism. For some spirits Washington death simply was not up to the task of expunging such unpalatable behaviors. While other spirits wore the white robes of purity, he and Lafayette continued to don their military uniforms to signify their nation' continuing struggle.[8]

More starkly, when Abraham Pierce refused a "parley" of spirits who had asked him to make his mediumship public, he was literally issued orders by the general. "Report yourself in readiness . . . to carry our messages of truth to the enemy's camp, with an offering of peace," he was told. "Take this as your commission." When Pierce still refrained, the general and his compatriots threatened force to make him comply and eventually acted upon their threat. "They commenced with redoubled vigor, like many persons chopping or cutting my body in pieces," Pierce wrote, and "my arm and hand were controlled by the spirits and the order was taken out of my pocket, and held up and shook in presence of the whole assembly . . . and I was compelled to read it." The handwriting on the document was unquestionably Washington's, he reported, though for Spiritualists the behavior could hardly be said to demonstrate spiritual improvement.[9]

In general, the logic of Spiritualist progress dictated that Washington's spiritual understanding of a sympathetically structured society would lead him to reject his mortal martial prowess. Like many illustrious spirits he did so by employing the evangelical formula of openly repenting his past through the public admission of sin in order to prepare for rebirth into a new, consecrated life, and he emphasized that the "rebirth" of the afterlife had allowed him to recognize his faults and relegate his militarism to the past. Through spiritual improvement Washington moved beyond violence to forms of behavior more in keeping with the precepts of sympathy. "I wish to bear my testimony to the truth," he exclaimed. "I wish to tell all that live hereafter, that peace is of God; that war is in opposition to His government." War, said the general, was the "most ungodly, and monstrously wicked pursuit known." Through such a process even Benedict Arnold and Aaron Burr had been reclaimed for morality and were welcomed by Washington himself into the pantheon of America's spiritual guardians.[10]

From this same spiritual perspective, and still enrapt with concern for the nation, Washington now repented his patriotism, which "takes the lives of its fellows without number; all its desires are bent upon the destruction of those that oppose his love of country, without stopping to look." A man who had epitomized moral circumspection in life, Washington was expected while dead to manifest the standards of a still more highly evolved spiritual behavior. Through the natural operation of sympathy, he asserted that he was now guided by "other loves that had taken root and had grown some," though still "very much choked with [his] educational and sectarian views." As sympathy broke down the divisions of life that impeded progress, the scales were lifted from his spiritual eyes.[11]

After death, spiritual growth swept away earthly distinctions of rank and all the divisions they entailed. "We are on an equality here," Washington claimed. "All honors in the bodily state, fall with the earthly tabernacle. . . . He that had been worshipped on earth, was on a level with the worshipper; he that had enslaved his fellow man, was on a level with the enslaved; he that had commanded armies, with him that was slain on the opposite side, in the conflict." To the Christian Spiritualist Eugene Crowell, Washington suggested that "earthly distinction and fame, unless based on sterling worth, are of little account" and claimed that there were many with high reputations in life who, upon dying, discovered their reputations were based on false premise and error. Yet few in the spirit world elicited more praise than high holy Washington, the man so lauded in life. While the stature of John C. Calhoun and Daniel Webster fell dramatically in the afterlife, Washington, Franklin, and Christ retained their laurels and, when seen at all, were universally discovered in the highest spheres. Those like Washington who had led lives in harmony with the principles of sympathy were "as highly appreciated and honored, and their eminence as generally recognized there, as here."[12]

Office, power, and public reputation meant nothing to spirits, who recognized only distinctions based upon the degree of spiritual development, and this, of course, was a function of time. The power and reach of sympathy assured progress to all and healing for the deepest wounds. The predeceased friends or relatives initiated the process of spiritual instruction for the newly departed and the process of reconstructing and perfecting community. Washington and Lafayette were joined by Jefferson, Franklin, and other Revolutionary titans, and even by Thomas Paine, the man who had accused Washington of "treachery" for forsaking him in a Parisian jail, their animosities erased through their newly acquired spiritual vision. When Paine died, according to Charles Hammond, he "was delighted beyond the capacity of human expression" to learn how the spirit world functioned. "I was not wholly a stranger in my new life, for I found a great multitude of spirits whom I had known in the body. . . . I was well acquainted with George Washington, Benjamin Franklin, Richard Rush, and many others. I saw spirits teaching them lessons of wisdom." Rather than social isolation, death represented the supreme cultivation of social ties: one retained connections not only with the living but with any and all of those with whom one had ever had affinity.[13]

The obligations to active assistance imposed by sympathy were no less felt by the great than the mean. In a vision of the afterlife, for instance, the former Methodist minister James M. Peebles was surprised to be greeted by Washington and Lafayette "and many others whose names I had venerated on earth." Wondering how it was that he merited such an honor, Peebles heard a "sweet voice as from the ether" say, "Serving the poorest of my creatures was serving me, the Creator and Father of souls": all selfless persons and reformers were united in the divine sympathetic nexus. The principle of mutual assistance included not only assistance in spiritual development but assistance in practical matters. While Franklin used his scientific genius to fashion the telegraph and other scientific apparatus,

Washington used his distinctive skills in leadership and governance to introduce political reforms, providing comforting assurance of his continued interest in the nation. Ever the organizer and leader, Washington took part in several spirit congresses designed to nurture, heal, and guide his beloved nation. James Peebles glimpsed him in a "Congress House of Justice" with Adams, Lafayette, and other "departed prophets, and many of the noblest of the great men of the last century," where they conversed on political economy and learned from still "higher unselfish intelligences" in the great chain of progression, gleaning ideas to be translated for application to earthly governments. "The spirit world is a counterpart of this [one]," Peebles reported, "only in the higher mansions of God, or spheres, as they are now called, everything seems more ethereal and peaceful."[14]

From the vantage afforded by his elevated moral vision, Washington sought to liberate the world from social divisions of all sorts and to translate the peace and purity of the higher realms to earth. Although he opined on politics generally, Washington's particular cause in the afterlife was the most explosive issue of the 1850s, slavery. To Isaac Post, Washington revealed that he intended to "loose every fetter, so that the oppressor will see the necessity of loosening the binds that fasten him to his bondman, as well as his bondman to him." Regularly, predictably, he and his spirit chorus assailed "sectarian" support for slavery and the manner in which sectarians employed Scripture to underwrite their claims. Through Nathan Francis White, spirits poetically implored Americans:

> Shake off your lethargy! take Freedom's part,
> And boldly strike against the tyrant might
> Which could derive you of your manly right.
> Leave not one hateful, damning link to bind
> The Body, or its rightful monarch, Mind!

For any individual to be free in this transparent, mutualistic universe, the spirits implied, body and mind—every body and mind—must be liberated.[15]

What distinguished Washington from his antislavery spirit peers like Calhoun and Jackson was that he could speak both from his position as a repenting slaveholder and as an uncontroversial national healer. Calhoun could rue his ownership of slaves, Jackson could cringe, but nullification and sectionalism were indelibly theirs. Washington's centrality in forming and stabilizing the nation placed him in a unique position to bridge personal culpability and national guilt. Indeed, Washington repented his ownership of slaves, but even more so he lamented his role in perpetuating the political basis for the slave power. Having allowing slavery to be written into the Constitution and having upheld it during his tenure as president, he cried: "I regret the government was formed with such an element in it; so filled with wretchedness, misery, cruelty, debauchery, and every wickedness that can curse both the oppressor and the oppressed. . . . I see that it is utterly impossible for Slavery and Liberty, for a great length of time to continue together." Drawing from the arsenal of evangelical rhetoric and figuring slavery as America's original sin, Washington likened his nation to the biblical Sodom and Gomorrah, asking rhetorically whether "boasting, sinful America" could escape the divine wrath meted out to those cities if it continued to ignore the "broken hearts of His slavery-crushed children."[16]

On the basis of messages from beyond, Spiritualists of the postwar years often claimed that the spirits had predicted and guided the course of the Civil War. Most famously, they pointed to Washington's 1859 message to the medium J. D. Stiles, in which he revealed that the spirits of the founding generation had witnessed the "fearful strides the institution of slavery had made" in recent years and rued that "at no distant day, it will lead to the dismemberment of this Confederacy of States, to civil war, commotion and bloodshed." Emma Hardinge claimed that Spiritualists were particularly desired as soldiers because they did not fear death, and she chronicled Spiritualist contributions to the war effort, ranging from the chaplaincy of John Pierpont to Thomas Wentworth Higginson's role as colonel of a "colored" regiment.[17]

More colorfully, Thomas Richmond described how a congress of spirits led by Franklin, Washington, John Quincy Adams, and William Penn announced a new dispensation "by which the wisdom and sympathy of the upper is transmitted to the lower world, to our conscious material senses," and precipitated the war as a means to end the worst sin on earth, slavery. At the request of these spirits, Richmond moved to Washington to lobby on behalf of the spirit congress, informing mortal congressmen that "God can never smile upon a nation, can never give permanent prosperity to a people, who ignore this immortal truth—the right of one man is the right of all men." On a regular basis he forwarded messages from the spirits' congress demanding, for example, that Lincoln "free and arm all the negroes in the Border States and that portion of Louisiana which you now hold in your possession."[18]

For Spiritualists a demand for immediate abolition grew from the belief that a sympathetic cosmos was so thoroughly interconnected that the "deadly influence" of slavery necessarily "extended widely," North and South, instilling itself even into the core of affective relations, the family, threatening the very stability of society. Washington's words to Isaac Post were uncompromising. "When the mind looks down one portion of the human family, it cannot feel that pure disinterested love which he ought. Oh, the heart burnings that the family circle must feel, as they witness licentiousness written in the complexions of the children around the plantation, telling of the uncontrolled passions of some of the lordly ones. If these was no other reason for wishing this system abolished, it seems to me this is enough."[19]

THE LIMITS OF SYMPATHY

Though vocal and unwavering in their demands, Washington and his antislavery comrades nevertheless exposed an inherent tension in Spiritualist reform. While Spiritualism was often tarred with the brush of radical reform by its opponents (and many of its supporters), radical reformers had no interpretive monopoly. Washington's position as the memorial center of antebellum white America transformed him paradoxically into a mercurial figure. White Americans of widely divergent, even contradictory, perspectives all traced a national past in which Washington loomed large: northerners and southerners each claimed a share; slaveholder and abolitionist held him up as their own; he was political partisan and political unifier. It was if all could agree on the centrality of the man, though none could agree on who this man Washington was.

Whatever their actual numbers in the movement, radical reformist Spiritualists faced a large body of fellow believers who remained apathetic or unmoved to action, and in some cases they encountered active apologists for slavery. Spiritualists of all stripes struggled with the meaning and limits of sympathy, the bedrock of their social philosophy, and in the end the murky boundaries hedging it in allowed both radical and reactionary to employ the same moral language of sympathetic mutuality while drawing diametrically opposite conclusions for social practice.[20]

The issue of the limits of sympathy extends at least as far back as Adam Smith, who proposed that the boundary of the nation-state marked the effective limits of sympathetic experience. Common interest and habitual contact, he reasoned, were unlikely to extend farther, and Smith even acknowledged that a certain countersympathetic schadenfreude might be possible. Although the "instruments of war" were disagreeable as agents of pain and suffering, when that pain was inflicted upon "our enemies," the result was pleasurable, for "they are immediately connected with the agreeable ideas of courage, victory, and honour."[21]

Writing Spiritualist harmonialism into the founding event of the American nation (just as he brought the founding generation into the present), Washington described how in 1776 a group of "noble minds" gathered "in a harmonious body" to draft a Declaration of Independence that offered "equal protection" for "the whole family of man, without distinction of sect, color, or caste" so that "*all* would find peace and protection, and dwell together in a Family of Brotherhood, as the children of One Impartial Parent should dwell." But even as Washington envisioned creeds, colors, and castes within the American state, he excluded others within its borders from the sympathetic community: the Loyalists. More importantly, as Robert Hare would demonstrate, at a time when the terms *race* and *nation* were interchangeable, the differential topologies of national and sympathetic communities could lead one toward, rather than away from, slavery.[22]

Despite proclaiming himself an antislavery man, Robert Hare, a confidant of the deceased George Washington and by any measure one of America's most prominent Spiritualists during the first decade of the movement, became the best known of Spiritualist apologists for slavery and hereditary inequality (fig. 8). An emeritus professor at the University of Pennsylvania, inventor of the oxyhydrogen blowpipe and an innovator in electrical apparatus, Hare was America's best-known experimental chemist during the first half of the nineteenth century and a member of Philadelphia's established elite, the son of a brewer and member of the state constitutional convention and the nephew of Thomas Willing, a signer of the Declaration of Independence and president of the Bank of the North America.[23]

FIG. 8. Robert Hare, portrait by Daniel Huntington.
(American Philosophical Society)

With talents defying boundaries, Hare was at turns a scientist, novelist, and poet, and he was a visible man within the city and beyond. His scientific and mechanical prowess earned laurels in England, France, and Germany, as well as the United States, and he was respected in conservative circles as a writer on finance, economy, tariff, and trade. From the time of the War of 1812, Hare propounded an unrepentant old-money ideology, extolling the virtues of wealth and social standing as a boon for society, and in their pursuit, he wrote, even the occasional self-serving excess of commerce bore positive social fruit. Absent of folly and vice (those traits endemic to England but not America), Hare insisted that commerce would provide "a more moral mode of accomplishing a contemptible purpose," carrying with it the seeds of self-betterment as it was constrained by the moderating influence of wife and child. "The money sought in youth with a view to sensual enjoyment," he argued, "is at a later age often applied to the maintenance of a family," and although the hunt for lucre retarded "the refinement of taste" and the "improvement of the understanding," commerce had the salubrious effect "of rendering venality and corruption less necessary." With the disciplining influence of sympathetic familial obligations and affections characteristic of this nation, "pecuniary extravagance" would be thoroughly checked.[24]

Wealth further benefited society by offering a means to exercise "otherwise latent virtues," for without means, a man may "produce neither much credit to himself, nor benefit to others." One need not fret that wealth produced an undue concentration of power in too few hands, but rather one should worry that "politically [wealth] has too little influence," and as if to prove the point, he noted that "the rich are with few exceptions every where in the minority." Only the wealthy could be truly independent and "averse from hard labour, or menial occupations"; only the wealthy man could provide comfort for his family and education for his children and "have leisure to cultivate his mind; or to contemplate or study, the beauties of nature, or wonders of the universe."[25]

Although he was a supporter and beneficiary of industrial development, Hare opposed the newer forms of industrial capitalism, excoriating free trade and the laissez-faire economics that promised (or threatened) social mobility and the unseating of the old moneyed elite. More than this, he was a virulent anti-Democrat, reviling revolutionary Republicanism, Jacksonianism, and the egalitarian tendencies of the Democracy, singling out Jefferson and "Jeffersonians" for a special round of rebuke. Perhaps for these reasons he clung to the party distinctions of his youth well into the 1850s, calling himself an unreconstructed "Washington Federalist" and siding with the nouveau Whigs reluctantly, if at all. Steadfast amid the leveling currents of the new nation, he lauded the natural aristocracy of intellect, ability, and family—all traits he associated with himself, all traits of his particular hero, George Washington.[26]

Long a nonconformist Episcopalian and opponent of sectarianism, Hare began his seemingly unlikely turn to Spiritualism only with "a view to refutation." Having read Michael Faraday's theory that the tipping of tables at séances was the product of involuntary muscular action by the human participants, Hare employed his mechanical genius to contrive a device to perform the *experimentum crucis*. Yet when he put the Spiritoscope into action, instead of overturning Spiritualism, he overturned his skepticism, and in 1854 he became the most celebrated convert to a Spiritualist community in Philadelphia that reportedly boasted thirty spirit circles.[27]

Hare soon unsheathed his pen and scientific sword for the movement, describing the grounds for his own conversion and the methods involved in his experimental confirmation of the facts of spirit communion. Along with Judge John Worth Edmonds and Wisconsin governor N. P. Tallmadge, no individual was more often cited by Spiritualists as proof that levelheaded persons of impeccable social and intellectual standing could investigate the spirits and find their truths convincing. The elderly Hare abandoned science altogether "for the investigation of truth," as he put it, "and act to draw attention in the Spirit world," taking his case to the floor of the American Association for the Advancement of Science, where he was roundly jeered. As he was quick to note, Hare occupied an exalted position in the mortal and the spirit worlds, "too much attended by High Spirits for evil ones to have access" and possessed of a mediumship "not suitable for the lower Spirits." In short, he was a self-proclaimed harbinger of truth.[28]

The importance of Hare's book *Experimental Investigation of the Spirit Manifestations* lies in its claim to being a dispassionate scientific analysis more than an enlightened revelation, anticipating the form of argument that would be associated with the psychical research movement during the last two decades of the century. But the book was also an important statement of Spiritualist philosophy in its own right, both explicitly and implicitly exploring the shape of sympathy in Spiritualist praxis. Predictably, Hare's earliest spirit communications consisted of loving messages from his father and two spirit sons—the core of his deceased nuclear family—describing their life of harmonious, mutualistic development, the "*universal* and *eternal* progression" they enjoyed in the afterlife, and the absence there of "sectarian or ecclesiastical feuds" and "metaphysical dogmas." Like any good Spiritualist, Hare's son Theodore made sure that the living were regularly visited, cared for, and instructed by "spirits highly elevated in love and wisdom," who even when "nearly forgotten" by their living loved ones hovered always near. Hare's was a world of transparent sympathetic unity, of connection, affinity, harmony, and love. In the development of his own Spiritualism, however, he soon transcended his family, discovering a particular personal affinity for the generation of the founding fathers. Thus began his extensive postmortem correspondence with Franklin and, above all, Washington.[29]

As he assured his readers, Hare was among the few Americans who could draw a direct affective connection to the nation's founders. Through his father and maternal uncle, he traced his lineage to the founding acts and persons of the nation, and working in Franklin's city in Franklin's university, he imagined himself as Franklin's "successor in Science" and intellectual heir as ingenious scientist and inventor and master of electrical practice. But it was Washington whom Hare particularly favored. "Washington and my relations were on terms of reciprocal hospitality," he claimed, and although he was only nine when the president died, he noted that as a boy he had enjoyed the president's company "on various occasions." This January/December relationship with Washington continued after death. Early in their spiritual partnership, Washington announced that he was gratified by a poem Hare had written in 1813 to commemorate the president's part in twice liberating the American people, first from the tyranny of Britain and second from the tyranny of French Republicanism. As Hare recited the poem, Washington effused over his postmortem friendship with Hare's father, avowing "a love" for the young Hare "commensurate with his worth."[30]

This dandling boyhood on the president's knee left an indelible mark. In Hare's eyes Washington was peerless, "preeminent among heroes for the purity of his character," for his "disinterested patriotism," and this purity was unblemished even by the unfortunate fact of slaveholding. Although Hare sided with many northern Whigs in styling himself a moderate "antislavery" man—at least in so far as he opposed the "excesses" of bondage and advocated a noncoercive, gradual abolition with full compensation for slaveholders—he never forgot that the peerless Washington had been a slaveholder himself when performing his greatest works. Indeed, Hare claimed to have derived his opinions on slavery directly upon what he had learned from the higher spirits, including Washington, Franklin, Calhoun, the "noted antislavery champion Isaac T. Hopper," and even from Jesus himself. The ideas that he and like-minded Spiritualists garnered were intimately bound up in a distinctive political economy, balancing a belief in racial and social hierarchy with a fear of the effects of unrestrained capitalism and reformist social agitation.[31]

Like many of his peers, Hare insisted that slavery was not the primary evil confronting the nation. Although it might well be a symptom "of a great moral and malignant disease," as a South Carolina Swedenborgian claimed, it was surely not the only one, nor even the most "fatal," but merely a "hepatic flush that tells of the disorder of far more vital organs than can be found on the face." Contrary to the garrulous spirits of the lower spheres, the higher and more perfectly knowledgeable spirits with whom Hare conversed recognized slavery as simply one more form of natural inequality, "a consequence of the general laws by which the affairs of mankind are regulated by God." The basis of a stable social order was the recognition of natural inequalities and their inscription within the system of the state.[32]

In some sense, Hare admitted, the Golden Rule (sympathy in application) dictated that slavery was undesirable, but in the wake of the Fugitive Slave Act and Bleeding Kansas, antislavery had become even more undesirable, even more bitterly divisive. Consequently, Hare applied the lash of blame squarely to abolitionist backs. Abuses in slaveholding, he argued, were mutually the fault of northerner and southerner, produced by the fear that slaveholders felt at the antics of abolitionists. Were it not for the threat of servile insurrection "excited by Northern sympathisers," he insisted, "the conscientious holder of slaves would doubtless feel happier at the adoption of a system reconcilable with morals, philosophy, and the religion which they profess." The "phrenzied" demagoguery of a Charles Sumner, he insisted, would only plunge the South into barbarism. "Who," he asked rhetorically, "would wish to convert our Southern territory into another Hayti, or to see the plantations of the South in the ruined state of those of Jamaca inducing the blacks to retrocede to that wanted barbarism, out of which, few African nations if any have emerged?" It was in this sense that a proslavery Swedenborgian pronounced that "the abolition spirit is the subtlest demonism of the age."[33]

Such sentiments were eagerly seconded by other Spiritualists, and particularly by a former minister of the Church of Christ from Tennessee, Jesse Babcock Ferguson. While many northern Spiritualists and social radicals rent their garments over the domination of one segment of society by another, Ferguson embraced domination, arguing that slaves "are utterly discontented, unhappy and worthless, except when in subjection to the whites." Northern agitation on the subject, he said, only exacerbated matters: if left to their own devices, without interference, southerners would improve conditions for slaves and eventually would emancipate (and colonize) those few who were capable of independence. As abolition clearly ran against the grain of an inherently unequal human nature, it clearly contradicted the divine order.[34]

As evidence for his position, Ferguson claimed that forty-five years of abolitionist agitation had done nothing to improve the plight of the slave. "It has only placed him between the upper and nether millstone," he wrote. "It has made him a fugitive in a foreign and, to him, inhospitable clime. It has intensified sectional prejudice, and brought on a fratricidal war of unprecedented malignity and desolation. And it has revealed the blunder, not to say curse, of American statesmanship, in that, with all its cry against slavery, it has made no provision for the outgrowth of the coloured man's capacity. Moreover, it has anew demonstrated that the slavery of a tribe or race cannot be abolished, because, like childhood, it is natural."[35]

While northern Spiritualists argued that in heaven no barriers could conceal thoughts or feelings and while they assailed all barriers separating persons on earth, Ferguson celebrated some barriers, those between the sections and those between the races, complaining bitterly that "the crying evil of the day" is the "disposition to intermeddle with every body's business but our own."[36]

The Civil War did little to alter Ferguson's opinions on slavery or the spirits. Although he later claimed to have done his "utmost to unite the South to prevent the war," when the war came, he used his "impetuous eloquence" to urge unity in its prosecution. This "Patrick Henry of a new revolution" preached to Confederate recruits headed off to war, escaped arrest by Federal authorities only by fleeing into exile, and claimed to have undertaken a secret, apparently self-appointed mission to England on behalf of the Confederacy.[37]

The war's end barely slowed Ferguson, as he turned loose his aggression on the Radical Republicans in Tennessee, warning of a race war and Jacobin clubs if they were not held in check, and insisting still upon the value of slavery for the enslaved: "We can never abolish slavery by civil enactment. We but change the condition from one of dependence upon the superior civil development of the white man to that of dependence on the bounty of chance, amid the fierce and intense rapacity which the vast rewards of skill and industry of modern material conquest have organized over the whole area of so-called civilization. To free without provision for his enlargement, is but to victimize the negro, and send him down to a deeper barbarism than any now marking his worst condition in slavery."[38]

The natural condition of slavery, Ferguson argued, had promoted sympathetic union in the nation by establishing mutuality between enslaver and enslaved, binding them in "a spiritual and heavenly union, making them brethren in Christ, and heirs to the same heavenly inheritance." In such a community progress would guide the advancement of both master and slave, together as one. Indeed, he defined slavery as a "condition of servitude" where "one comparatively civilized people, may hold another of absolutely inferior civic attainment, in hereditary bondage . . . until at least the inferior shall become, in some degree, capable of the sustained efforts and persevering toil of a free government." This condition in many respects paralleled the Spiritualist vision of the superior spirits of the higher spheres controlling mediums for the benefit of the morally and spiritually destitute. In this regard, slavery became a fundamental instrument of progressive design, and if that design was thwarted, Ferguson, like Hare, insisted that Africans would be "utterly discontented, unhappy and worthless, except when in subjection to the whites."[39]

The Swedenborgian physician William Henry Holcombe added his brand to the fire in 1860 with an argument rooted firmly in structures of belief common to both Swedenborgians and Spiritualists. No less than it did for Ferguson, slavery emerged as a positive good, but it was Holcombe's particular genius to imagine the principle of correspondence as justifying, even requiring, slavery. To begin with, Holcombe enlisted the polygenic claim that the races were the products of separate creations, but in Swedenborgian fashion he argued that earthly races resounded with spiritual correspondences. Earthly races, he said, represented the degraded descendants of the beings created in a series of divine interventions. "Celestial man," the first and most primitive, had decayed into both Africans and Indians; "spiritual man," the second creation, devolved into Asians; while whites were the descendants of the third, or "natural man." These races existed in a discontinuous hierarchy reflecting their level of civilization, moral capacity, and spiritual advancement, with Africans falling short in every regard. Celestial beings originally had enjoyed "open communication" with the deity, and although they lacked literature, science, and government, "nature was an open mirror to them." In time, as Swedenborg described, they fell prey to sin, and in a cataclysmic change corresponding (in Swedenborgian terms) to changes in their internal state, many died, while a few had their spiritual faculties awakened. The celestial remnants of this debacle—Africans and Indians—remained "grossly sensual and barbarian" in their nature, childlike, lighthearted, simplistic, credulous, and timid.[40]

The differences between races were thoroughgoing and ineradicable, ingrained through separate creation and separate histories. Skin color, merely one measure of the gulf that existed between them, was laden with moral freight. In correspondential terms Holcombe argued that "perversions of charity would be represented by a lurid red, copper or bronze color, and perversions of truth by a dark or black color," with obvious implications for the character of Indian and African, respectively. More to the point, he contended that the laws of heredity were firm and inescapable, and because the African was "derived from the third, or deepest hell," it should be clear that "no exertion of his volitional or intellectual faculties can ever deliver him from his bondage."[41]

At this point the notion of slavery as a positive good blossomed. Sounding much like Robert Hare, Holcombe suggested that slavery benefited Africans by bringing the "*sensual-corporeal* principle" of their natures into "obedience and subjection to the *natural* or *scientific* plane of the white man's life." In slavery the African's "hereditary torpor is dissipated" through a spiritual influx from whites, and "the sphere of order, justice, and active use into which he [the slave] is inserted [becomes] repugnant to his attendant evil spirits, and they measurably leave him." Citing the decline in the population of free blacks in the 1850 census, Holcombe maintained that the discipline that whites imparted on black lives was necessary to their continued descent; without it, free blacks would disappear as swiftly as Indians. Acutely aware that notions of sympathy and unfettered intercourse led many Spiritualists to oppose slavery, Holcombe conceded that "the bondage of white man to white man, or of black man to black man, is fraught only with evil," but he assured his readers that sympathy between white and black was impossible because Africans "think, feel, and act differently from us in every thing. There is an impassable gulf between us." Physiologically, mentally, and morally the races were discrete, and in his opinion nothing more could be done. "Missionaries can do nothing," he wrote; "commercial intercourse can do nothing; external forces can do nothing."[42]

Hare's version of these riffs on the theme of positive good was carefully attuned to Spiritualist exigencies. Hare agreed with Washington, Franklin, and Isaac Hopper, who announced that ending slavery was "manifestly . . . impracticable" and perhaps even undesirable. Because "no person," he wrote, "would deem it reconcilable with morality or religion to make war upon the slave states in order to force emancipation" and because slaveholders could not be persuaded to divest themselves voluntarily, Hare insisted there were few options available for ending slavery.[43]

But why call an end to an institution so beneficial to all concerned? Rejecting "Jeffersonian" assertions that slavery degraded whites, Hare asserted that slavery, the true wealth of the nation, had benefited them both individually and as a country. The leisure that slavery made possible for southern whites had enabled a degree of cultivation of mind and manners found nowhere else, which made slaveholders, in Jesse Ferguson's pregnant phrase, superior to any "in the education of the affections [and] in the true knowledge of things." According to Hare the lessons of American history demonstrated "that many of the great and good men drew their birth first in the slaveholding states," including, of course, Washington and the other peerless Virginians of the Revolutionary generation. When enslaved, blacks were brought under white influence where at last they could be elevated culturally above barbarism. In contrast, whenever they had attained freedom, blacks had shown themselves incapable of self-governance or of fending for themselves and had proved their irredeemable inferiority. White control and tutelage were necessary for black betterment, even to the limits of their capacities. "Instead of working to abolish or check slavery," Hare suggested, "philanthropists" would be better put to "exert themselves to meliorate it" and let it run its course.[44]

Washington and the higher spirits predicted that the persistence of slavery eventually would "meliorate the condition of the African race," no less than the white, and Hare proposed a system by which slavery could be ended without loss to either. Innately inferior, blacks could be cared for "as so many minors" and provided with an appropriate education "to give them that subordinate menial condition which[,] as it must belong to one of the races[,] is more appropriate for the inferior race." A sort of Owenite community could be founded in which slaves (freed or not, he does not specify) could be trained in the menial manual arts and menial social status and held "under a control consistent with tutilage . . . where there could be sufficient exterior constraint upon that selfish individuality which have rendered the efforts of Owen and other philanthropic communists abortive." Then, perhaps, a few of the better sort of slaves might be returned to Africa to redeem that continent spiritually. "Let them, and their posterity, improved by their American education," Hare wrote, "vindicate the pretentions of the woolley head and black skin, in the clime appropriated to their race by God."[45]

Jesse Ferguson had no hopes of reseeding Africa for its betterment but was just as adamant as Hare that slavery benefited slaves. It was not simply that they were unhappy outside of servitude or that it had delivered them "from cannibalism and all the abominable barbarities of the lowest idolatry of the darkest region on the face of the face of the earth," but American slavery had placed them "in a relation of greater physical comfort than any other laboring class in the world." Comfort for the master, comfort for the slave: a rising tide of comfort lifted all boats. While abolitionists invoked sympathy and an abstract sense of racial justice to argue for the liberation of slaves, Ferguson and Hare argued that a proper understanding of sympathy led to the preservation of the peculiar institution for the economic and social benefits that welled forth from a slave society. Each believed that he "advocated [slavery] no less in the interests of the African race, for whom he has a true and generous sympathy."[46]

But these benefits were only a part of the equation. Hare began his assessment of the benefits of wealth by citing the lion as the paradigmatic example of the adage, "Wealth is in fact one species of power." Although the lion lacked human forms of wealth, his natural talents ensured that he was wealthy indeed, "since every creature within his reach is in effect as much his property, as the sheep in the fold are the property of the owner." Like the lion or the shepherd, ownership and control were the natural goals of humanity, and because wealth was beneficial, so too was control, as long as it was accomplished with paternalistic restraint. "Were it deemed a merit, than otherwise," Hare suggested, "to have a well organized, well fed, well housed and well clothed family of negroes, how much happier would it be."[47]

On rare occasions, Hare confessed, the inequities of the slave relation led to excess, and he acknowledged the moral affront posed by such situations. Yet the hallowed Constitution, as he was quick to point out, unequivocally sustained the moderated form of the institution Hare advocated. "The idea of holding human beings as property, as we do quadrupeds, is revolting," he admitted, "but the 'holding them to service,' in the words of the national Constitution, is widely different." Furthermore, Hare doubted that slavery could be reduced to the cruel and craven domination described by abolitionists; like wealth, even its excesses were productive of good. Labor relations inherently entailed inequality, but slaveholders, unlike industrialists, bore an inherent sympathetic interest in the well-being of their property and therefore were less inclined to exploit their workers. Just as the sympathetic union of marriage and family moderated the excessive wealth-seeking behavior of youth, the sympathetic union of master and slave would moderate the excesses of power, and "until the situation of free labourers, admits of a more favourable illustration," Hare concluded, "slaves in the Southern States have little to gain by an exchange of situation with them." If on some future occasion slaveholders chose to manumit their slaves, Hare hoped that the former slaves could be brought north to be employed in industry, assuming subordinate positions befitting their limited abilities. There, placed in closer contact with whites than would be possible in the South, freedmen could be further instructed and controlled to their benefit, while their labor could be used to benefit the North as it had the South. There, a sympathetic proletariat, they would improve industrial relations as well.[48]

At the national level Hare argued that the greater community stood to gain from the recognition and maintenance of proper race relations. "When slavery exists in a country," he asked, "does it not follow that subordination is indispensible to the welfare of the community?" In essence, slavery—or at least racial subordination—offered the most effective means of healing the divides of an industrial economy. Wealth is indeed power, unmistakably, and is desired and sought after by all reasonable men. In recognition of this state of affairs, a true sympathetic nation included—demanded—some sort of slavery for the benefit of those who, like the lion or white man, possessed the means of exerting their power.[49] A powerful government in the hands of the powerful few was a thing to be desired:

> The secret lies in this[:] that a rich man under an absolute government being more at liberty to do as he pleases, than a poor day labourer in a republic, a man will rather be *rich in a monarchy* than *poor in a republic*. There is hardly a poor man in this country of boasted freedom, who would not go to any monarchy where he could enjoy an estate nor is there any rich man to whom the offer should be given to retain his wealth and live in a foreign monarchy, even that of despotic Napoleon, would not prefer the latter alternative rather than work as a clerk, or official or operative for maintenance dependent on his personal daily exertions. . . .
>
> It is manifest that very few of those who call themselves Christians act as if they really believed in a future state. . . . They so palpably neglect his injunctions respecting wealth and resistance to blows as to pursue a course diametrically opposite, being not only intollerant of a blow but actually aggressive at the same time making the attainment of wealth a primary object of their exertions. . . . Were slaveholders spiritualists, they would readily strive to carry out the schemes which I have proposed, which have the sanction of the higher inhabitants of the Spirit world. The holder of slaves would feel that his position in the Spirit world would be more elevated in proportion as his treatment of his slaves should be more consistant with the Golden Rule. The slave perceiving his master thus acting like a father, would return a filial devotion and thus each would labor for the other's good. Vastly more work would be done by the same number of labourers with more economy and the master would be enabled to clothe, feed, and house his subordinates proportionably better.[50]

What distinguished Hare's arguments on slavery (or Ferguson's, or Holcombe's) was the degree to which he promoted social and racial hierarchy. Rigid systems of social ordination based on natural inequalities, he claimed, were the foundation for a stable and peaceful political order, congruent with the natural desire for wealth (power). His arguments were fundamentally Spiritualistic not merely in incorporating spirits but in his use of sympathy as the primary means of making sense of social relations. Yet where many antebellum Spiritualists entertained thoughts that "all the races compose one universal brotherhood" and that sympathy was ubiquitous and unlimited, Hare was fundamentally concerned with the sympathetic limits, unwilling to admit the most radical interpretations of sympathetic congress or to fall in too closely behind the democratizing spirit.[51]

As a spiritual cartographer Hare was intensely interested in the question raised by Adam Smith of how far sympathies could extend. Forged by proximity and exchange, sympathies produced a community comprised of a nested set of more or less powerful sympathetic subcommunities, all crosscutting but all bound by emotional and economic exchange. At some point, however, because the power of sympathy attenuated at distance, community frayed and lost its power to bind. Smith condemned the efforts to extend sympathy beyond these natural limits, condemning "those whining and melancholy moralists, who are perpetually reproaching us with our happiness" and our "natural joy of prosperity" in this unequal world. In the redshift world of the 1850s, with distance always receding, the question of boundaries acquired an added significance.[52]

For Smith a concern with the power, cohesion, and stability of the state led him to circumscribe the nation with a heavy border, but in the American racial climate, Hare and his cartographic allies discovered that other borders, unstable and shifting, required mapping as well. Although the higher spirits attached an importance to "the friendship, the affection, and the ardent love" between "congenial minds or souls"; he asserted that "they seem to recognize love as something which cannot be felt by all to all." Not everyone could participate in sympathetic commerce, and it was absurd to attempt to extend it beyond its natural pale. "Sympathy between the parent and child, between husband and wife, and likewise occasionally between brothers and sisters, or such friends as Pylades and Orestes," he wrote, "may be so strong as to induce the risk, if not the loss of life, but this sympathy cannot be self-induced. . . . The most that can be done is to act as if we did love, and consequently sympathize, so as to feel the pains and privations of another as if they were our own. . . . But were the sentiment to be felt universally, or even generally, there would be such a cutting up of our time, service, or attention, that, as respects any individual in particular, it would be nugatory, and might as well not exist."[53]

In part a restatement of Adam Smith, Hare's idea is rather more important in reformulating sympathy as a strategic natural resource of restricted availability, a resource requiring a calculated expenditure. In this economy sympathy and benevolence must be cultivated, but the careful application of social and emotional resources required that it be circulated only within the terrain demarcated by the natural limits of human skin and human power. "Does it not argue a want of discrimination," he asked, "to treat love as a sentiment, to be entertained toward all other mortals by mere volition?" Would Christ, he asked, enjoin humanity to love all when the capacity for love "manifestly varies through organization and education" as widely as the dog varies from the wolf, one with the capacity for civilization, the other weighed down by an unchanging and unchangeable barbarity. For Hare and like-minded Spiritualists, transracial sympathy was an affront to the divinely inspired order of nature. "Were his organization and education dependent on himself," he wrote, "it might be reasonable to say to a human being, Love your neighbour as yourself, love your enemies; but how can that Deity who determines man's race and his parentage, and of course whether he be a savage or a civilized man, whether a Thug or a *real* Christian, if such a thing can be,—how can that Deity require a being to do that which is irreconcilable with his passions, opinions, and habits, derived from nature and education, as well as the examples set by those around him?"[54] In all its inequity, racial biology, in effect, reflected the divine will that structured emotional capacities and social potentials.

Borrowing the primary assumption of American anthropology that Africans were hereditarily inferior, Hare and his cartographic allies mapped a nation of constrained sympathy in which blacks were variously within and without, capable of sympathetic commerce with whites only under specific conditions consistent with their natural inferiority. Naturally and irredeemably inferior, no degree of progressive development could produce equality, but when subordinated and controlled, they could be incorporated within the nation, participating with the superiors within the emotional and financial systems of exchange. Ferguson was most explicit. In the absence of slavery, blacks would regress, as he insisted had occurred after emancipation. "The reason is clear." In all of America, "not a county, not a township has as yet been set apart for the enfranchised negro—not a place where he can enjoy social equality—not one where his ignorance and even colour does not expose him to enormous trespass." Blacks, he concluded, could never be incorporated into a community with their superiors except as slaves, and when left to fend for themselves among whites as political and social equals or alone without them, they could never form a true community. The result was a choice between progress and regress, inclusion or expulsion.[55]

Similar concerns over the ability of blacks to participate in the sympathetic nation plagued even the more radically inclined Spiritualists. Having assured A. J. Davis that Africans would one day "work in the sunshine of gladness" and "barter with consumers" on their own, that they would one day become "an *independent* Nation!" the spirits equivocated on whether the race could be "nationalized" in America. "This is not yet known," they said, "but we perceive that their development depends upon this destiny." White Americans must not expel them, Davis was told, and they must be given justice and freedom. Then, if they chose of their "own subsequent genius and individual attractions" to leave, whites should support their decision financially.[56]

For Ferguson and Holcombe the sympathetic nation required slavery; for Davis, justice; for Hare, merely subordination. But all agreed that a commingling of commerce, power, race, and community formed the nation, and all shared in the sense that sympathetic rapport was embedded within the inequities of labor relations. Highlighting the boundaries of race, their mapping had the added effect of obscuring the systematic violence and oppression of slavery by secreting it behind the borders of nature, benevolence, and sympathy. To cut slaves "off from a race of masters with whom there is now a fellow-feeling in sorrows and joys," Ferguson wrote, was to sever relations in which there is "a mutual dependence and affection which calls into play all the finer emotions of our nature." To cut them off would simply reduce slaves to "aliens from our hearts and home."[57]

6

Invisible World

THE NEW YORK *Herald* pulled no punches during the convention of "Southern Loyalists" in 1866. "Blacks and Whites," it howled in headline, "Free Lovers, Spiritualists, Fourierites, Women's Rights Men, Negro Equality Men and Miscegens in Convocation!" Understandably, the thought of southern Republicans clamoring for radical change was hard for any dyspeptic Democrat to stomach, but even more than its stark political message, what begs comment in the headline is its odd congeries of -isms and -ites. With an impressive economy of word, the *Herald* conjured images of a far-flung subversive cabal, pitting Spiritualists in the middle of a chain of radicals bent on subverting the nation. For many Americans Spiritualism evoked the specters of women's rights, abolitionism, and racial equality and threatened to alter families and marriages, schools, churches, and prayer, and even diets, for without dietary change, one Spiritualist avowed, "all progress will be to a greater or less degree cramped, warped or stunted."[1]

The connections between Spiritualism and reform and the fears they conjointly elicited are hardly new territory for historians, who in the past several years have created a cottage industry of spinning together speaking with the dead and speaking from the dais. Although the cross-fertilization of Spiritualist discourse and radical ideologies of gender has been explored repeatedly by historians, who have concluded that the Spiritual rostrum was a significant, though not unproblematic, space for the propagation of "feminist" views, few have addressed the equally powerful connection between Spiritualism and the antislavery and racial-equality movements, even while acknowledging that a remarkable number of prominent abolitionists were intrigued by or committed to Spiritualism. In 1857 William Lloyd Garrison proclaimed himself a "firm believer in the reality" of Spiritualism, and to varying degrees he was joined in his belief by Sarah and Angelina Grimké, Lydia Maria Child, Gerrit Smith, LaRoy Sunderland, James Freeman Clarke, and others.[2]

Spiritualists asserted that their reformist influence reached into the halls of Congress, and a few did their best to besiege Washington during the Civil War, not with swords but with pens urging absolute liberty, the vigorous prosecution of the war, immediate emancipation, and full civil rights for former slaves. According to both opponents and proponents of the movement, even the White House was infested with Spiritualists. One critic asserted that Lincoln was a "spiritualist of the abolitionist school" and insisted that "unlike our old fashioned presidents, who were compelled to consult the constitution," Lincoln descended "in a secret hole of the White House" to consult "a *rapping* table," which served as his "law, constitution and gospel." It was the spirits, the writer claimed, who plunged the nation into war, demanded racial equality, and insisted against all reason that "all must be free—untrammeled and unrestricted." Spiritualists themselves hardly disagreed, claiming to have held séances on Capitol Hill and to have delivered messages for the president and his wife . . . no doubt from the Lincoln bedroom.[3]

The cumulative effect of such claims and counterclaims has been to weld Spiritualism firmly onto the structure of social reform, so firmly that one historian insists "it is fair to say that there was not a single early spiritualist who was not also a reformer and abolitionist." The seams of this weld have been reinforced by the starkly instrumental claims that trance speaking and spirit messages were merely a means—conscious or unconscious—of justifying unpopular political agendas, a convenient way to take up the cudgel of reform while deflecting the blows of opponents.[4]

As I have suggested, even on the surface these assertions beg further investigation. If a Hare or Ferguson did not exist to muddy the equation of Spiritualism and social radicalism, one might still inquire how spirit messages could possibly be effective in advancing any agenda. Fit to reject self-interested claims, Spiritualists routinely questioned spirit communications with which they disagreed, while for non-Spiritualists, spirit messages represented nothing less than the toadstools of enthusiasm. More tellingly, nearly all of the public abolitionist-Spiritualists came to antislavery before adopting Spiritualism, and nearly all had long careers of public speaking without the aid of spirits. Within the antislavery ranks, too, there was strong sentiment that the "the whole matter" of spirit communion was nothing less than "some form or other of human credulity or human imposture" that might embarrass or cripple the movement. Like many of his peers, Charles Fox Hovey felt that although "*the truth* can harm no cause," this might not be said of "error." More importantly, the increasingly sophisticated understanding that historians have brought to the role of religious belief in sustaining antislavery sentiment should cause us to reexamine the link between Spiritualist discourse and racial ideology and suggests the desirability of moving the debate beyond the pure instrumentalism that has prevailed.[5]

At a certain level the question comes down to black and white. The Civil War was both a watershed in the Spiritualist movement—a period of great change theologically and ideologically—and a watershed in American thoughts and feelings on race. Dramatic changes in race relations had begun during the antebellum years, as working-class whites began to internalize a profound sense of their own racial identity, bound up with a shift from experiencing class-based solidarity as "not slaves" to one predicated on being "not black." But in the postwar period, after a half decade of carnage over the issue of slavery and with the ramifications of the extension of suffrage and civil rights to former slaves opening to view, the once abstract issues of race now acquired a concrete political meaning. Simply put, for white Americans racial thinking became an integral part of life.[6]

New Orleans, home of the largest community of Spiritualists in the American South, was the site of a particularly protracted and violent struggle over the direction of racial change, and although the city is clearly sui generis with respect to its history of race relations, it was in many ways a bellwether for changes affecting American society at large. The moderately flexible three-tiered system of social stratification that was endemic to antebellum New Orleans, that pitted Creoles (persons of mixed race) in a middle ground between white and black, collapsed suddenly and catastrophically during the postwar years into the rigid two-tiered "American" system that recognized no shade apart from white and black.[7]

For Spiritualists, obsessed with the identity of the self and the structures of American society, issues of racial identity had never been far from the surface. As racial barriers, North and South, began to ossify after the war, and as the meaning of sympathy began slowly to slide, many Spiritualists followed the lead of Robert Hare in incorporating racial incommensurability into the material and spiritual worlds. Spiritualists of color concurrently traversed the ground from a period of expanded horizons shortly after the war to the post-Reconstruction realities of drastically curtailed possibilities. In the process they carried on an extended conversation with white Spiritualism, appropriating and reshaping it into a set of beliefs predicated less on sympathy than on charity in an expanded sense, a tacit surrender to the inevitability of social inequality. For whites, in ways that could not be foreseen, black Spiritualists became a part of the invisible world here on earth.

SYMPATHY AND SENSE

The emotional heart of antebellum Spiritualism beat in the torso of an open body, a "self" reflected in the Spiritualist belief that all individuals interpenetrated one another and affected one another's lives. This cosmic system provided a sense of interconnection and belonging and fueled a sense of personal responsibility for the problems of others. In one of her numberless entranced lectures, Cora L. V. Hatch captured the feeling of the antebellum spiritual body over and above its implications. "Worlds on worlds and systems on systems, which extend out into space far beyond all human comprehension, bear the closest relation to each other, and not one could be destroyed without the derangement and consequent confusion of the whole. God has constituted the Universe so, that from the smallest atom to all those orbs which fill the boundless space, there is a perfect unity and a dependence upon each other."[8]

Embedded in the conception of the self as porous, unbounded, and mutualistically engaged, sympathy created an emotional topography that enabled individuals to parse out and navigate the complex, confusing, and rapidly shifting social structures of mid-Victorian life. Harmony and disharmony, intercourse and barriers, were more than mere words for Spiritualists; they were powerfully experienced emotional states, and those social structures that impinged upon the unboundedness of the body proved most problematic, emotionally, politically, and socially, and cried out most urgently for reform.

Conceivably, at least, sympathetic navigation was available to all, regardless of race. Although Robert Hare and Jesse Ferguson busily remapped sympathy for social stability, expelling all but nonresistant slaves from the sympathetic nation, the antebellum myth of Spiritualism held that its ranks were filled with the "Women's Rights Men, Negro Equality Men and Miscegens" of the New York *Herald,* the wide-eyed, long-haired radicals who promised to build a "grand co-operative society" in the flesh, whose spirits taught that "a white man cannot do injustice to a black man without injuring himself, and that in the same ratio that he sins against the divinity of the human he is sinning against the majesty of the Divine in heaven." The editor of the Spiritualist *Tiffany's Monthly,* Joel Tiffany, predicted that if Spiritualism became widely practiced, "there will be an end of dissipation and vice. Selfishness will be converted to love. War with its long catalogue of crimes and woes will cease. Slavery and oppression will die. Fraud and deceit will be no more. Man will be redeemed, and the kingdom of heaven will come, and the will of God will be done on earth as it is in heaven." Spiritualist sympathy provided the intellectual and emotional spark that promised to light the damp fuse of the millennium.[9]

Yet all the talk of universal brotherhood, all the rhetoric of antislavery and civil rights, translated into only a handful of African Americans at the tilting tables of the northern states. Although there was a remarkable freedom of religious expression and participation in Spiritualism, given the lack of central authority, and although Spiritualist practice bore at least superficial similarities with West African worship of ancestors, African Americans showed relatively little interest in the spirits. This is all the more surprising because since the First World War a highly syncretic version of Spiritualism has, in fact, flourished in African American communities, where it has been interpreted as a means of coping with the stresses of racial oppression and social stratification.[10]

Evidence of African-American participation in spirit circles is not entirely lacking: a few individuals did take up the Spiritualist challenge to experiment and decide for themselves, but fewer still remained within the fold for very long. Paschal Beverly Randolph, a New Yorker of mixed race, toured for over seven years as a Spiritualist trance lecturer, healer, writer, and reformer in his own mold, but in 1858 he broke with the movement and renounced it, passing into Rosicrucianism, occultism, and "sex magic." In his recantation Randolph claimed that various "excesses" of the movement troubled him—particularly its dalliance with free love—and he discussed the even more troublesome bogeys of centuries of enthusiasts, those omnipresent, obsessive evil spirits.[11]

Predictably, there was a strong Spiritualist backlash against Randolph after he left the fold, even though he never denied the reality of spirit communion. Spiritualists accused Randolph of trying to resuscitate a floundering career as a lecturer by desperate means, and the *Spiritual Telegraph* bitterly asserted that his "prominence as a medium or Spiritualist has been confined chiefly to his own estimation." Emma Hardinge added uncharitably that the loss of Randolph meant little to the movement, snidely insinuating that he would take any publicity he could get "and was glad to accept anything short of negro minstrelsy." From the mouth of one of the national voices of the movement, this stinging assertion carried considerable weight, and Randolph's near exclusion from the Spiritualist lyceum circuit thereafter suggests that Hardinge had found her mark. At another level, though, Hardinge's statement does more; it hints at how the politics of race might be made to work uniquely against an African-American believer whose opinions diverged from whatever was defined as the Spiritualist norm. Walking a perilous course, Hardinge stopped just short of claiming that in rejecting Spiritualism, Randolph became a spurious black man—a minstrel sham—and by so doing, she was able to maintain her self-professed alignment with the "true friends of the Blacks" (those who eschew minstrels) while rejecting the black man himself. Ironically, but perhaps not coincidentally, Randolph made conflicting claims throughout his life about his own racial makeup, sometimes claiming, sometimes denying that he had any African blood at all.[12]

The very brief list of African-American Spiritualist investigators might be extended to include others—most prominently Sojourner Truth—but at best the brevity of the list provides an indication of how little interest there was. During the Civil War, Emma Hardinge did her best to pad the list by citing a conspicuous number of seers among the "contraband" refugees in Tennessee as Spiritualists, but the fact remains that in the North, African Americans never adopted Spiritualism to any great extent.[13]

The spirits of African Americans were only slightly more inclined than the living ones to attend spirit circles. While Indians repeatedly communed across the grave and white spirits were the norm, relatively few African-American spirits spoke, and many of those who did prattled away in comic dialect, delivering messages that conveyed anything but abolitionist or egalitarian ideas. On the eve of the Civil War, Rike, a poisoned slave from Accomack County, Virginia, delivered a typical message to Francis H. Smith: "I am right smart happier here dan dar. De blessed Lord looks on de cullared folks as well as de dear masters." Although the intent seems to be that the lowly will be cared for in the afterlife, Rike's inclusion of "dear masters" implies that temporal relations had no long-term implications for the afterlife—an opinion that nearly all antebellum Spiritualists would accept. Yet set off against the contention that men and women of all classes would be elevated in the afterlife, the brevity of Rike's statement establishes a troubling equivalency between master and slave that deflates the political and moral meaning of slavery, robbing it of its brutality and veiling the systematic inequality and oppression that were integral to the peculiar institution.[14]

Other enslaved spirits verged more completely on the minstrel mode than Rike and seemed just as concerned with averting their eyes from the issues of racial violence and domination. A recently deceased "slave from Richmond," Sam, expressed himself delighted with death but confused with the changes. "Oh, bress de Lor, massa, I'se free, free, free Massa, whar dis place? I never was here, massa. It can't be so—it must be Richmond, massa. Oh, dear massa, I'se 'fused. . . . Massa has got most fifty niggas. They teach me to speak, to write, to read, took care ob me when I was sick. I used to brush massa's coats and boots; but I wanted to be free. Massa say I should be when I dead—so I'se dead and free too. . . . I don't know what to say massa, for I'se 'fused."[15]

In communicating his feelings, Sam ended by saying, "Yes, I'd like to go on the old plantation, massa," coming far closer to the minstrel ideal of the happy slave nostalgic for his old home than to the pitiful victim of white sentimental literature, more palatable to the sentimental paternalist ethos of proslavery agitators than the sentimental literature of antislavery. Sam's list of the benefits of slavery included education, health care, and (it appears) a light workday, and while he tempered his enthusiasm by asserting that he wanted to be free, he pined for his old plantation. Furthermore, in Sam's use of the term *massa,* it is not possible to determine whether he was employing a generic term to refer to an implicitly white reader or was addressing his own "massa." In either case, the effect is to suggest that God cared for both slaves and masters—"massa" was right about Sam's future state, "massa" asked the questions, and it was to "massa's" plantation that he longed to go. More pointedly, the social relations experienced in life— "massa" as owner of the plantation, as provider and controller—seem unaltered by death.

NEW ORLEANS DIVINITY: HENRI LOUIS REY

Emma Hardinge was concerned that a fear of northern ideas would inhibit the southern spread of Spiritualism, and so she was surprised to find during her visit to New Orleans, one of the capitals of slavery, that the movement was thriving there among both the American and French communities. "New Orleans divinity" was already a common term used to signify the sort of unabashed, irreverent heterodoxy that might foster Spiritualism, but when Hardinge visited in 1859-60, the reasons for the unusual degree to which Spiritualism flourished were rooted specifically in the politics of race and ethnicity.[16]

Although statistics on antebellum Spiritualist adherence are notoriously unreliable, given the lack of meaningful standards for assessing who ought to be counted, the available data indicate that Louisiana boasted an unusually strong community for the South. For comparison's sake, Uriah Clark's *Spiritualist Register for 1857* tallied 240,000 Spiritualists in New York State—a healthy 6 percent of the population—with Massachusetts (6%) and Ohio (4%) not far behind, but the southern states were largely a spiritual(ist) wasteland. Only Louisiana with 20,000 Spiritualists (1.7%) and Tennessee (10,000; 0.9%) boasted substantial Spiritualist populations in terms of raw numbers, and for Louisiana it appears that the majority were concentrated in the Crescent City.[17]

In attempting to assess the significance of these figures, one swings from the unreliable to the speculative: there is tantalizing but inconclusive evidence that unlike their northern peers, southern Spiritualists were buoyed by African-American support. During her mission to the South, for example, Hardinge encountered an entranced slave on the plantation of one of her hosts, Colonel MacCrae, who communicated messages from Mac-Crae's deceased son. Although this might seem a risky enterprise for a slave to undertake, the effort was well received by the colonel, who accepted its authenticity based on the personal nature of the information conveyed. Even more conjecturally, the incident hints that such encounters might not have been limited to New Orleans, for Hardinge noted that the medium came originally from North Carolina, and his arrival on Mac-Crae's plantation appears to have been recent enough that all assumed the slave would have known nothing about the conditions of MacCrae's son's death.[18]

New Orleans, however, provides stronger evidence for the existence of a stable, independent African-American Spiritualism. During this same tour Hardinge was introduced to a Creole spiritual healer named Valmour, a powerful medium who, "possessed of some independent means of his own," donated his services to the world. A colleague of Valmour's, Henri Louis Rey, recalled the meeting with Hardinge as a dramatic one: as Valmour was walking past the Odd Fellow's Hall, Rey reported, he was seized with a spiritual influence and was compelled to enter the auditorium. Instantly Hardinge recognized a sympathetic affinity with Valmour and cried, "Let that Brother come up here to me, to give me strength to speak, he is full of electricity."[19] Whatever the conditions of their meeting, Hardinge was sufficiently impressed with Valmour and his circle to state that "either the noble Creoles are determined to take Spiritualism by storm, or the spirits are determined to take them." In either case, she was correct.[20]

The circle of Spiritualists headed by Rey and Valmour first gathered in about 1857, comprised of a core of relatively well-to-do Francophone Creoles of Roman Catholic origin, persons of mixed race. The distinctive social and intellectual position of Louisiana Creoles has sparked intense interest among historians over the past decade, and the system of racial ordination in antebellum New Orleans had many nuances. Unlike the rigid, dichotomous system of black and white found elsewhere in the United States, in New Orleans the races were arrayed in three tiers, with some mobility between, and each tier was further subdivided by allegiances based on ethnicity, class, and nationality.[21]

Between whites (American and French; immigrant and native born) occupying the top rung and blacks (enslaved and free) at the bottom was a

middle rung comprised largely of Creoles of mixed race and various national affinities. Rodolphe Lucien Desdunes, for example, himself a New
Orleans Creole, recognized a distinct difference between the "Latin Negro" and the "American Negro," neither of which category mapped clearly
onto phenotype. "One hopes, and the other doubts," according to Desdunes. "Thus we often perceive that one makes every effort to acquire
merits, the other to gain advantages. One aspires to equality, the other to
identity. One will forget that he is a Negro in order to think that he is a
man; the other will forget that he is a man to think that he is a Negro. These
radical differences act on the feelings of both in direct harmony with these
characteristics."[22]

The Spiritualist Creoles of New Orleans were fed mostly from the Latin
Negro stream. Many enjoyed some of the lesser ensigns of whiteness—a
higher education, a refinement in culture—and some were substantial
property holders, even slaveholders. Yet as a group they vigorously rejected and resisted the imposition of distinctions or legal barriers based
purely on color or race. Although they might form elitist organizations,
such as the Société d'Économie, of which Henri Louis Rey was a member,
these were based on profession (and therefore class) rather than race. It
would be far too simplistic to claim that the subsequent history of Creole
radicalism in New Orleans and their formidable and resilient resistance to
racial oppression grew out of either their experience as liminal beings, be-
twixt and between American racial categories, or their Spiritualist sense of
the self as unbounded, but it would not be remiss to suggest these conceptions of the self resonated, supported, and sustained that radicalism in a
manner that transcends any single dimension.

As might be expected, given the flow of speakers and ideas from the
North into this port city, Spiritualism in Creole New Orleans initially drew
heavily on northern influences, and to a marked degree on French influences as well. Northern Spiritualist periodicals circulated in the city, and
northern emissaries, including Thomas Gales Forster, Emma Hardinge,
and James V. Mansfield, tried their hand there. Although New Orleans
Spiritualism bore some distinguishing features, including a stronger tinge
of (and against) Roman Catholicism, a different suite of communicating
spirits (including Catholic priests and religious figures), and of course, a
different language, Rey recorded communications that in most regards

could have been heard in any northern séance. New Orleans spirits such as Père Ambroise described the fate of the spirit after leaving the body in terms nearly identical to those used by northern spirits, highlighting the division between spiritual and material bodies and the role of sympathy in binding the system into a whole. "When we detach ourselves from our material bodies, we enter into the invisible world, each in accordance with the manner in which he had conducted his earthly life. We have different societies according to the sympathy which lead such and such spirits to unite. Fraternity exists among us, except among those who are dominated by the material."[23]

Just as northern spirits assured their listeners, southerners remarked that each spirit who required instruction received it, and all spirits progressed rapidly through the spheres, even the infant whose *carrière* was cut short by death: the infant "attaches himself to a sympathetic soul," Rey was informed, "who guides him throughout life, to whom he manifests himself. That voice which counsels you, which suggests beautiful thoughts to you, is his." Spirit instructors and a concern with the fate of infants were thus not unique to New Yorkers and New Englanders, and the parallels extended to the insistence that the afterlife included all, with no election, no eternity of torment, no wrathful, punishing God, and they extended too to the outspoken anticlericalism of the New Orleans circles, though their wrath was reserved primarily for the Roman Catholic Church.[24]

Above all, the unmistakable Spiritualist self, in all its electricity and physicality, could be found animating nearly every séance. Looking back on the early days when the circle was open to the public, Rey felt that the presence of mere curiosity seekers had impeded the progress of the circle, because the curious "established by their desires currents that were as different as they were varied, which destroyed the harmony of the circle." Only later, he argued, when the circle was more mature and limited to a harmonic core of experienced Spiritualists, were members able to make substantial spiritual progress, more unified and harmonious as a body, more in keeping with the notion of themselves as "one grand co-operative society."[25]

The Rey circle was still immature when the outbreak of the Civil War forced its suspension. Like many members of the Creole elite, Rey volunteered for service in a Confederate militia unit, the Louisiana Native

Guards. Louisiana had a long history of military participation by free persons of color, extending back to the French and Spanish colonial periods, but the thought that free persons of color would choose to fight for the preservation of racialized slavery is, to say the least, perplexing. After the war a veteran of the regiment, Charles W. Gibbons, testified that he had volunteered only out of fear for his life and property, but others may have identified with their region, may have thought they might enhance their social position, or, as slave owners themselves, may have enlisted out of economic self-interest. In any event, the interstitial position of the Creoles of New Orleans made such service more likely, rather than less.[26]

A twenty-nine-year-old clerk when he enlisted, Rey was commissioned a captain, a reflection of his high social standing in the Creole community. His brothers, Armand (drummer), Octave (lieutenant), and Hippolyte (corporal), joined him. Posted in New Orleans, the unit was never allowed to perform meaningful duty—they were for show, not action—and they suffered in comparison to white regiments in being ill outfitted, minimally armed, and possibly mistrusted. Toasts he presented at a Christmas celebration in 1861 provide a small window on the effect this treatment had on officers like Rey and his friend André Cailloux. Raising his glass, Rey hailed "the Revolution which broke the chains of Young America, which shook off the yoke of the Mother Country, and permitted her to take rank among the first nations of the world." He then added another toast to "the present Revolution" and "all Revolutions—for they give birth to the progress of man, and lead him on the way to true fraternity." Ambiguously, the toasts seem simultaneously to celebrate the Confederacy and to threaten it.[27]

In April 1862 Federal forces seized New Orleans, and whatever their orders from the Confederate authorities, the Native Guards stacked their arms—hiding some from the Federals—and remained. Aware of their status in the Confederate military, the otherwise unidentified Colonel Labatut is reported to have told the men, "If I have advice to give you, it is to return to your homes, because they mock you, that's what they do!" The new Federal commander in the city, Benjamin Butler, initially harbored no more intention of using African Americans as soldiers than had the Confederates, but a shortage of manpower and military necessity overcame his reluctance, and he negotiated with a delegation of officers of the Guards, including both Henri and his brother Octave, to tender their services to the Union. Through their intervention three regiments were raised during the fall of 1862, Henri Rey and Cailloux were appointed captains in the First Native Guards, Octave Rey became a lieutenant in the Second Regiment, while a third brother, Hippolyte, received a commission in the Third.[28]

On paper Butler insisted that only those who could prove free status would be allowed to serve in the Guards, but many slaves did enter the ranks, and slaves may even have comprised a majority of the Second and Third Regiments. Joseph T. Wilson, a historian and veteran of the Second Regiment, claimed that "any negro who would swear that he was free, if physically good, was accepted."[29]

With Rey already poised on the perch of radicalism, his command over slaves galvanized his views on race, and by November 1862, if not before, he was actively imagining a panracial alliance in the service of racial liberation. "Come visit our camp," he wrote to a comrade; "in parade, you will see a thousand white bayonets gleaming in the sun, held by black, yellow or white hands. Be informed that we have no prejudice; that we receive everyone into camp; but that the sight of salesmen of human flesh makes us sick; but, since we know how to behave, though Negroes, we receive them, completely concealing from them the violent internal struggle that their prejudice forces us to wage within ourselves."[30]

During Butler's administration of the Department of the Gulf, the First Regiment saw its first active duty during one of the most violent engagements of the Civil War, Port Hudson. Although the siege of Port Hudson was little more than a sideshow to the more important campaign for Vicksburg, it took on a significance for both North and South as one of the first major engagements involving black troops. The carnage sustained by the black regiments was viewed by supporters of arming slaves as proof of their capacity to act as soldiers and men and was equally viewed by opponents as proof of their inability. In either case, the First Native Guards was one of the regiments in the forefront of the assault on May 27, 1863, seeing twenty-six of its number killed in action, including two officers, Cailloux and a sixteen-year-old free black lieutenant, John H. Crowder. Cailloux's death drew particular attention in the press for the gallant manner in which he had comported himself, urging on his troops even after his arm had been shattered by shot. After lying on the field for several days because the Confederates refused to allow burial details near the black bodies, Cailloux was recovered and interred in an elaborate public ceremony. It is unlikely that either Henri or Octave Rey was physically present at the assault: records indicate that Henri resigned on April 30 for reasons of health, while Octave was one of a number of officers in the Second Regiment who had resigned in March "for reasons of prejudice."[31]

REY'S RECONSTRUCTED CIRCLE

Returning to New Orleans, Henri revived his Spiritualist circle, and both he and Octave took up the struggle for racial equality, aligning themselves with the most radical clique among the city's black Republicans. From 1868 to 1877 Octave served as chief of the New Orleans police, and Henri served as a Republican state representative in 1868–70. The postwar years were as turbulent as any New Orleans had seen, bounded by a deadly race riot and massacre of pro-suffrage activists on July 30, 1866—during which the police, aided by civilians in Confederate uniforms, beat, stabbed, or gunned down dozens—and by a violent race riot in September 1874.[32]

Adding a particular twist to the threat of racial violence was the gradual collapse of the three-tiered antebellum system of racial ordination to the two-tiered, "Americanized" system that eventually was codified in Jim Crow. Creoles were legally and socially designated as black, and any semblance of fluidity in racial definition was annihilated. In the face of increasing oppression, radical Creoles responded in the press, at the ballot (when possible), and in the courtroom, imploring persons of color in New Orleans to resist falling prey to resignation and complacency and to remain united in opposition to racial oppression. They responded, as well, with an expanded awareness of a racial common cause with black Louisianans and with an imposed awareness of the necessity of mutual interest and mutual response. The need to refrain from the squabbling that divided English- from French-speaking persons of color in the city and rich from poor thus became a common refrain. Although in hindsight the juggernaut of segregation and racial subordination appears unstoppable, the Reys stood in the vanguard of resistance to the Americanization of race relations in New Orleans, with their Spiritualism lending support and solace, providing an intellectual and moral structure to their struggle, and just as critically, providing a physical point for like-minded radicals to meet.[33]

Within weeks of returning home, Henri Rey and his circle began receiving communications from the dead and departed, and almost immediately the Creole martyr Cailloux returned to appoint himself their guardian. "They thought they had killed me," he wrote, "but they made me live. . . . I will be the torch that will guide you, it will be I who receive you into our world if you die in the struggle, so fight! God desires liberty, our brothers have it, equality will come later, it is true, but in all structures there must be a first stone . . . there must be victims to serve as steppingstones on the path to liberty."[34]

The reasons that Cailloux assumed the role of spirit guide for the circle are deceptively simple. He was, of course, a comrade who had died under arms, falling heroically in a conspicuous display of gallantry, bearing sympathetic connections with his Spiritualist *amis* on many levels, as Creole, as soldier, as Spiritualist. His appointment had other advantages. A cigar maker before the war, educated in Paris, Cailloux was also respected for his "polished manners and confident air." In a eulogy he was praised as "the idol of his men a true type of the Louisianan," having defended "they integrity of the sacred cause of Liberty, [and] vindicated his race from the opprobrium with which it was charged." But most importantly Cailloux had proudly maintained that unlike nearly all of the other officers in the Guards, he was of pure African descent, "the blackest man in New Orleans." He was the living (now dead) embodiment of a newly imperative identification with an African heritage but also of the Creole tenet that distinctions based solely upon race or phenotype were anathema; this man, the blackest in New Orleans, was a martyr for the cause and the exemplification of the virtues cherished by southern white society as much as Creole society. In their effort to annihilate the boundaries dividing New Orleans society, Creole Spiritualists first set their sights on annihilating the boundaries among persons of African descent.[35]

In many ways the revitalized circle picked up very much where it had left off in 1861. The spiritual afterlife retained a northern tinge; it was still sunny and studded with sympathies and affinities. One spirit described the spirit world as one of unified, endless progression and the satisfaction of desires, with spirits living in the "most perfect harmony . . . bounded by laws which they cannot violate and which control them with neither effort nor violence." Every spirit progressed, as always, without "torment, and without the least bit of jealousy or envy," and every one received whatever education was necessary. "We have houses for every taste," the spirits added, "every desire, all arranged in an admirable, intelligent, and harmonious fashion. Each receives that which is due him, and exists with the sublimity of new organs, prodigious new sensations, infinite, admirable, appreciable, and experienced with all the power, perfect and delicious."[36] Furthermore, these spirits continued to assert that "nothing is hidden, because nothing can be lost" in the spirit world. In other words, Creole spirits, like northern ones, were still able to penetrate and apprehend the inner thoughts and emotions of other selves.[37]

On a more personal level, Henriette Lavigne, the sister of one of the members of the Rey circle (several Lavignes served in the Native Guards), underscored the role of sympathetic exchange in supporting political perseverance. "Patience," she counseled, "continue your admirable work; it is your fortune. Get past this bad road, abandon all of your errors, nourish your heart with gentle thoughts, then your spirit of spiritual joy, of good, and charity, share your pain with those have none, and find solace in your sufferings."[38]

In other ways the Spiritualism that emerged in Rey's circle after the Civil War began to differ significantly, and increasingly, from northern white Spiritualism, and to differ in ways that suggest how the Creole community had begun to mobilize and adapt Spiritualism to their own religious, social, and political ends. Although the differences are for the most part ones of emphasis rather than kind, they become progressively more marked and more consistently stake out a unique territory. Among the most distinctive innovations found in postwar Creole Spiritualism is the belief in the operation of what might be called a wheel of fortune. While most northern antebellum Spiritualists argued that there was no punishment in the afterlife for mortal malefactors—and Creoles generally concurred—Rey's spirits repeatedly emphasized a subordinate refrain that the change in status accompanying death leveled all members of society, bringing the mighty low and the despised into respectability. The spirit Daniel Webster remarked that his experiences as a spirit left him feeling obliged to forgive his "earthly brothers," and he admitted that the laurels with which he had been blessed in life had left him feeling superior to others. "But what a sudden change I met with when once I was divested of my material envelope," he sobbed, "and when I perceived that I was nothing more than all my brothers. Yes, my friends, I pardon those whose reason is still kept in darkness by good many causes. I cannot help by so doing when I come to consider the most learned of men are the very ones who profit of their knowledge in order to keep their fellow brothers in such a state of ignorance." The ultimate tyrant, Napoleon, was similarly direct. "Oh, kings," he exclaimed. "You who believe yourselves masters, disabuse yourselves; you are but slaves to your pride. You, the first on earth, will be last here, and like me, you will regret the royal mantle you draped over your shoulders."[39]

In reimagining the basis for social relations among the living, the spirits were relatively evenhanded when they explored the views of the oppressing class, which included political tyrants, racial oppressors (Calhoun, Clay), and northern supporters of racial oppression (like Webster, supporter of the Compromise of 1850). The Creole circle went further than their northern counterparts, however, in eliciting the views of the oppressed class. In messages from fallen women, criminals, and slaves, the spirits ascribed temporal fate largely to social factors rather than intrinsic merit. "Do not condemn the fallen woman," begged one spirit, "because her fall is often the fault of society through its injustices." Reflecting on the fate of these despised persons after death, Sylvia, a slave who had entertained "false ideas of virtue" when alive, argued that "as long as he had not been a criminal" the slave "always receives a luminous crown from the Lord and a prompt redemption, which is worth a great and magnificent retribution."[40]

The cosmic economy of white Spiritualism grew out of a notion of mutual uplift, an eternal progression that elevated all spirits who wished to better themselves. Although Creoles accepted some of the basics of this model, their experience as subordinate members in a highly contested but hardening system of racial stratification may have made such optimistic approaches less alluring than the promise of cosmic equity. While some northern Spiritualists seemed to entertain an afterlife in which happy slaves gained liberation and lived side by side with their oppressors, the Creole Spiritualists imagined the mighty brought low before the feet of the slave, rueing their past.[41]

The Creole Spiritualists of New Orleans further differed from northern whites in attaching the principle of charity to sympathy as the primum mobile of the spirit world, in part, perhaps, reflecting a Roman Catholic influence. Not coincidentally, Saint Vincent de Paul assumed a large (and increasing) role in transmitting messages exploring the social meaning of charity. "Charity," he insisted, "will guide you in all your actions. . . . Charity will make you tolerant toward those who live in error." In Spiritualist terms charity was not taken to mean simply the gift of material goods by superior members of society to subordinates. "Charity does not lie in the alms given," according to Saint Vincent, "but in the generosity of spirit which makes you pardon instead of condemn." In operation charity could transform the leveling that was promised for a future, spiritual plane into a leveling in the temporal, earthly state. For the disempowered, disunited, and imperiled, charity offered a more effective means than sympathy for catalyzing social change by rendering the relations of exchange in more concrete terms, identifying what should be given to whom, defining the skein of moral indebtedness. Moreover, it drew upon a long Christian tradition that promised easy translation into non-Spiritualist contexts.[42]

These alterations of northern Spiritualist theory provide a small taste of the social content of the messages received under Rey's mediumship. No less than their northerner counterparts, Creole Spiritualists insisted that the identity of the individual continued after death, and the individual's identity and position in the struggle for racial justice were critical to interpreting that individual's messages. While a variety of spirits communicated throughout the 1860s, including relatives and friends, famous Frenchmen and Louisianans, the circle received powerful, outspoken messages from comrades in the Native Guards who had died "like a dog" in the brutal fields of Port Hudson, as well as those who had died of disease. When Colonel Dreux, the first Confederate officer killed during the war, reported, "We fought for nothing," the spirit Cailloux retorted, "We fought for something."[43]

Spirits like these and others associated with the struggle for racial justice maintained a running commentary on the course of political events in the 1860s. Toussaint L'Ouverture assailed both political and religious despotism, John Brown ("the American Jesus") addressed racial leveling, and Abraham Lincoln spoke of the fate of the nation. Their messages often addressed specific political issues, always framed within Spiritualist notions of cosmic justice and order. During a time of intense struggle over the future shape of the state and its institutions, the urban novelist Eugène Sue came back from the dead to give his opinions on the need to recognize the demands of the minority in forming a government and on the need to reform hospitals and systems for poor relief, while W. R. Meadows, a man murdered in the riot of July 1866, warned his opponents: "The hour of reward has struck for the suffering blacks. . . . You can put off the hour, but you cannot stop it. Mixed schools will come, the sooner the better for you; the punishment of your crimes will be according to your resistance to the law of Justice." Creole spirits packed a punch.[44]

The New Orleans riot of 1866 scarred the circle, as it did all of mixed-race New Orleans, not just in adding the voices of Meadows and his fellow victims Dostie, Lacroix, and others but in lending a more desperate and angry tone to their messages. The spirit of Dostie castigated the recording secretary of the circle for failing to record his first missive, delivered within days of the riot. Dostie suggested that fear of discovery had cowed the circle into submission, but he assured them that victory would be theirs, that there was no need to hold back. Dostie, like the other victims, cajoled and encouraged the circle into the public expression of their views.

The martyrs of racial justice returned frequently in the postwar years, particularly after major crises. Seven months after his death, Lincoln came to address the circle:

> Courage, brave children, do not doubt for an instant that you are of God; you are all of him. Is it your fault that God created his children with different colors? Ought the wicked to direct His work? No, a thousand times no; they must not, because it is He alone who is master of His creation, and not men, his children who he created to serve him, to adore him to love him like the best of fathers. . . .
>
> I assure you, my children, liberty will reign on earth, because it was born of heaven; it is God who made it, not men. Men must restore this work to how they found it, in its place, or they will suffer tortures, cruel wars, revolutions, assassination of one and all, and the slaveholders [*chef des chaines*] will be found hanging from the gibbet where they sacrificed so many of their poor black brothers who did nothing to them, in order to enrich themselves, to treat them well to nourish them in indolence and idleness.
>
> Courage, my brothers. God watches over all of you. You will be compensated for the suffering you have endured, you, as well as your children. But they will be happier later, because liberty will bring about calm and change hatred even to fraternity.[45]

The cumulative weight of these messages, however, goes beyond mere encouragement to continue the struggle and does more than simply elucidate the meaning of charity. Until at least 1871 the spirits explored the formation of cross-racial alliances to combat oppression and restrictions of all kinds, political, religious, and social, seeking to maximize the scope of the sympathetic community. Within this Creolized version of the northern antebellum fantasy of "universal brotherhood," all would be Creole, and race would disappear as a socially divisive force. The spirit of a Union general during the Civil War, identified only as Williams (possibly Thomas Williams, killed at Baton Rouge in 1862), resorted to a more mystical rhetoric than was usual among spirits. Williams, a white spirit, claimed that the members of his "invisible army of Progression" knew neither North nor South but only "humanity and one flag for all and every one." Humans were not created to be brutes, either oppressors or oppressed, but to search for justice and equality. "Harmony must be inscribed among the stars of the Union which adorn the Flag," he continued. "The stars and stripes must and will protect all the citizens of the Great Republic. In the broad and beautiful land of universal Brotherhood and Love, we are watching the men of strong heart and who love freedom of thoughts for all; none but them will be admitted to battle and help us in the great work of progression; the wicked will stand aside, weeping over their past errors; but when truth and Light will enlighten them, we will ask them to come and join us in the struggle for Justice against Blindness of thoughts."[46]

This theme was continued in messages from Montezuma (opposing Roman Catholic priests), Pocahontas, Piloho ("Many Americans here, but brothers"), and other Indians, who included other races in their plans as well. The Indian spirit Poloah exclaimed: "Long live liberty, long live spiritual fraternity, with its splendid bonds that unite Chinese, Hottentots. There are brothers here, in every meaning of the word. We all smoke the peace pipe, and the tomahawk is buried forever, as a memory of barbarism." God commanded harmony and love, he insisted, and the spirits obeyed.[47]

During Reconstruction the spirit R. Preaux implored his fellow whites to surrender their egotism, to renounce once and for all the "fratricidal war" they had waged as they spoke "of Liberty amidst slavery" and as they forged "chains while shouting about oppression." Given their history,

Preaux asked, how could whites speak of the despotism of Reconstruction. "You speak of your chains," he complained, "but, Cain, what did you do with your brother? What do you still wish to do to him, notwithstanding the lessons of the Past which ought to have enlightened you, for they have been written with letters of blood."[48]

Preaux unhesitatingly noted that the hypocritical white backlash against civil rights was met by the Christian generosity of the "Black Man." "Vengeance has not put the incendiary torch in his hands," he argued; "he did not outrage anybody, he remained a black Jesus, flogged, tracked, dragged as beast of burden from state to state: these black brothers have awaited the hour of deliverance, and they did remain free from stains, from hate, from vengeance!" The spirit implored his brothers in white flesh to act in a similar spirit, not to reject their "black brother," who "belongs to God the same as you" and who "is entitled to the same rights as you," but to accept them within the larger community of affect and law. The spirits demanded acknowledgment of the contributions and suffering of black and mixed-race people and a recognition of the moral value of their suffering.[49]

Together African-American and Indian spirits, joined by a select group of white spirits, envisioned an activist call to transracial unity. In the compressed language of celestial poetry, one spirit announced that although he had been called "Black in the land of America," in the spiritland his hands were pure. "I look with joy from Africa," he wrote. "No Americans, to spirit land / Are sent," but he presented himself, forgiving and hoping, knowing he was right, and

> From darkness, light
> I received
> Never deceived
> Are men in the spirit-land.

The poet begged the "White men of America" to change their ways and to

> Join the sons of Africa
> In love we live
> In love forgive
> White men
> Black men.[50]

Signing himself "a Black man once," the poet adopted a name significant in light of the spirits' comments on the future of the races. In the culmination of this experiment in transracial unity, using terms evocative for persons of mixed race, the spirits of Lamenais and John Brown separately revealed that "the fusion of races will take place little by little," with Lamenais adding that the result would be that "antagonistic elements will harmonize and concord will triumph over disunion." Like white Spiritualists, Creoles insisted on the endurance of personal identity after death but implied that all—black and white—would become Creolized "White men / Black men" and accepting of the divergence of physical identity. Antagonisms were to be resolved in part by a leveling in which "the proud will be brought down. . . . Castles will crumble. The great popular voice will be heard. Reason will triumph over injustice." The divisive problems of race as practiced in America would dissolve only as race itself dissolved, only as all men became black men, once.[51]

Not every spirit accepted that the races would blend in the afterlife; indeed, some insisted on the celestial significance of race, though far differently than Hare or Ferguson. The old nemesis Henry Clay, architect of the reviled Compromise of 1850, returned from the grave to concede that the social and political ascension of blacks was inevitable, and he confessed that he now recognized that each race would play a role in shaping the future of the reformed nation. Each race, he argued, contributed uniquely to the "mysterious element controlled by the spirits" and

> leads the bar of Progress to a triumphal end—these different races constitute the strength of the country, because all of them are compelled to work for the amelioration of the human specie: each one being interested in the safe guard of its interests in particular, in guaranteeing the most extensive and equal rights to each one, whoever he may be.
>
> The question is solved; the Black shall reach where his faculties call him. . . . He is the master of the situation, and will command it.[52]

Clay's genius was to graft a theory of competing interests onto the standard demand from charity, arguing that the majority must respect the rights of the minority. In bold terms he outlined a positive-good argument for the existence of race: each race played a unique role in the progress of the world, each looking after its separate interests for the aggregate good of the species. The black race, he noted, had made unique contributions to this nation, having "gas-welded together the different parts of the union" with their blood, and as a result blacks were now tasting the first fruits of their labor. "In his new position," Clay claimed, the black man "is acquiring DOLLARS, which, in the American mind, constitute the pillars on which everything rests." Having progressed from being the objects of exchange to becoming full participants in exchange, having been the corporeal substance of national unity, blacks were now being integrated more completely into the financial economy and must therefore, Clay said, be accepted by whites as full members of society.[53]

Pragmatically, the spirits of slaves and other oppressed persons received and demanded justice in the afterlife, but in the interests of harmony and unity, they carefully eschewed vengeance, arguing, as Rey had, that they must conceal and subdue their inner turmoil in the interests of harmony. A former slave, John Jones, insisted:

We do not desire to retaliate. . . .

Bury the past, bury the hatchet, oh! men! and be united to each other, in order to prompt Harmony in the heart of each and every one. . . .

Liberty is now for all in Louisiana, you will be all united as we are here. . . .

I was a poor slave of man, but now a pure Spirit of God, looking to the Great Work of Redemption. . . .

No chains, nothing can forbid me to write my thoughts.

I am free!!! Where are you, slaves of Passions?[54]

The products themselves of miscegenation, Creole Spiritualists envisioned a spiritual future in which all were "Miscegens," all were Creoles. In a spiritual world in which a sense of cosmic justice and sympathetic recompense held sway, Creole spirits lit a path to a future in which racial distinctions evaporated but racial worth was underscored. The experience of wartime service on behalf of the enslaved and the hardships they endured during the early Reconstruction struggle for civil rights had catalyzed Creole Spiritualists to reimagine a social system in which solidarities could be entertained across races and could serve as a basis for political mobilization. Their vision was an actualization of the Spiritualist body: a social body in which no barriers limited the flow of sympathy of individuals, charity obliged the powerful to act on behalf of the weak, and all were made to recognize a commonalty of interest. Creole Spiritualists achieved this world not by partitioning parts of their experience, as northern Spiritualists did, but by a radical fusion of all elements, each with its own peculiarities and strengths, into a grand harmonious whole.

SUSPENDED REWARDS

The protracted struggle over civil rights in Louisiana had many dramatic moments but few sharp turning points. The recalcitrance of white opposition to racial equality, coupled with their effective legal and political maneuvering, gradually shut the door on any possibility of racial justice in the nineteenth century. The riots of 1866 and 1874 were shocking, painful, and disheartening to the Creole residents of New Orleans and dulled the optimistic edge to their thoughts on race relations during the early and mid-1860s. Along with the formal end of Reconstruction and the adoption of the "Redeemer" constitution, they signaled the gradual victory of the supporters of racial segregation and subordination.

The riot of 1874 may have been particularly painful for Henri Rey, for his brother Octave was the acting chief of police at the time, and it was his forces that spilled so much black blood. For Rey's circle the frustrations of repeated political failures and the exposure to recurrent violence showed in changes in the style and content of the messages they received from their departed friends, revealing a reluctant, and forced, accommodation to the new social order. As the promised fruits of Reconstruction died on the vine, Creole Spiritualism was transformed from a religion of social action into a religion of resignation that offered solace by plucking the only plum in sight: the promise of a future of equality, despite the present of oppression, terror, and pain. After 1874, and perhaps earlier, the messages received by the Rey circle become more and more removed from daily life, more and more restricted to heavenly, rather than earthly, concerns and compensations. The circle's registers are filled with elaborate instructions on how to conduct séances and how to manage a harmonic circle but contain fewer and fewer of the radical missives that illuminated the immediate postwar years. Instead, the spirits turned to an insistence that harmonic circles be closed, shut off from open intercourse with the general public in order to ensure the total sympathy of the participants and to exclude any disharmonious elements. Like white Spiritualists, though for drastically different reasons, Creole Spiritualists sought to circumscribe their sympathetic community around the remapped boundaries of race.

The world described by the spirits of the mid-1870s remains recognizable
in its general form, but amid the messages extolling charity and sympathy
are others that make it clear that these sentiments operated over a vastly reduced range. In 1877 Lunel, a regular visitor to the circle, could still insist
that everything in the spirit world "exists in a natural sympathy and currents
of attraction" and that love and charity reigned supreme, but he added:

> There are natural consequences to a state of unhappiness of the soul which do
> not permit it to exist in the middle of those who revel in the glorious state. . . .
>
> It is impossible for the spirit unhappy in the darkness of his soul to exist in
> our luminous societies, where all are impressed and act in accordance with the
> laws of love, devotion, and fraternal assistance.
>
> There is the "law of attraction" which carries each individual into a society
> natural to his tastes. The mask of hypocrisy falls before the piercing eyes of the
> spirit, which is no longer obstructed by the material which once enveloped it.[55]

In the fate of dark spirits lay the change. Among the luminous sympathy
made all transparent and harmonious, but it did so by exclusion. While
sympathizing souls unite, others—the dark-souled and miserable—withdrew elsewhere, to parts unstated, tacitly segregating the afterlife for the
harmony of the spiritually advanced.

Another spirit, Paul Bertus, encouraged mortals not to fear for their
rights in the future, for "they will be recognized and maintained." Deferring to the afterlife would bring its rewards, he claimed: "Oh! Cry not, my
children, if you know Spiritualism, you will wear your martyr's crown with
patience and resignation, without hate, without envy, without speaking ill
of anyone. . . in spite of your blood, spilled in profusion, your hands have
remained pure." To the "pariahs of the world," he promised a sort of
Franco–New Orleanian schadenfreude, a world in which he could ask,
"How many of you will be happy to have been oppressed, when seeing the
lamentations of your oppressors here [in the afterlife]. Pardon your enemies; they will learn here what they have done." But unlike the spirits before him and despite all his spleen, Bertus offered only future compensation and neither present political activism nor the hope of earthly
justice.[56]

Having their faith in the institutions of earthly government returned with violence and exclusion, some spirits held out a hope in the protections afforded by the government of the afterlife. After promising that all would be profitably employed in the afterlife, a "Luminous Brother" contrasted the institutions of death with those of life. Among the living "societies" were "organized for the guarantee of each one against the encroachments of those who are unfortunate by their passions and unjust pretentions," while among the dead societies were "constituted of the love and charity of those who compose them," geared toward the advancement of all in "mind" and "soul." Among the living societies exerted control by "forced obligations by laws which command," while the dead "exist by conventions always respected, and by laws which impress each one of his duty." Within these institutions of the dead, the "Luminous Brother" asserted that the rights of the minority to dissent were respected, even if the minority on earth fell too often prey to the "reflex of the mass, their desires, wishes." In the afterlife, he insisted, "to deny a representation to the minority, would be . . . a monstrosity in the elevated social state in which we find ourselves."[57]

The version of the afterlife advanced by Lunel and Bertus is marked by the segregation of oppressor and oppressed and an admission that sympathy was of limited efficacy in regulating earthly behavior. As I suggest in the next chapter, their version of the afterlife strikingly parallels versions of an apartheid afterlife advanced by northern white Spiritualists in the 1870s and mirrors the changes taking place throughout American society. But unlike white versions, the messages describing the Creole afterlife characteristically drift into a mystical language promising deferred justice through direct spiritual intervention, seeming to imply that if change could not be brought about by human intervention, then they must await the divine. One spirit alerted Rey to a spirit army being assembled to carry on the struggle. "It is a great liberating army formed in battalions, whose material bodies mouldered into a pile of dust centuries ago, but who built a luminous pyramid with their spirituality to light the route for humanity. They fight in the ranks of reason, strengthened by charity, and sublime in the devotion that guides them. . . . It is an army led by God which watches eternally. Empires fall, kings disappear; but it is there, always there at the post of honor."[58]

Whether or not this invisible army was to replace the active struggle that Rey and his fellow Spiritualists had long waged, it formed an easy road into quietism and social inaction; in light of the demonstrable failure of social action on earth, justice and equality could simply be placed in the hands of the unseen. Fueling this impression are messages from the old charitable stalwart, Saint Vincent de Paul, extolling the virtues of self-abnegation, "the precious jewel in the crown of the Elect." According to St. Vincent, in self-abnegation "there lies the force in his mission; it is there that his charity becomes sublime."[59]

By the last years of Reconstruction, the spirits who encouraged, consoled, and abetted the Creole veterans of the Native Guards in seeking to transform New Orleans, those who entertained prospects of transracial union and racial amalgamation and who preached racial self-awareness, had taken a muted tone, leaving justice in the hands of the dead. In the face of years of white political intransigence, in the face of frustration, violence, and oppression, Creole Spiritualists turned inward, away from the notion of an unbounded self toward a dissected, race-conscious selfhood. It was not the end of Creole radicalism or Creole resistance to racial oppression—that lineage passed directly from the Rey brothers through Rodolphe Desdunes—but in these changes was the end of effective Spiritualist resistance.

7

Shades

Race has, of course, been a characteristic American obsession.
—PHILIP J. DELORIA, *Playing Indian*

FOR A MODEST FEE clients of the National Developing Circle received a small packet of "developing paper" surcharged with an electric energy guaranteed to produce wondrous results. A simple touch, it was reported, had reduced one recipient to a fit of uncontrollable trembling; the paper had burst spontaneously into flame in the hands of another without being consumed, had reinvigorated the wasted limbs of the crippled, soothed the infirm, and it promised to cure "every variety of sickness or disability." It was, as the mediums of the circle announced, a benediction to humanity, the latest gift to mortal health from the spirits of the American Indian.[1]

The developing paper was revealed to the mortal world in 1879 when a barely articulate Indian spirit appeared to the Philadelphia publisher James A. Bliss. Blackfoot, the descendant of a line of medicine men stretching back centuries "before the pale-faces had found a home in America," had inherited his forefathers' healing powers and wished to "impart *their* magnetic influence to whomsoever might need it." Thus he set about instructing Bliss in the arcana of transforming ordinary blotting paper into an electrical panacea, coaxing, cajoling, and finally tricking the young publisher into folding a few specimens into outgoing issues of his periodical *Mind and Matter*. Like magnetic Deerslayers, Blackfoot and his "vast number of Indian assistants" then tracked the currents left in its postal wake to enter directly into the homes of the spiritually and physically afflicted, intent on applying their healing arts. "Where paper go," the spirit spokesman, Red

Cloud, said, "Blackfoot go; go quick." From New Hampshire to Nevada, spirit Indians displayed their skills in tracking, pursuing the paper to the promise of health restored.[2]

Blackfoot's magnetic physicians were only a ripple in a rising tide of spiritual Indians that crested in the decades following the Civil War, when spirit Indians grew so numerous that they supplanted fathers, mothers, sisters, or brothers as the stereotypical spirit guide. As white Americans rued (or celebrated) the vanishing Indian in novels, plays, poetry, and song, as they swilled "Indian" tonic and drank their patent medicines, Indians became ever more visible as spirits, leaving the perplexed antispiritualist investigator H. H. Furness wryly to observe that "there is no Cabinet, howe'er so ill attended, but has some Indian there."[3]

Whether lurking within a darkened cabinet or hawking tonic, the essence of the "Indian's" identity transcended death. Just as white spirits retained their talents and prejudices beyond the grave, Indian memories and emotions were translated into the afterlife in undiluted form. Red Jacket remained the orator, Samoset the leader, and Pocahontas the altruist and intermediary. Even the more mundane spirits were vested with their own unique histories: Vashti, the spirit control of the medium Fannie Conant, remained very much the little Piegan girl that she had been when her family was massacred along the banks of the Yellowstone River in 1869. The memories accrued and the affective bonds forged in life remained with them, but unlike whites, Indian spirits bore the attributes of an entire race. Every spirit Indian was, in a sense, Every-Indian, stripped to the essentials.[4]

It goes without saying, perhaps, that given the paucity of firsthand acquaintance with living Indians among white Spiritualists, much less affective connection with them, spirit Indians drew upon the deep and polyvalent traditions of Indian representation in the popular culture of white America. On stage and on the page, in the fraternal lodge and political mob, the "Indian," as Philip Deloria suggests, helped whites to "imagine and materialize distinctive American identities." Playing Indian was one way to solidify and express "new national ideals," to revel and rebel, to claim the native landscape and "liberty" as their special province (and providence), and later it was a means of fording the rising stream of "modernity."[5] The whooping, dancing, and pranking of a Honto, Wickahee, or Santum, the Indians who sprang from the Eddy family cabinet in Vermont, or the antics of Shanny, sister of Pocahontas, who would "cut up dido in high Injun style" and "squeal and dance and jabber Injun magnificently," all owe a palpable debt to Red Face stage plays. In their "true Indian" behavior, their mimicking of white men mimicking red-speak, their long and tragic soliloquies on the demise of the race, and their noble critiques of the dominant (white) political culture, the spirits wallowed in two centuries of "the white man's Indian." Beyond their value as entertainment, these Indians resonated with the Spiritualist experience, forming an implicit critique of modern white society. In their "pure" state they were the focus for a nostalgic yearning for the simple, organic relations that had been corroded by technology and modernity, their impact intensified by their unique ideological association with the American nation and the American people.[6]

Spiritualist Indians, however, conveyed an additional dimension emanating from their place within a broader anthropological system of race. While the seams of materializations cabinets burst with Indians, it seemed curious to H. H. Furness that "departed black men, who might be supposed to be quite as unsophisticated as departed red men, have hitherto developed no such materializing proclivities."[7]

Had Furness continued, he might have noted that the dynamic and timing of the Indian influx fulfilled the specific needs of a post–Civil War generation of whites struggling with the conspiracy of Darwinian theory and the political reality of emancipation that thrust the issues of union with nonwhites—sympathetic, political, ethnological, and biological—to center stage. They proliferated in death because they performed a vital function for the living within a racial system that facilitated an adjustment to a universe of constrained sympathetic reach, becoming as much the healers of sympathy as they were sympathetic healers.

In this chapter I take three excursions into post–Civil War Spiritualism in an attempt to conceptualize the changes in race, emotion, and nation. Following a tour of the post–Civil War afterlife to review the changes in heavenly geography, I turn to the Indian healer as a focal point for analyzing the Spiritualist version of "playing Indian" (or more accurately, from their perspective, "being Indian"), and finally, to a discussion of the formal efforts of Spiritualists to grapple with the fundamentals of Darwinian theory and the ethnological dilemma: resolving the genetic relations and systematic ordering of the human races.

When Allen Putnam asked in 1872 whether color or complexion could be found in the afterlife, the answer was admirably clear. "Yes, relatively," a spirit answered, "since it does not proceed from the external, but comes from the internal to the external, it must of necessity be deep-seated." Because race was "incorporated with the entire physical life of the being, and more than that," was "part of the spirit-body—belongs to that—therefore the spirit-body is affected by it; is colored by it, if you please."[8] Race was the spiritual core of identity.

THE RACIAL GEOGRAPHY OF HEAVEN

The heavenly cartographers were kept busy during the 1860s, drafting and redrafting the borders of the afterlife. Few antebellum Spiritualists would have predicted such a massive boom in employment, having argued that once spirits were divested of the prejudices, distrusts, and divisions of mortal life, they would enter a new-mown world in which "all comers are welcome" and in which, as one Spiritualist wrote, "it made no difference from what nation or kindred they came—Egyptian, Jew, or Hottentot, civilized, barbarian, or savage: all were welcome." Sooner or later the influence of that cosmic force, progress, would ensure that the boundaries of mortal life would fade.[9]

Yet spirits such as the one who spoke to Allen Putnam gave a new lease on the cartographic (after-)life, as race became the resilient exception to the border wars. No less an authority than Benjamin Franklin pronounced that in heaven, as on earth, "the white man has his characteristic; so has the African, so has the Indian; they are alike distinguishable here." Although many writers agreed with B. T. Young that the "kingdom of heaven" included "all nationalities and creeds," drawn together by the "sympathy of minds" and "like belief," the spiritual haunts of these nationalities and creeds and their circles of acquaintance became the subject of intense Spiritualist scrutiny. By the late 1860s all of the dimensions of race in the mid-nineteenth century—not only Putnam's "color and complexion" but language, nation, and culture as well—had imparted a distinctive geographic order onto heaven that cut across the spheres.[10]

The first sign of this new order was the demarcation of a distinctive heaven reserved specifically for Indians. There, in their "happy hunting-grounds," Indian spirits enjoyed an Arcadian America whose scenery and appearance were "as natural as those of earth, and far more beautiful," a landscape diversified into "grand forests, hills and even mountains." The Christian Spiritualist Eugene Crowell reported that spirit Indians enjoyed the completion of their domestic circle, each living "in his wigwam with his squaw and papoose," each taking part in the essential activities that made an Indian man a man: he "has his canoe," Crowell explained, his "bow and arrows, his horse and dog, and chases the deer, as he formerly did here, the only difference being, that, whereas when here he hunted from necessity, there he engages in the chase for sport, with no intention of destroying life, and without the ability to do so if he were so disposed." The insistence upon their proclivities for the hunt underscored the inferiority of Indians in the Scots stadial model of sociocultural development: their reliance on hunting for sustenance, though reduced to a spiritual analog that inflicted no suffering, placed them on the lowest rung of the *scala cultura*.[11]

Geographically, Indian status was well marked. Almost unanimously Spiritualist cartographers insisted that Indians inhabited a sphere located in the lowest realms of heaven, with some declaring that this sphere was lower even than the one to which the most dissolute whites were drawn and others arguing that this was the sole sphere available to Indians at all. In their isolated hunting ground, Indians conducted themselves as they had for centuries, fearing technologies such as steam and rail when they were introduced or taking a naively gleeful, uncomprehending, childlike pleasure in them. The spirit Winnebagos, for example, rebounded from their initial apprehension at seeing their first steamboat, amusing themselves by testing the speed of their horses by riding alongshore, whooping and shouting away.[12]

The cultural inferiority of Indians, Crowell cautioned, did not signify spiritual inferiority, for "in respect to character," the Indian heaven was "entitled to ranks among the higher heavens." A Spiritualist chorus agreed. One of the first mediums to invoke spirit Indians, Charles Hammond, proclaimed (with a hint of sarcasm) that the "untutored inhabitant of the forest" occupied "a higher position, and a purer circle" than the "murderers, liars, thieves, robbers, misers, winebibbers, gluttons, and many others" who proliferated on earth. Herman Snow, who became an important medium in San Francisco, added that these "simple, unsophisticated sons of the forest," these men "into whose glades the light of civilization has never dawned," exemplified a moral state to which cultured, civilized whites might aspire but seldom attained. These "unlettered children of the forest" bore an interior perfection that the temptations of civilization and technology had eaten away; they were the perfectly natural man before the doleful divisions of modern life, the noble savage who occupied a region that was itself the perfect expression of American nature.[13]

The blood of living Indians was steeped in savagery and spiritual purity. "Childlike" by nature, at least in their "original condition," "unsophisticated and simple far beyond the ordinary white man," living Indians were said by the Spiritualist publisher Samuel Terry to be uniquely open to spirit influence, so much so that he maintained that all Indians were Spiritualists "in the sense of believing in a life after this." Their medicine men were all "more or less mediumistic or clairvoyant," and like a child, even the average Indian possessed a naturally enlarged sympathetic capacity that permitted a casual familiarity "with the phenomena of spirit manifestations," enabling them to converse with spirits "whenever and wherever [they] meet together."[14] When insulated from the seductions of modern life and the encroachments of "churchianic" excess, living Indians continued to look "not to man's, but Nature's Architecture and Architect." Only in their native state could they continue to worship from the heart, "not in accordance with the forms and expressions of the few—nor the many." These primitive men were the Primitive Church incarnate.[15]

For all their rude, uncultivated habits, Indians were thus held up as spiritually superior to whites. Though lacking "the educational discipline of the present age of the world" and burdened with "superstitious ideas," they possessed "clearer and more beautiful and Christian conceptions of the True God than many minds who rank higher in point of intellectual ability." Naturally, humans learned through their "intuitive faculties, which are receptive to truths," and apprehended the divine in all things. The result of Indians being Indians, according to the medium Mary Theresa Shelhamer, was that in the "red man's happy hunting-ground," tranquillity reigned. Intertribal animosities evaporated there, where the various tribes "mingle together and dwell in unity." In the Indian spirit realm, there is "no hate, no anger, no fears disturb their minds; they grow in harmony, and gain that strength of mind which they send back to aid and assist the pale-faces through their chosen mediums." It was a region "where no foe disturbs him, where no storms can come," and although whites were permitted as visitors or missionaries ("who delight to teach the red man, and whom he in turn listens to with reverence and love"), as Shelhamer insisted, too, it was a region that remained "exclusively an Indian country."[16]

By the late 1860s it became increasingly clear to Spiritualist cartographers that every race and nation, not just Indians, enjoyed its own unique heaven peculiarly suited to its individual needs and desires. As early as 1853 A. J. Davis advised that the hemispheres of heaven were divided into six societies, "each being characterized by a different race of spirits, ruled by its own affinities, with different habits, in different stages of moral culture." These societies, "differing as one star differs from another, or as the different notes in music," were "sub-divided over and over again" by finer and finer degrees of affinity. While Davis emphasized spiritual unity in 1853, after the Civil War the essential distinctions of race began to acquire momentum. "Everywhere" in the afterlife, the medium S. G. Horn reported, "peculiarities of race still exist," and everywhere sympathy drew like to like, "the Hindoos and Turks each retaining their peculiar marks of character, colour, and development, though possessing less arbitrary forms of government"; Englishmen were joined to Englishmen, and Bushmen presumably to Bushmen. Near earth's Africa, Horn discovered that spirit gorillas, which "possessed a species of soul" and the rudiments of a "spiritual existence," joined other gorillas to live "quite by themselves," eking out an afterlife that was "advanced a little beyond the animal, more like the barbarous tribes of Africa." These refined apes were "especially friendly," living in huts and eating only fruits and grains. To the east pagodas abounded, and the spirit Japan and China thrived in "a high state of civilization," conducting friendly relations with the American dead. Even their religions persisted. "Mahomet and Confucius have both their followers in this world," Horn observed, "as men, mortal or immortal, seem bound to follow some ideal teacher."[17]

Eugene Crowell concurred that "national distinctions and boundaries exist in the heavens, as here," but Crowell asserted that the signifiers of race eventually would lessen (though never quite disappear). Although a "Negro there is still a Negro," Crowell claimed that both "Indians and Negroes, as they progress, constantly assimilate in appearance and character to the white race," becoming "blended with the whites" in the highest spheres. Eventually blacks became "as white, beautiful, refined, and intellectual" as any Caucasian.[18]

But few shared in Crowell's vision. Most postwar Spiritualists insisted that because nationality and race (as much as these were distinct concepts) supplied the strongest, most natural sympathetic bonds, they were singularly resistant to change after death. Carrie Twing stated bluntly that the notion "that a negro is white in spirit life, is antagonistic to nature's laws," for if, as Spiritualists had long maintained, personality remained unchanged by death, "it would be out of place to see the color of an African changed while he still retained the thick lips and flat nose of his nation." Although Twing admitted that "spirits from different races and colors" visited other regions of the afterlife, she insisted they are always "much happier to have their spirit homes with those of their own kind."[19]

Race ran longitudinally through the spheres, and neither physical differences nor emotional connections would change significantly. Recalling Adam Smith's admonition against the degrading habit of extending sympathy to lessers, Benjamin Franklin pointed out in the 1890s that although the spirit world was daily besieged with "hordes of wild spirits from Asia, Africa, and Europe," not to mention "the fanatics of India, the savages of the forest, the murderers, drunkards, and half-idiots that swarm the earth," this did not indicate that sympathy with them was warranted. "Receive each according to his degree," he advised, "and do not form a spiritual friendship with those who would tempt you to drink, swear, or act untruthfully."[20]

Racial penetration of the body, material and spiritual, was a law of nature, immutable, that extended even to a cosmic scale. Moving away from seeing race and culture as functions of the external environment, postwar Spiritualists increasingly saw them as manifestations of a deeper, sympathetically determined interior state. They were in effect replacing environmental determinism with a pastiche of interior drives and sympathetic determinism, the tangible manifestation of which was an apartheid of the spheres that, as Annie Cridge and A. J. Davis discovered, held true even on distant planets. When Cridge and Elizabeth Denton (the mediumistic sister and wife of William Denton, respectively) psychometrically toured Mars in 1869, they discovered four races that like the races of earth populated a unilinear gradient of development. At the top was a "Caucasian" race with skin of a "beautiful *pink,*" bearing beautiful heads marked by the phreno-logical virtues of firmness and veneration and by large organs of intellect and morality. At the other end of the scale, Cridge saw a race that was "al-most black," with bodies covered with hair, and below this, an even more inferior race that was difficult to perceive, perhaps because it was so for-eign. Obscure as it was, it was clear that this race was "dark colored,— very dark," though Cridge added she "should not call them black." Com-pared with the Caucasian Martians, this race had small heads, "even in proportion to their small bodies," and displayed signs of the irremediable cultural inferiority. "They do not live in houses," she wrote; "they are the most inferior race of human beings I have yet seen."[21]

Andrew Jackson Davis's visions of the afterlife also ventured to "far-distant planets" and their "infinite variety of radical personal character-istics and temperamental differences." In their disparate homes Davis ob-served that these extraterrestrial spirits "carry upon the life within their faces, as well as in the secret chambers of their affections, the effects of life upon the globe that produced them." Interiors mirrored exteriors, but on different planets as on earth, culture and race were the "natural exponents of the interior realities of the societies of men and women."[22]

INDIAN PHYSICIANS

Nowhere were the interior realities of being Indian better revealed than in their capacity as healers. As the National Developing Circle and countless advertisements in Spiritualist periodicals attested, spirit Indians were the finest naturopaths known to the mortal body. For generations before the seductions of modern life, Indians had lived a "nomadic and simply natu-ral life," acquiring a "peculiar knowledge of herbs, plants, and earthly pro-ductions" and an intuitive awareness of the "manifold healing balm that the earth generates in her bosom," which they now used to prescribe "rare and invaluable medicaments for the cure of disease."[23]

Predictably, for all their diagnostic skill and intimate knowledge of materia medica, the ultimate key to the Indian reduction of pain lay in the power of sympathy. One spirit explained that the "law of sympathetic at-traction" drew all spirits to the sick and suffering, leading them to bring their mediums into "strong and harmonious rapport with the debilitated body." By thus establishing a "chain of sympathy between the medium and patient" and "causing the former to take the disease of the latter," they were able to identify and treat "the region of pain and distress."[24]

Indians were always the most responsive, most capable of physicians, seldom restricting themselves to the treatment of simple physical pain. Where Adam Smith had promoted sympathy as a social palliative, Indian spirits manipulated both physiological and social sympathy to manufacture a mental instrument for the diagnosis and cure of all pain, individual and social. If there was an Indian medical specialty during the 1860s and 1870s, it was the treatment of the social malady of racial animosity. From Emma Hardinge and James Peebles to Jesse Babcock Ferguson and Fannie Conant, Spiritualist mediums and writers drew attention to Indian spirits who, having shed their material bodies, shed with them the confinements of racial antagonism, thereby restoring a harmonious balance between the races (fig. 9). With the clarity of spiritual vision earned in nature and enhanced by death, Indians renounced their personal histories of suffering at the hands of whites and shed their resentments for the mantle of repentance, altruism, and reconciliation.

As the nation was fragmented and reassembled during the Civil War, discussion of the reconciliation of personal animosities assumed a cardinal importance in the Spiritualist literature. The spirit Hamilton was spotted seeking his Burr, Arnold and André together sought out Washington, Lincoln was seen walking arm in arm with John Wilkes Booth, and Robert E. Lee and a host of dead Rebels conversed with the Yankee dead in postmortem amity. Yet Indians were uniquely identified as a class of spirits dedicated to personal and collective reconciliation. Unlike the prototypical spirit child or parent of the 1850s, the harmonizing efforts of Indians led them into congress with persons whom they had never known at all. Indians came to the tilting table as Indians, with race forming a significant element of the sympathetic connection. The Indian who worked through the medium James M. Peebles had never known him in life, but his mission was clear. This stately Indian, Peebles said, had "long ago washed the warpaint off from his face, broke his arrows, unstrung his bow, and put white feathers in his hair." He had recast his die as a "peace Indian" who prom-

FIG. 9. Spiritual drawing of White Feather, Indian spirit guide of the *Banner of Light*'s medium Fannie Conant. (Frederick Currier Photographic Collections, William L. Clements Library, University of Michigan)

ised personally to assist Peebles whenever he was present, and whenever he was away, he assured Peebles that it was only because he was "with the Indians and the white men, away off towards the sun-set, trying to make them love one another and be happy."[25]

Such devotion to mediums, their companions in intermediation between heavens and earth, was the Indian norm. Emma Hardinge believed that Indian spirits "delight to work out a new and beautiful mission for themselves, in guarding and protecting the toiling mediums," and as Spiritualists often attested, their record was impeccable. When the home of Allen Putnam grew uninviting to the better sort of spirit due to the loitering of a dead and miserly "Chinaman," it was a nearby band of Indians who intervened, greeting visitors as they approached the door, countering the Asian's hostility with hospitality. "*These* Indians are a noble band," Putnam crowed, his mediumship restored to order as the Chinese spirit was "softened, expanded, refined, and beautified, in the copious and gentle rays of a mother's love, mingled with those of a charity which knows no race, color, or condition." Even the hardest-hearted of living Indians, a veritable Black Hawk, was softened in the spirit world. Where once "pale-faced spirits found little welcome at his council-fire," this repentant warrior now welcomed all with open arms and spiritual gifts.[26]

The spiritual balms from Indian hearts flowed over more than mediums. In attending to soma, spirit, and society, Indian benevolence flowed over all members of the white race and beyond. When the spirit of a four-year-old "colored" child arrived in heaven, for example, suffering "from scorn and neglect" because the "taint" of its "origin seemed to follow even into the spirit-life," it was a "band" of Indians who came to the rescue. "With rough comicality, music, and dancing," as Herman Snow described the scene, they induced "a cheerful harmony," and after they had established conditions sufficient "to answer a somewhat higher purpose," gradually "a change of influences took place." A white and motherly woman was attracted, and although she harbored a lingering earthly revulsion over the child's complexion, she took it as her own, whisking it away to join her throng of adoptees. "Here the hitherto homeless one," Snow concluded, "will no longer feel or know of a distinction founded solely on race and color," here the effects of a fractured family were healed by new affective bonds forged along the natural, sympathetic lines of motherly care.[27]

The ministrations of spirit Indians stimulated the reciprocity of white spirits and white Spiritualists. Mary Dana Shindler encountered two white missionaries so devoted to their charges in life that long after death they chose to remain "with their dead Indians." In life the mediums of the National Developing Circle extended "an open and sympathetic interest to all spirits coming to us in the understanding of Truth irrespective of race, nation or color" and claimed already to have received spiritual returns from "the Indian, African, Egyptian, and Persian." Likewise, the antislavery veteran Giles B. Stebbins informed a Japanese diplomat that "millions" of Americans were willing "to accept truth from Pagan or Christian, and in a sense of 'the sympathy of religions' and the spiritual fraternity of the race," while Hudson Tuttle exclaimed that it was a characteristic of Spiritualism to grow from contact with other races and creeds. "Like the bee," he wrote, Spiritualism drank "nectar from the poisonous nightshade as well as from the fragrant rose, it absorbs the truths of Catholicism, of Mohammedanism, of Buddhism, of Philosophy."[28]

The relics of disdain harbored by Tuttle for the poisonous sects were not translated to the heavenly "Hall of Brotherly Love," where the clairvoyant medium Josiah Brigham could see "the Indian," now pacified. The lingering discord of life had been sapped by racial reconciliation, and now, in heaven, a peaceful Indian could be seen

> listening to the "big words" of wisdom as they fell from the lips of the "pale-faced brother." Without fear and trembling he sat at his feet, listened to the sweet counsels he breathed, heard him tell of the Great Manitou whose love extended over all, whose Big Heart throbbed with the tenderest affection for every child, and who welcomed all to a seat in His Eternal Wigwam. Joyfully my eyes feasted in that sublime spectacle,—that holy, heavenly picture of harmonial communion! It brought to mind the prophecies of the past,—the dawn of that glad Millennium-Day, when the lamb shall lie down with the lion, the kid with the wolf, and brethren live together in peace, harmony, and love, with none to molest, nor to make afraid.[29]

Such harmonial Indians, Brigham explained, were constantly involved with white spirits in promoting mutual spiritual advancement and were essential cogs in forging a sympathetic link between the most refined spheres of the highest heavens and the lowest and most degraded. Brigham witnessed Indians assisting Benjamin Franklin as he tried out a new machine he had designed to shower "DEFECATED ELECTRICITY" for the benefit of the unenlightened. As Franklin and Isaac Newton took the helm, concentric circles of Indians gathered beneath, with Samoset, Osceola, and Pocahontas at the center and still other Indians farther below, awaiting the "flood of inspiration" and the chance to distribute it to the spiritually needy.[30]

When it lurched into gear, Franklin's machine drew "vitality from surrounding bodies, and from the forces of the ethereal atmosphere," and it issued "forth a splendid flood of light." Joining hands and singing to induce harmony (as many Spiritualists did in séance), the Indians were "united together again by a small, subtle chain, as thin and delicate almost as air," sympathetically completing the circuit from the highest heavens to the lowest. The harmonious interaction of white and red bodies combined produced an irresistible healing current, with Indians as the essential intermediaries. "Released from the trammels of sectarian prejudice and bigotry," Brigham concluded, "there was naught in the way to prevent the full outflowing of the natural affections and sympathies, or to hinder the flood of intelligence they were sending on an errand of peace and love." According to Pocahontas, that paragon of interracial cooperation, the machine produced a union of selves in which every thought became "the reflex of a combined band," the exemplification of a high order of sympathetic union. Another Indian, speaking through Samoset (no less a paragon than Pocahontas), implored the less enlightened to "tread with us the walks of a higher life" and to "dwell with us in those beautiful wigwams, ever smiling with the beauties of harmony, of love, and of charity."[31]

As clearly as any Spiritualist, Brigham situated the work of racial reconciliation and spiritual renewal squarely within the context of the American nation. For Brigham, racial harmonization took place through distinctively American symbols, beginning with the genius of Franklin, the arch benefactor, patriot, and inventor, and extending through the united bodies of Indians, who were not only symbols of the American nation, as Philip Deloria has suggested, but who were specifically responsible for fostering the survival of the earliest European colonists. Just as characteristically, and just as symbolically, Brigham's critique of white behavior and his formula for mutual advancement did little to disturb the relations of power between whites and Indians: whites remained in positions of control, doling out "big words" and designing the machinery of enlightenment. Indians were the hands, and perhaps the hearts, but whites were the head.

Whatever else it implied, the healing capacity of Indians in spirit communion signified the presence of powerful interracial sympathetic bonds, so powerful, as Eugene Crowell noted, that "there is probably not a medium for physical manifestations where an Indian spirit is not a principal, if not the principal operator." In healing and materialization séances in the United States, where the spirit body appeared visibly and where the intimacy between spirit and medium approximated the highest states of sympathetic union, Indians, but not Africans, Asians, or other "lesser" races, abounded. When a medium was possessed by any spirit, Crowell explained, "all the movements of the body and limbs of the medium correspond to and are but the reflected movements of those of the body and limbs of the spirit," and when a medium stood before an audience, he added, the "rapport of the spirit speaker with the medium is so intimate that he perceives each person in it, and hears what may be said as distinctly as if he were personally present in the flesh." With Indians, such intimacy was essential to the healing process.[32]

For believers, the experience of this sort of "playing Indian" was therefore conceptually distinct from the many other varieties described by Philip Deloria. In minstrelsy, stage plays, fiction, revelry, or rebellion, playing Indian worked from a white interior expressed through a "red" exterior, while materialization proceeded from a "red" interior toward the white surface. The self-conscious artifice of minstrelsy and street theater and the play between reality (white) and projection (Indian), between alternate forms of power, were met by an insistence of bodily and emotional merger: the tangible white medium collapsed into an equally tangible Indian possessed of his or her own distinctive history. With "eyelids closed, and all power of action . . . suspended," the white medium entered into a potentially transgressive surrender to the red other, the white tongue refusing "its office" while the red prattled on, a miscegenation nearly unthinkable between white and black but one that became the rule between white and Indian. Nor was the impact of such merger blunted in the face of mediumistic fraud. Whatever the intentions or beliefs of the medium, the audience experienced a true interracial fusion, if only vicariously.[33]

That both the experience of fusion and the assertions of Indian spiritual superiority were inevitably coupled with the signifiers of cultural inferiority, however, lends support to David Roediger's claim that for whites, dressing Indian (that lesser form of possession) "usually involved a conscious declaration of whiteness and white supremacy." Spiritualists who became Indian emerged with a sharpened sense of racial identity that accompanied the step into cross-racial liminality and the certain return into a white-born skin.[34]

It is particularly notable that this affirmation of white identity and superiority was enacted through symbols that had been singled out by Spiritualists as peculiarly divisive and troublesome. Excursions into Indian heaven shone a light on modern technology, religion, material culture, and economic relations, offering alternative readings of cultural change that paired the utopian vision of perfected industry, commerce, and society seen in the highest civilized spheres with their rejection in the equally utopian, racialized, and decidedly savage "happy hunting-ground." The Spiritualist heavens and the noble savage within them provided a means of identifying and challenging the most divisive effects of modernity and incorporating them within whiteness; they performed a social-critical function and simultaneously offered a means of accommodation, and perhaps resistance, to what seemed the inevitable march of progress. Technology, industry, and commerce became white.

The anthropologist Michael Taussig has argued that contemplation of the savage is interesting in part because "such looking is in itself a form of theorizing society and historical process," including the historical process that Spiritualists called progress. Taussig interprets the mimicking and embodiment of the colonizing other by tribal populations as an effort to capture or co-opt the power of the imagined other. "To give an example, to instantiate, to be concrete," he suggests, "are all examples of the magic of mimesis, wherein the replication, the copy, acquires the power of the represented." In Spiritualism, as in formal ethnography, the power relations are reversed: the dominant group embodies and mimics the subordinate, and the peculiarly intimate embodiment of Spiritualist possession results in the consumption and knowing of the subject represented, a way for the Spiritualist to "yield into and become Other," to acquire the essence of the Indian for their quotidian lives.[35]

Whatever this heart of redness was, this thing acquired, possessed, and co-opted, it was negotiated through the sympathetic bonds that united Indian and white. The absence of family connection, of racial or intellectual affinity, precluded the ordinary channels of sympathetic congress, for Spiritualists were repeatedly assured of Indian otherness in each of these regards. Instead, the sympathetic bond that connected Indian and white inhered in the American landscape and its synecdoches, the nation and national characteristics. As Jill Lepore argues was the case in red-face drama, these bonds became tacit calls for Americans "to become Indian, to take on their unique American inheritance, thereby distinguishing themselves from Europeans and European culture."[36]

But the double edge of savagery was never distant, and just as the noble savage was consistently paired with the ignoble, the spirit Indian stood both as a critique of contemporary white culture and as something atavistic, inferior, diminishing, and quite often threatening. Indian land became the particular point at which the intimate and forgiving face of spirit Indians met with another, seemingly paradoxical face: the angry, resentful, and violent. Ever sensitive, Eugene Crowell concluded that Indian behavior in the afterlife was not, in fact, always productive of racial harmony. Despite their healing ways, spirit Indians harbored resentments that occasionally burst forth, the unresolved relics of bitter injustice suffered in life. "America is the Indian's native soil," he explained; "here he has been defrauded, insulted, and massacred. He is revengeful here, and for a while at least after entering spirit-life, he can be no less so." The result, Crowell concluded, was that most murders in the mortal world were instigated by "the spirits of slain or starved Indians," who hovered about and influenced the more "mediumistic" mortals to commit crimes in order to "gratify their revengeful feelings upon the pale faces."[37]

From Osceola laboring with Ben Franklin to Black Hawk, Red Jacket, Tecumseh, and King Philip, the most relentless opponents of white encroachment and the most confirmed nativists crowded the séance room. These were not generic Indians to be donned and doffed, but men (almost invariably men) with distinctive and well-known histories of familiarity with European ways and beliefs and equally well-known histories of resisting and rejecting both outright. But the meanings of this resistance are not self-evident. Although in the twentieth century the spirit of Black Hawk has become enshrined within Black Spiritual Churches as a symbol of and encouragement to the resistance to racial oppression, among white Spiritualists of the previous century, the savagery of a Black Hawk served quite the opposite purpose, working in two distinctly different ways to excoriate whites for their behavior, while at the same time absolving them. Placated and reconciliatory, newly converted to the ways of peace, a dead Black Hawk pardoned even the most recent sins of whites, even as he proclaimed those sins for all to hear. A self-described advocate for the Indian, James Peebles could not refrain from commenting upon the disparities between white and Indian behavior, condemning whites not only for their actions in the past but for their ongoing violence and greed. "Is justice, is philanthropy, dead?" he demanded. "Is progress a dream? and sympathy a mere historic legend?" Yet Peebles removed the fangs from this asp, insisting that Indians were even now "returning good for evil," coming back from the dead with "balms of healing, and words of love and cheer," as if nothing in life had mattered.[38]

To Emma Hardinge the stoic, all-forgiving behavior of Indians reflected a fundamental spiritual truth. "It is a glorious indication of the bright transfiguration which death effects in our human weaknesses and vices," she wrote,

> to find that the red man, whose highest earthly virtue is revenge, and who, according to the short-sighted policy of human calculations, might reasonably be expected to return in the spirit of an avenger for the intolerable wrongs his race has endured, almost invariably performs, in the modern spiritual movement, the high and blessed function of the beneficent Healer. . . .
>
> Hapless ignorant beings, nay, whole tribes that have been despoiled and cheated by Christian cupidity, out of land, home, and life itself, now seem to be the most prominent of all returning spirits, in practically illustrating the lesson which the Christians so glibly teach and so wantonly falsify by their deeds, namely, to "overcome evil with good," and forgive those who know not what they do. It is one of the strangest and most instructive of lessons—this relation between the white man and the spirit of his "savage victim."[39]

At the most basic level, the abundance of forgiveness and the displacement of justice to the afterlife passed for a sort of antinomian ticket out of collective guilt. Indian leaders like Black Hawk, Powhatan, Thunder, Logan, and Little Crow were erased as figures of resistance, only to reappear as the ultimates of forgiveness, dedicated only to "shedding their healing magnetisms and peace-influences upon the inhabitants of earth," sharing the healing secrets of generations of Indians with those who had inflicted the greatest harm. For a man hanged only a decade before in one of the greatest mass executions in American history, Little Crow seems remarkably composed, demonstrating the power of sympathetic healing and the mastery of emotional control, but also the possibility of Indian erasure.[40]

Vanishing, as Philip Deloria has emphasized, was integral. Like their literary counterparts, spirit Indians gave vent to the sentiments of personal and collective loss, railing against the violence and injustice of their lives. The wide and white appeal of the death speeches of a Logan or Metamora lay in their denouement, as Deloria writes, during which dying Indians "offered up their lands, their blessings, their traditions, and their republican history to those who were, in real life, violent, conquering interlopers." The key was not merely the forgiveness granted but the ideology that claimed that Indians were a vanishing race destined for an extinction that would further obscure the brutality of dispossession by relegating it to the past tense and to a natural (and simultaneously sociocultural) inevitability. Spiritualists extended the reach of this formula by framing it within a morally compensatory cosmic system that punctured the last vestiges of rage at injustice. Jesse Ferguson was not the only Spiritualist to reject original sin when he announced that "neither you nor I ever felt *guilt* for Adam's transgression, or any man's transgressions over whom we could not have exerted influence." No recompense was needed because Indians were already gone, or soon would be, and their postmortem forgiveness was complete.[41]

Indian fury, as Eugene Crowell demonstrated, could be simultaneously legitimated and displaced, and the more it was rehashed, the more it allowed the fiercest implications of white complicity in suffering to be entertained, while at the same time sapping it sympathetically of force. When memories of white atrocities caused the spirit Big Bear to lather himself into such "a condition of intense excitement and indignation" that it appeared he would inflict "serious injury" upon the medium or the audience, Crowell defused the situation by showing him how misguided his anger was. With the aid of a wiser Indian spirit, Crowell assured Big Bear that "many white persons had received even worse from other white persons, and from Indians" and calmed him by pointing out the "injustice and cruelty [that] were daily witnessed all around." Cruelty and savagery were individual traits found in white and Indian alike, natural and inevitable and not the exclusive property of either. Commenting that Big Bear's "squaw" and children were now delighted with their death in heaven, Crowell emphasized how "wicked" it would be for Big Bear "to cherish such feelings against any human being," adding that earthly anger "can only prevent your advancing in spirit-life, for just as long as you do this you cannot progress, and it is for you to throw off all such feeling and do your duty like a man who is determined to conquer them." In Crowell's critical equation, emotional control and progress were cause and effect in a single logical chain.[42]

When the spirits of slaves were brought into the formula, this wishful persuasion grew rapidly more complex. Few mediums offered more fertile soil for investigating the quadratics of race than the proslavery Tennesseean Jesse Babcock Ferguson. From the time of his conversion to the spirits in 1854, Ferguson was a magnet for Indians. In his first Indian encounter, as he later recalled it, he had been dozing by a fence when the crack of an invisible ax startled him as it smashed into the railing above his head. Having heard the near-fatal blow, his terrified and conveniently clairvoyant wife reported seeing a "noble looking Indian Chief" looming over, and after receiving reassurance from the spirit of the noble Theodore Parker that she would not be harmed, she allowed the Indian to speak through her. Given voice, the chief declaimed:

> We, my dear sir, as a nation, have been driven out, before the face of the White Man, to live among the beasts; therefore, little is expected of our nation. There are many of us, rest assured, who are much more capable of Civilization than many of your own nation; yet, we are driven forth from the presence of the White Man. He would have been calculated to civilize and train the mind of the Red Man, had he approached us properly from the first. We would not then have worshipped our images. The bow and arrow, the tomahawk and scalping knife would not have been our emblems of justice, had he placed before us the true teaching. We need pure teachers, among our nations. Such teachers, let me tell you, as are sent to the Red Man, only make him worse—more corrupt.— Ah! when they leave the civilized portions of the world, they think they can do pretty much as they please among savages. We see and behold them with scorn and irreverence. We cannot reverence them. They are more savage than we.[43]

Flensing the skin of civilization to expose the savage interior of the nation (putting words to the life history of the murderous Albert Tirrell), Ferguson's chief persistently contrasted his nation with the nation that had supplanted it, the nation of white America. In order to subsume Indians, he contended, whites had expelled them with the aid of slaves, and neither the introduction of Christianity nor that of civilization had lessened the devastation of their lives.[44]

Instead, Ferguson's Indians proclaimed that every act of interracial violence was the product of white duplicity and their injustice in labeling Indians as savages and "unfit for earth" solely "because the tinted semblance decks" their "form." Puncturing the ignoble version of the savage that fitted him out as "a furious foe, ready to bare my breast to the impending storm; ready to protect the hearth of wife and little ones," Ferguson's Indian insisted upon his humanity and his right to the same affective, familial structures as whites, decrying the inferiority imputed them by the white mind and the behaviors said "naturally" to be theirs as mere pretexts to annihilation. "Speak you of his crude, untutored nature?" one Indian asked. "Who made him so? Let the white man tell the tale. Let him record, in letters of living fire, the many hearths desolated. Let him speak of the decline of mighty nations, that once roamed through this broad and extended plain. Where are they now? This is a problem for humanity to solve. Has some shaft, from the hand of God, missed its aim, that these damning feuds recoil not around the paternity they bear? No: 'Tis but the death-knell of the representations of that infinite justice and infinite mercy encircling all." Mercilessly local and personal, persistent, complaining not about abstract injustices but about deprivation of the very land on which Ferguson lived, these Indians fairly roiled with rage. "If my own nature were allowed to burst forth, with all its vehemence," one said, "it would create an ocean, whose waves would ascend to heaven, and deluge the infatuation of the White Man."[45]

Exposed by the angry Indian, this infatuation was nevertheless carefully circumscribed within the orbit of vanishment: the injustices were past, irrevocable, the Indians gone, and furthermore, Crowell's equation between the control of emotion and spiritual progress still held true. That Ferguson's Indians contained their anger—barely—was both entirely consistent with the stereotype of the stoic Indian and a central factor in Ferguson's racial cosmology. His Indians betrayed a sense that the surrender of savage to civilized was a process continually imperiled by backsliding and atavism. In the year in which he announced his commitment to Spiritualism, Ferguson proclaimed his faith in the "law of human development, happiness and glory" that he witnessed in the "progression from brute nature to the elements that make the human organism" and in the "progression from feeble infancy to maturity." But the progress for which Ferguson yearned ("Aye, I love the word; I almost worship the idea") was fragile and threatened.[46] For progress to occur, man must acknowledge the link between emotional control and spiritual destiny, must master desire and insulate himself from the atavistic emotions welling from within. If not, Ferguson warned, "our appetites and passions, misdirected and uncontrolled, become like voracious serpents winding their loathsome length in tightening cords around our capacity for pure desires and holy works, and spreading their blighting slime over every flower of faith, love and hope within us. Our evil propensities follow, like rabid dogs, along the pathway of every footstep we make towards the divine and eternal good. Beware, then, of serpents; beware of dogs."[47]

And for Ferguson the rabid dogs were African, they were beings who, unlike the Indian, were incapable of either restraint or self-governance when freed and whose spirits sang only hosannas to their "liberators" or, like the spirit Oliver, longed simply for a banjo and for "dancing and patting 'Juba' in real negro fashion." Were not all races "men and brothers," a spirit Indians asked (echoing the antislavery motto). "Has the Indian one God, and the White Man another? Has the Negro the same claims to that common Paternity you bear?"[48]

For Ferguson the answer revolved around the dichotomies between red and black, free and enslaved, independent and dependent, irate and docile, and it involved a complex interplay of internality and externality, of emotion and excess. Symbolically the nonwhite races represented alternative futures for whites, linking white, black, and red in a causal and genetic emotional nexus. Blacks could be made internal to the nation only when disciplined within the financial economy and brought within the sympathetic orbit of their superiors, and when they were not, they were consigned to be "aliens from our hearts and home," a moral and physical peril that required a surgical excision. But tied to the American soil and psyche, Indians were sympathetically joined to whites, as victims but also as Americans, as healers, as missionaries. Their nation could not endure the white onslaught, but once it had vanished from the earth, their land became white land, and the immaterial spirit Indians could safely be incorporated in a way that the all too material Africans could not. As the midpoint in two diametrically opposed historical trajectories, white Spiritualists like Ferguson imagined themselves enmeshed with Africans and Indians, able to ascend or descend accordingly, to master emotion and complete the sympathetic nation or to descend into unrestrained savagery.[49]

DARWIN AND THE SPIRITS

In 1860, when the comic magazine *Punch* lampooned the controversy over Darwin's unsettling new theory on the origin of species, it did so with a cartoon depicting a gorilla wearing a sandwich board emblazoned with the phrase "Am I a man and a brother?" In these few words the magazine captured the threat that Darwin's damned idea posed for man's place in nature, at the same time raising the question of the place of nature in man. By linking a disquiet over natural selection with the well-worn antislavery motto "Am I not a man and a brother," *Punch* hinted that somehow this new theory spoke to old practices of racial ordination, suggesting that it was not just the genealogical threat of the African ape that proved so disturbing but the threat of the African man.

Far from being the first to promote an unflinching evolutionism, Darwin was mining a deep, though not uncontroversial, vein of thought, a vein mined independently by his contemporaries Robert Chambers, John Fiske, Lewis Henry Morgan, and most prominently (from the Spiritualist perspective), Alfred Russel Wallace, the staunch British Spiritualist and codiscoverer of natural selection. To many of Wallace's coreligionists, natural selection seemed to offer a material counterpart to the spiritual processes they had been hawking for over a decade, including progress, gradualism, and natural law. Yet others, including Wallace himself, were less sanguine. Amid the pre-Mendelian squabbling over evolutionary mechanism and the nature of inheritance, Spiritualists assumed a range of positions on evolution as diverse and conflicted as those of their Protestant counterparts, tacking from wholehearted embrace to bitter rejection. They displayed consistency only in their obsession with what might be termed the ethnological dilemma of evolution: the vital and difficult question of what natural selection meant for the origins of humanity and human races, how these had changed, and how they related to the divine.[50]

In his attempts to recapture the valence of evolution in the mid-nineteenth century, the historian of anthropology George Stocking has repeatedly emphasized the extraordinary flexibility of the concept and the very different boundaries that it encompassed, particularly when applied to the study of human racial variation. Although Darwin catalyzed the acceptance of evolutionary thought in the formal scientific canon, in the absence of any workable theory of inheritance, natural selection struggled for its very existence. Until the rediscovery of Mendel at the turn of the twentieth century, natural selection was nowhere as popular a theory for accounting for descent with modification as Lamarckism (the inheritance of acquired characteristics), and several prominent theorists upheld ethnological and polygenic theories of race based upon very different mechanistic allegiances. Ethnological evolutionism, basing phylogenetic reconstruction upon comparisons of cultural practices and institutions, reached its apex of popularity between 1860 and 1880, while polygenism, the proposition that human races can be traced to several discrete origins, retained its attractions almost into the twentieth century.[51]

At least in the extremes, these four approaches were theoretically mutually exclusive. Polygenism and Lamarckism, for example, represented what Stocking calls "two enduring alternative attitudes toward the variety of mankind," with the polygenist assertion that human races were created separately seeming to preclude any form of transmutation juxtaposed against the Lamarckian allegiance to common ancestry and the transformative potential of internal tendencies. Among nonelite evolutionists, however, including nearly all Spiritualists, these approaches were interfertile, with evidence for the origins of races garnered eclectically from physical structure, language, religious practices, internal tendencies, and "character." As a result sociocultural evolution became mechanistically and historically aligned with biological evolution in a way that made the study of either pregnant with implications for both. To imagine being American, being a scientist, a Christian, worker, or human being, was to imagine being part of a grand historical process and an overarching social and cosmic order. For James Peebles, Hudson Tuttle, William Denton, and Andrew Jackson Davis, the four Spiritualists whose interpretations of Darwin and the ethnological dilemma I chart here, human variation and human potential were key concerns.[52]

Beneath the rock of Darwinian theory, Spiritualists struggled with two major, countervailing tendencies. On the one hand, natural selection offered a material gloss on the spiritual processes that drove the afterlife. On the other hand, it was framed in a competitivist architecture and unforgiving hypermaterialism that clashed with spiritual harmonialism. Notoriously agnostic, natural selection failed to acknowledge the sorts of internal progressive tendencies and forces favored by most Spiritualists (and most non-Spiritualists), leaving them gasping at the supposed gaps in Darwinian logic. Thus while the erstwhile abolitionist, trade protectionist, and social radical Giles Stebbins admired Darwin and his "mastery of physical facts," he lamented the failure to "open his soul to interior ideas" that consigned Darwin to see only "the external," to see mere "matter and force and law, not mind and design." Until it accounted for the role of mind, natural selection could never be more than "external and imperfect." For Stebbins it was spiritually self-evident that "the intention of nature" was nothing less than "the perfection of man": "star-dust, and crude matter and all lower types of life prophesy him," just as mortal life prophesied the spirit life to follow. Where Darwinians discerned evolution "as the working of force and law in the transfiguration of matter," for spiritual scientists "evolution is the Divine method, the positive power of mind using and guiding force and law, not merely to lift rock and clod to finer forms and higher uses, but also to guide man up the spiral pathway in an unending progressive development. By so much as immortal man is greater than the clod he treads on, spiritual science is greater and more complete than all merely inductive methods which only touch matter and ignore the soul in man, and the Soul of things." Once such sentiments were introduced into evolutionary theory, Stebbins felt, "it will be perfected, and will be the helper of a deeper religious faith."[53]

More committed to scientific rationalism than Stebbins, Epes Sargent found an immanent, theistic evolutionism particularly appealing for its potential to bridge the material and immaterial. The startling ability of spirits to appear and disappear at will in materialization séances, he reasoned, indicated that the universe was governed by "a concretion of forces" that might still be little understood but "the trunk-force of which," he insisted, was "the Divine Idea." Although the facts of Darwinism were largely "in harmony" with Spiritualist conceptions of the natural order, Spiritualism offered deeper insights that verified the profound fact that "the idea must ever precede the organism." Any attempt to prove this idea "by purely physical means and processes" was doomed to failure and error. In short, strictly materialist approaches to evolution could never account for mind or spirit.[54]

Disdaining the "dark, doubting materialism" of natural selection, James M. Peebles concurred that the "Physical man" of Darwin could never illuminate the deeper realities of "Spiritual man," any more than the shadow could reveal "the substance," or the cover, the book (fig. 10). At the root of natural selective theory, he argued, was the illogical proposition that nature produced a "procession from the seen to the unseen, from matter up to mind; thus making the lesser produce the greater." Was it possible, Peebles asked, for "unconsciousness to go up into consciousness; for the chilliness of death to ultimate in life; and for the animal to unfold into the Caucasian?" Darwin might believe so, but Spiritualists could not. "Spirit is causation," Peebles insisted, the result of a "divine force superior to matter or any attribute of inert matter," and Spiritualism "puts spirit, as the energizing principle of the universe, first, and considers matter as the residuum of spirit-substance." Yet despite holding such opinions, Peebles was a committed evolutionist, a monogenist who believed that the human races were, in some sense, Lamarckian manifestations of a single, pure human type. All of the races, he insisted, "whether Africans, Indians, or Aryans, constitute one brotherhood" that sprang from a single precursor hundreds of thousands of years before.[55]

Like Darwin, Peebles analogized the process of human diversification to artificial selection, substituting coffee, roses, and turkeys for Darwin's pigeons and dogs to demonstrate how quickly organismal change could be produced. Since the appearance of the first human (an event left explained), Peebles believed that a series of geological events had partitioned the races biogeographically. The slow divergence that followed the sinking of Atlantis and a maze of subsequent migrations left human populations responding independently to local environmental stimuli; however, none of these changes could obscure their essential unity. Arrayed along a unilinear scale of development, the races were crowned by the Caucasian and

FIG. 10. "The Spiritual Pilgrim," James M. Peebles.
Frontispiece from J. O. Barrett, *The Spiritual Pilgrim: A Biography of James M. Peebles* (Boston: William White, 1869).

floored by the Bushmen of Africa, the wretched Patagonians, and the "black men" of Australia, who lacked even the rudiments of a home to testify to their humanity. Culturally, Peebles argued, even the rudest attainments of the rudest races distinguished them from the apes. No ape could learn to speak, but even babies in Australia babbled; no ape had thoughts, used fire or tools, or cooked, but Africans could. Physically, too, a chasm separated humans from apes: humans alone possessed the phrenological organs of "hope, veneration, conscientiousness, ideality, and spirituality," and more importantly (evangelical missionaries notwithstanding), all of the races of humanity possessed a native consciousness of the immortality of the soul.[56]

Despite his willingness to accept the seamlessness of humanity, however, the seamlessness of Darwinian theory disturbed Peebles when viewing the larger fabric of life. "I will not pronounce it impossible," he wrote with sharp tongue in cheek, "that Carlyle and Emerson made their way up through fire-mist, protoplasmic jelly, billowy lava, granitic incrustations, creeping vegetation, and patriarchal monkeys, to manhood: but I fail to trace the steps." For Peebles evolutionary potential was restricted within "type," the Platonic and biblical ideal of each species, the "eternal entities" toward which every organism tended, but that could never change. Darwin's pigeons were a marvelous demonstration of descent with modification, Peebles admitted, but they said nothing about the production of new species or the alteration of type, nor were they the product of "some inherent power in the plant or animal themselves" or the "infusion of some new element or invigorating principle." Environmentally induced, such variation was merely epiphenomenal and could conceivably proceed in any direction at all with no impact upon interfertility (then, as now, the most common definition of species). To illustrate his case, Peebles noted that on his visit to southern Africa, he observed even the purest descendants of European settlers beginning to assume African characteristics, growing "more rounded in features, and sluggishly heavy," and "as inclined to be indolent, like the Hottentots." Influenced by the environment, human phenotype could shuttle from black to white and back again, but humans remained human.[57]

Peebles insisted, therefore, that "evolution is true," but only in the analogical sense that the "life-germ" within all living beings—the Divine Idea of Epes Sargent—served as the "groundwork and conditions for the influx of new and greater spiritual forces, whereby it is enabled to expand in the directions of its natural tendencies." The natural, sympathetic propensities that guided progressive change, facilitated by the influx of higher knowledge from the spiritual spheres, found their direct counterpart in the physical world.[58]

The "unfoldment" of the life-germ in humans, as Peebles saw it, produced cultures that resembled a truncated version of the stadial histories of the eighteenth century, a tripartite ethnological schema connecting the savage ("an individual thoroughly selfish, an Ishmaelite, a restless wanderer, a rude hunter, living by hunting and fishing, and upon spontaneous fruits and nuts"), through the barbarian pastoralist, to the civilized agriculturalist (the divisive *Homo commercialis*, the apex of civilized man for the Scots, was not admitted into Peebles's divine scheme). From observations made during his world tour in the early 1870s, Peebles concluded that the varieties of humanity filling these sociocultural categories were all in flux, constantly in motion, with nations "ever rising and descending as do waves upon fathomless oceans." Where the massive mounds and ornate temples dotting the landscapes of the Mississippi Valley and Southeast Asia bespoke the ancient presence of grand civilizations, only sad, savage relics could now be found. But not only did civilizations disappear, they merged. Everywhere Peebles looked, miscegenation ruled. The cultures and religions of the "Malays" and "Americans" showed notable affinities, and Malays themselves appeared to be the product of admixture between Africans and Mongolians. Only the primary colors of humanity, the Mongolian, African, and Caucasian, sat somewhat apart, but no race was firmly fixed in time, space, or cultural status.[59]

For Peebles the root of all human cultures was planted in Africa, and the pinnacle in the Aryan Caucasus. Comparative ethnography, aided by spiritual input, led him to conclude that the purest of languages, Sanskrit, was ultimately African, and that Africans were the rootstock of all races. Shocking as this might seem to his readers, who could no more imagine the African man within their lineage than Peebles could imagine the African ape, Peebles urged them not to "shrug the shoulders at the mention of Africa," for "neither Congo nor Congo negroes constitute all of Africa," nor were all "Ethiopians" possessed of "thick lips, a flat nose, and short, knotty hair." There was great phenotypic diversity on the continent, he insisted, and the African explorer David Livingstone discovered that Aryans still resided there, or at least the "fading remnants of this fairer race, degenerate descendants of the original African Aryas," a people who were "tall and slender, olive complexioned, and as intelligent to-day as the peasantry of Britain." The Aryan germ survived on the continent, hinting, as Peebles maintained, that whenever the "Negro element" came into contact with Mongols or Malays, or any other superior race (and they were all superior), "it melts away much as do wild animals before civilization."[60]

Driving these changes, whether biological or cultural, was an internal force, steeped in spirit(s). If "spirit is causation, force, life," Peebles concluded, then "all existence constitutes a magnificent unity. The soul is the man; and this soul, a divinely etherealized portion of the Infinite 'oversoul,' did not 'descend,' or more properly, come up, through ascidians, apes, and baboons; nor did it in any sense originate from matter." Teleologically, the divine order produced an evolutionary process that culmi-

nated in the Aryan—the "first of the blood-spilling nations," as one ancient spirit revealed—who in turn extinguished the lesser races. Politically,
Peebles identified himself as an opponent of the extermination of American Indians and as a believer in the unity and equality of all races, yet his
ethnology is tinged with the essentialist and inegalitarian. Most fundamentally, like most Spiritualists, his ethnology transformed race into an etherealized and spiritualized concept as well as an essential state of being, the
product of a divinely directed sympathy that imparted order and history
on the natural world. The spirits and spiritual tendencies created a material
universe that operated through the lines of racial descent.[61]

Hudson Tuttle was as eager a monogenist as James Peebles, but he departed from the Spiritual Pilgrim in devoting himself equally and zealously
to Darwin (fig. 11). A sophisticated, largely self-educated student of evolutionary biology, Tuttle firmly believed that despite the difficulties inherent
in the analysis of human history, the ethnological dilemma was soluble.
Like nearly all Spiritualists, he viewed the universe as a single, mutualistic
organism bound by sympathy, in which the worlds of science, nature, and
culture were all facets of the same reality. Employing the proper analytical
tools, he reasoned, one could demonstrate that the entire range of biological and social diversity was the product of a single Darwinian process. "We
know that the universe is a unity of forces," he wrote, "that the realm of
life is guaranteed throughout its vast extent by the fixed principles, which,
applying to all beings, to the highest and the lowest, bind them together,
and infallibly point to a common source." Sympathy was the force, and ultimately, he argued, Darwin was the source.[62]

In the *Origin and Antiquity of Man*, Tuttle envisioned sympathy on the
broadest scale as spiritually uniting all of creation, with humans having
two distinct lives, organic (or vegetative) and animal, which, as "intrinsicly
blended as these are," were clearly "governed by distinct and wholly separate laws." On their organic side humans reached down to the plants, becoming "brother with flower, fruit, and tree" and bearing their "closest relationship with fucoids of the sea, palms of tropic climes, and alpine
pines." On the animal side evidence for common origins was overwhelming. A laundry list of homologies ensconced the Order Mammalia firmly
within the Class Vertebrata, ranging from the numbers of embryonic ver-
tebrae and the conformation of the limbs to their "ultimate" (chemical)

FIG. 11. Hudson Tuttle. Frontispiece from Hudson Tuttle,
*Arcana of Spiritualism: A Manual of Spiritual Science and Philos-
ophy* (London: James Burns, 1876).

compositions. Tuttle insisted that it was simply "absurd and childish" to
deny organismal unity.[63]

When it came to the races of humanity, uniformity was even clearer.
Like Peebles, he argued that "nowhere can lines of demarcation be clearly
drawn, so imperceptibly do the families of mankind blend at their circum-
ferences," adding that "there are no race marks which are reliable; and
those thought permanent, undoubtedly are so only by the equilibrium established between man and his externals, of which they are the expression." As for color, the universal emblem of race in America, Tuttle found
it unreliable as a marker. The immense variability in skin tone within a
population and the presence of innumerable "intermediate gradations"
rendered color of "little value" for delineating the history of races, and
furthermore, he insisted, skin color was merely a function of pigments be-

tween the "cutis and cuticle," so shallow that it could literally be lifted off the surface. Phenotypically, he wrote, "all the races flow together at their borders; and it is at the centre, and not at the margins, of their broad streams that distinctions are discernible.[64]

Tuttle therefore dismissed Buffon, Kant, Blumenbach, Samuel George Morton, and the other disciples of polygeny. Races were too "united in one great plan" to accept that they might have sprung from separate creations, and only an obsession with "color, form, and all the accidental effects of conditions" had led previous anthropologists astray. Searching for a more stable basis for a racial taxonomy, Tuttle turned to the comparative philologist Friedrich Max Müller. Having immersed himself in Müller's analysis of language families, Tuttle concluded that linguistics provided a surer estimate of human history than any physical marker because language, as "the expression of the mind, is less influenced by conditions than the physical form." In essence, language was a nearer guide to the internal tendencies of mind than the body could ever be. Through Lamarckian or Darwinian adaptation, physical form could change rapidly, but because language was not "fashioned by rules of men," it was more stable; "it grows by rules established in the constitution of mind; it is not created by reason, but by growth." Growing in accord with the laws of sympathy and progress, language revealed the structure of the cosmos.[65]

Although the racial taxonomy Tuttle arrived at bore a superficial similarity to competing taxonomies, his five races were subtly distinct. His Oriental Negroes (Australians, Melanesians), Africans ("Caffres and Hottentots"), and Aryans (Europeans, "the ruling race of Hindostan," and scattered others) were largely, though not unproblematically, congruent with Blumenbach's Malay, African, and Caucasian, respectively. By phenotypic standards, however, his other races were thoroughly heterogeneous; the Semites (Hebrews, Arabs, Armenians) and Turanians (American Indians, Chinese, Hindus in part) brought together peoples of disparate complexion, body type, and character. To make matters more difficult, Tuttle implied that his taxonomy had both synchronic and diachronic dimensions. The positions of the races in the scale of cultural advancement corresponded to their relative times of divergence from their common ancestor, an idea reflected in the frontispiece to the *Origin and Antiquity of Man*, a tree diagram of linguistic relations (fig. 12).

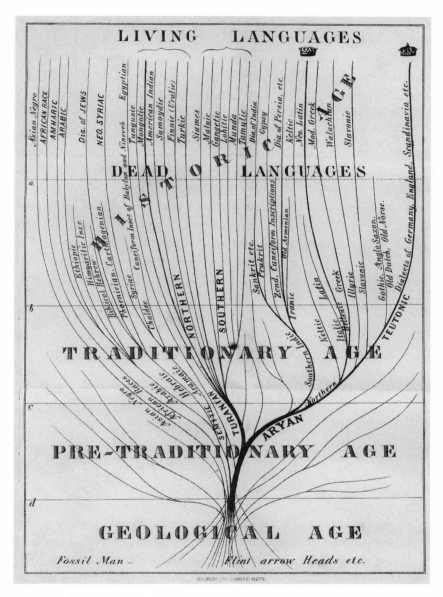

FIG. 12. Chart of racial relations. Frontispiece from Hudson Tuttle, *The Origin and Antiquity of Physical Man Scientifically Considered* (Boston: William White, 1866).

In translating this linguistic taxonomy into a broader theory of sociocultural evolution, Tuttle began with the premise that thought preceded word ("for a word is a symbol of an idea") and with the proposition that as thoughts expanded, humans necessarily developed new words to express them. This essentially Lamarckian mechanism implied a relative plasticity of words that was paired, in turn, with a strong conservatism in grammar: vocabulary fluctuated, but grammar remained fixed. Once a race had achieved a degree of cultural advancement that allowed for the acquisition of "a permanent speech," Tuttle claimed, "the essential elements of that speech are retained more tenaciously than the physical characteristics of the race." The lowest and most primitive races in the scale of being—the Oriental Negroes and Africans—possessed languages so primitive that they could not even be connected "with the great stem which supports the other races." As they were "cast off before the fixation of speech," these races possessed languages beset by "constant flux," continually erasing the traces of their own heredity in a chaos of perpetual change.[66]

Stepping up half a racial rung to the Turanians, Tuttle confronted the savage directly. For the most part Turanian languages were less vulnerable to rapid change, but because "the ideas of savages are not complex . . . but as simple as those of children," Turanians attempted to express themselves "simultaneously by a single effort or word." The result is a linguistic tendency toward "agglutination or polysynthesism," the concatenation of words of disparate function into confused and ungainly assemblages. North American Indians, Tuttle argued, were typical, their savagery marked triply by agglutination, the lack of a written language, and the absence of significant civilizations, other than those in the optimal climates of Peru and Mexico.[67]

As progress continued and as greater clarity was needed for greater thoughts, human populations discovered the need to distinguish different parts of sentence and speech and to distinguish action from that which was acted upon. The Chinese were still too tied to barbarism to have attained this level, and English retained dim traces of its own "original polysynthesism," as witnessed by the words that serve doubly as nouns and verbs, "as fly, an insect; fly, to move through the air." But English and the Aryan languages had indeed progressed, their growth emerging from a social need, a need for expression, clarity, for establishing social and affective bonds among a people.[68]

When savages began to aggregate into tribes, Tuttle wrote, each went their own way in speech, adapting to the peculiar circumstances in which they lived (the mountains, sea, or deserts), each seeking to express the thoughts and feelings specific to their environment. Although tinged with Lamarck, language growth was unmistakably a sympathetic process. "It appears complete," Tuttle wrote, "as the work of one man grasping the wants and feeling of all other men; yet we know by the records of history that it has been built up by the conjoint labors of all men, laboring unknowingly, as bees building in harmony a beautiful and mathematically constructed comb. The philosopher coining a new word to express the scarcely defined shade of meaning he wishes to convey, the playful chance misarticulation of the child, the word of wisdom, the rude utterance of the boor, the polite language of refinement, the slang of the street, even the voice of the wild brute, is incorporated in this structure."[69]

Like sympathy, language bound disparate elements of human society through the need to express and share sentiment, growing by the same principles of mutuality and progress and resulting in each language becoming "a perfect harmony" unto itself, each one bearing evidence of "the deep foundation of their [common] structure!" Like sympathy, too, language sought to expand to the farthest reaches, to become all encompassing, "to become cosmopolitan." As the means for travel became available and the facilities for "mutual interchange of thought and commodities" were perfected, "each language grasps to itself all others. Each race learns the thoughts of others; and how can the new thought be better expressed than by the words by which it was first conveyed?" Language grew by exchange, by "expansion of mind," diversifying by precisely the same process as the "chain of living beings revealed by geology." In the early stages, Tuttle reasoned, one organ had sufficed for all purposes, but "slowly other organs form[ed] to meet various requirements."[70]

Only after the divergence of the Aryan languages from the Turanian did the Aryans (and Aryans alone) attain the degree of permanence of language associated with the highest levels of cultural attainment. In looking down upon the lesser races and lesser languages, Tuttle identified weaknesses that prevented the free interchange of sentiment, thus ensuring cultural stagnation. Some savage languages, like ancient Greek, had quite perfect structures, yet their sheer complexity led them to be stereotyped, imbued with ideals of "beauty, sweetness, strength, and power" but incapable of expressing more advanced concepts. All of the lesser races were static to some degree, but just as Oriental Negroes and Africans epitomized the lowest stages of humanity, devoid of any cultural attainment, just as the "lower" Turanians formed the purest examples of undisciplined, undirected flux, the Chinese ("higher" Turanians) were the quintessence of racial stasis. The Chinese language had remained mired in the land of monosyllables, "almost immovable" due to its "early fixture in the sacred writings of Confucius. . . . A better plan to fetter and stagnate thought cannot be imagined. Literary progress was unthinkable until the whole orthographic system was overthrown for a phonetic alphabet, an event which, Tuttle wrote, "will not occur until forced on them by a conquering race." For such static races there was no hope of improvement. A sudden "deluge of wisdom" could do nothing to "elevate the rude Hottentot to the level with the enlightened European mind," for "such a change would entirely change the being, and a mind so changed would lose its identity with the rude, undeveloped being."[71]

Darwinian sentiments transformed such stasis into a death knell. In Tuttle's opinion natural selection and the Malthusian limitation of resources implied "not a battle," he wrote, but a "silent combat between the weaker and the stronger, in which the weaker eventually perish." In a world incapable of supporting the abundance of life-forms produced, humans were not immune. There was "no break, no chasm, but a perfect and complete series" between the highest apes and lowest humans, just as there was an unbroken series between the lowest forms of life and the apes, and the laws of hereditary descent led each population to "breed true to ancestral forms." The ape would therefore remain an ape, and although humanity was clearly seated at "the head of the animal world, as the perfected fruit of incomprehensible millenniums of its growth and progress," it was equally clear that the African would remain an African, the Semite a Semite, and the Aryan an Aryan. When "crowded into narrow spaces like the Grecian or Italian peninsulas, and subjected to excessive competition," Tuttle wrote, "superior civilizations flash out, the admiration of all coming time," but stronger and more advanced races eventually would drive the weaker to extinction as part of the natural, sympathetic plan.[72]

Yet even this bleak assessment was too rosy for Tuttle, for even if the primitive races staved off extinction, they were perpetually losing ground to their superiors. "Progress is in a geometrical ratio," Tuttle asserted; "the more enlightened a nation is, the greater will be the rapidity of progress." Like Peebles, he insisted that contact with Aryans would lead inevitably to the extinction of savages, a fact corroborated by the inexorability of white imperial and national expansion. Only the "inaccessibility" of Turanian lands preserved them from domination and extinction, and "even the lower members of the Aryan" race were vulnerable. Whenever "the European-Aryan meets the effeminate Indo-Aryan," Tuttle argued, "the latter is subjugated to the genius of the former. The Aryan is a proud and energetic race. Already its members talk of making their dialects the universal tongue." Teutonic Aryans had already extended their empire around the globe; it was the "great historic race of the present, and around it gather the ruling nationalities of the world." In America the "fate of the Indian, who requires three thousand acres of forest for his support, is easily foreseen when he is brought in contact with the European, who by agriculture can maintain himself on a single acre. So speedily does he vanish, that it can scarcely be said that he offers any opposition to the invader." Like a comet guided by the gravitational pull of sympathy and progress, the races of humanity were led by a bright light, followed by a disintegrating, fading trace. The extinction of lesser races was hardly a fault, barely resisted, but merely a function of spiritual design.[73]

Although Tuttle was pure in his monogenism, there is a tendency in his writing that became more explicit among his peers. Although the races shared a common ancestor, Tuttle argued that they had long been separate, and the distinctions among them were becoming more pronounced, rather than less. In the hands of two self-professed social radicals, William Denton and Andrew Jackson Davis, these tendencies blossomed.

A geologist, socialist, and all-purpose agitator, Denton derided anything smacking of "orthodoxy," including scriptural authority and the biblical story of creation (fig. 13). Surveying the history of life, psychometrizing fossils and communing with spirits, Denton saw the traces of natural law operating to promote change within type but found no evidence that Darwinian laws could explain the origins of human mind or soul. He barely hid his further feelings about Darwinism. In his satirical anticlerical tour through heaven with the recently departed William Lloyd Garrison, he joked that he saw Satan taking "advantage of Darwin's discoveries in natural selection," producing new breeds of locust to plague the earth. Darwin and disaster went hand in hand.[74]

Refusing to cede primacy to either Darwin or Scripture, Denton settled on a merger of naturalistic and spiritual modalities, arguing that nature was best understood as the product "of an unseen, but ever active . . . intelligent spirit." Human experience, as he saw it, demonstrated that this spirit was impersonal and distant, acting invariably by invariable laws, and it was

FIG. 13. *Denton's Illustrated Scientific Lectures*. Poster. In addition to his work as a writer and publisher, William Denton was a popular lecturer on historical geology. (American Philosophical Society)

therefore more parsimonious to assert that humanity arose by "natural processes" of the sort "which we may reasonably suppose are still at work upon our globe," rather than by any form of divine intervention.[75]

Recent discoveries in paleontology, Denton wrote, confirmed Samuel George Morton's claim that as long as there had been humans, there had been races. But unlike his predecessor, Denton extended racial differences back into the diverse prehistoric, prehuman world of Neanderthals and Cro-Magnons, arguing that all of the modern races had advanced, un-mixed, from these "ape-like brutes" along independent lines. Furthermore, equally distinct and long-lived fissures separated the major families of languages. Despite their best efforts, historical linguists could find no common root for modern languages, and the major linguistic families could never be joined. Basque would ever be Basque, with no relation to any other tongue.

Such discoveries posed a paradox for Denton. Phenotype and language were deeply rooted and fully independent, yet all of the races had evolved from prehumans into modern humans in precisely parallel fashion. To Denton this paradox signified the workings of some essential, spiritual tendencies. Within all humans lay the innate capacity for forming language and for other traits of character. The organs of phrenology ("as much a true science as geology taught by Sir Charles Lyell") were particularly re-vealing of these tendencies, pointing toward the "perfect man, toward which the human race has been moving from its start, and that is des-tined eventually to be perfectly embodied in man, when the fruit of the tree of life is fully ripe." With "unguided variation" insufficient and divine intervention unpalatable, Denton proposed that these internal, "inherent forces" had provided a "spiritual direction" that drove the races toward this material and spiritual ideal. Where Darwin proposed, for instance, that sexual selection explained how men chose the most beautiful women with whom to mate, and vice versa, leading to a progressive beautification of the race, Denton saw an inbred aesthetic, an internal sense of the perfect hu-manity toward which all were drawn. With these and other lines of ev-idence, according to one reviewer of his writings, Denton provided Spiri-tualists with "many cogent reasons" to believe that the "the essential begets & directs the material, that the shell is not the egg, nor the bark the tree; that the origin of thought, the spring and course of action come of deeper & subtler forces than mere surface phases of being disclose."[76]

The godfather of harmonial philosophy, Andrew Jackson Davis, took such internally driven polygenism further down the visionary path. A staunch antislavery advocate in the 1850s, Davis was a magnet for theories of race, but like a magnet, he exhibited the polarities of attraction and repulsion. Favoring immediate manumission and the arming of slaves during the Civil War, he wrote that he rued the day that America won the Revolution but "inherited" slaves. "Our greatest national success," he wrote, "which gave us the power to overthrow the mastery of England—gave us also mastery over millions of Africans." For him the political history of the nation was chained to the history of slavery, and the American character was forged in a conjunction of black and white. The "moral, political, social and civil degradations" inflicted upon blacks exerted a corresponding influence upon whites and led, in Davis's formula, to the inevitability of Civil War.[77]

Preoccupied with thoughts of heredity and racial essentials, Davis sounded familiar themes in proposing that the races were the scions of blood, brain, and spirit. Blood was the common inheritance of all but was manifested most acutely in Africans and Malays, consumed with "passion-fed fires and gehennal impulses," and above these sat the brain races with their "calculating selfishness." At the top the spirit races represented the future: Caucasians (alone) fought "wars of Thoughts, of Ideas, of Principles" and one day would "be conquerors . . . masters of the races of the human world." Clearly, he wrote, "the Mongolians are not conquerors; the Africans are not; the Indians are not, but are, in fact, passing away."[78]

But elsewhere Davis advanced a more novel interpretation of the divine creation, envisioning it as an etherealized binary fashioned into a grand cosmic spiral. This spiral, or more accurately this double helix, simultaneously represented the opposites of science and art, male and female, Caucasian and African: one strand, the African, commenced along the "left side of humanity," while the Caucasian commenced from the right, and from such opposite beginnings, "the opposite races work leftward and rightward in all countries and in all history," as did male and female, science and art, producing cultures and characteristics of correspondingly divergent qualities. The elements of each strand were yoked, mutually implicated. "The negro is artful and emotional," Davis wrote; "he represents nature in her senses; the Caucasian is nature in her brains and organs. The first manifestation of taste in the female nature is surface ornaments, display. . . . The masculine commences with the brains and works into the senses, and scarcely ever gets out of them." For Davis the ultimates in themselves were incomplete but worked toward common fulfillment. "If more men," he wrote, "were out of their senses—in their superior condition—and had arrived at Art, 'the world would be the better for it.' Woman commences leftward and works rightward. She begins in the heart of things and expands and reaches to the surface-plane from which man started."[79]

The fusion of femininity with blackness and masculinity with whiteness, so common in other ethnologies, was integral to Davis's philosophy. Based on dichotomies, however, the helix on which he constructed his system had little room to include Mongols, Malays, and Indians. These supernumerary races thus sat interstitially between black and white, male and female, rendering them either sexless or hermaphroditic as the case may be. These "transition races" were "bridges, which connect the two sides of humanity," uniting the "masculine and feminine in ethnology, and in the interior attributes of opposite races," the interior characteristics of each having been shaped by its position in the cosmic helix with respect to the binary strands. It was clear, though, that the transitional races were irrefrangibly alien to both black and white, never coming into significant contact with either. The domineering "sentiment and emotions" of the Africans, their love of the sensual pleasures of the surface, were not conveyed to the Malays, whom Davis analogized to "the Rhodent." The mind of the Malays, he claimed, "seeks to live on others" and "chooses a dark abode and burrows in the ground." Whether hailing from North America or Asia, Indians were another animal, represented by "the squirrel and the raccoon, and the animals that live like them in the forests." "They will live and they will die together," Davis wrote. "When Nature gets old enough to destroy all of the animals that live on nuts and acorns and berries and fruits of the field and the forest, and when she also destroys all that live upon the flesh of other animals, then will she be also old enough to seal the destiny of the Oriental as well as the western tribes of the streams and wildernesses."[80]

The extinction promised to the Indians by each of Davis's peers was thus promised to the Malays and Mongols as well; the natural, cosmic order having no place for the liminal or indeterminate. These static, interstitial beings were relics of the past, as static as Tuttle's Chinese, while the polestar of Davis's future pointed toward the Caucasians, the race that "pursues all parts of nature by science, and lays all existence under heavy tribute." By his nature ("he" being defined as masculine), the Caucasian "subjects the world to himself," dominates the other races with whom he comes into contact, and points the way to "the higher race to come." The Caucasian "expands into the universal Yankee . . . expand[s] by means of his encroachments and infringements, all over the inhabitable globe." This distinctly American type, this pinnacle of creation, could not look back: the universal Yankee could not regress culturally, and his influence would expand irresistibly to raise the lesser races about him or would drive them to extinction in the process. "The American does not become Europeanized," Davis insisted, but the African might well become "Caucasianized in his habits, tendencies, and aspirations," that is, whenever a Caucasian opened those black "eyes to behold the temples of learning and of universal progress."[81]

But it was only after death, after all of the races had settled in Summerland, that the full sympathetic potential of this helical system came to pass. In death the "ultimates of every race . . . establish a community or a world of their own" (that spherical apartheid again), and there Caucasians visit each of the lands to "mingle with all classes and families," spreading sympathetic tidings, shedding the light of superior knowledge. Through visitation with lesser races, the Caucasian mind developed, linking him "sympathetically with all other races and brotherhoods." As a result the ends of the helix finally met; "the negro and the white man—that is to say, the African and the Caucasian, as left hand and right—are coming eventually together, and will friendly face, like palm and palm." Davis advised, however, that the races would not become "affiliated and amalgamated," for "the moment the opposite races touch perfectly, that moment they take separate rooms in the Father's house. They work for each other and through each other without affiliation or loss of individuality."[82]

In fact, as Davis made clear, the ends of the helix would never meet, because the African could "never fully understand the Caucasian, nor the Caucasian the African, and "the races that come between these extremes will be neither understood nor tolerated." Each race would strive along in its parallel career, never meeting, never comprehending the others, the balance of nature ensuring that the left hand and right were preserved, but that the intervening, interfering transitional races would find no place. "Only the Negro can prosper in copartnership with the Caucasian," Davis wrote, while the Indian inevitably "drops outward and goes away from among the races."[83]

Translating these concepts into political practice was not easy, but Davis began with the assertion that "inequalities are as natural as equalities." Ringing of Hobbes, he insisted that in a proper society "all are but parts of one harmonious whole," forming one organic body. As "the feet and hands of society in the South," blacks were as "essential to the great workings and ends of the infinite plan as you are," but they would remain always as feet and hands. "All efforts to fix human beings upon a social level of life and government," Davis insisted, "are illogical and impracticable." Men and women could never become "alike in any of these great spheres of action," nor, by implication, could white and black, "and yet," he wrote, "the divine principle of Love gives to each an equality of existence to the extent of his or her capacity."[84]

From monogenism to polygenism, support for Darwin or denial, Spiritualists sprawled across the anthropological map, offering almost nothing new to the debates over the transmutation of species or to ideas on the origins of humanity. Recasting arguments from the scientific and popular literature, borrowing liberally, if not always coherently, their views on race represented a singular, highly refined distillation of ideas common in American culture, ideas about the shape of the emotional world as it was transformed by practices of race. Bred in bone and soul, Spiritualist race was essential, eternal, ethereal and with sympathy formed a multitiered ethnological system far more effective than any simple binary at justifying and consoling their white audience, far more flexible and adaptable to the changing political, ideological, and emotional demands.

As Spiritualists attested, the end involved extinction. Late in the century, Hudson Tuttle proclaimed that the "peculiar phase" of Indian abundance was "passing away" from Spiritualism, and their spirits were disappearing as rapidly as their brethren in flesh and blood, falling out of the sympathetic orbits of whites. The days of communing with the lowest rank of spirits, he felt, were over now that the higher and more reliable intelligences could be drawn into communion. The result was "most desirable," he wrote, and their disappearance in the "capacity of doctors is also to be congratulated." Their vanishment was the last knell of the sympathetic era.[85]

Conclusion

IN THE WAKE of the Civil War, the spirits spoke as often as they ever had before, but their silence prevailed over words: defying both critics and historians, the half million souls that littered the landscape from Pennsylvania to New Mexico remained resolutely mute. Although fifty years later the regiments of the dead poured forth from Flanders field in such fervent response to the "neurotic" desires of "grief-stricken parents" that they left Houdini gasping for the "health and sanity" of the nation, the Civil War dead remained almost inert, unheeding of the living. For every soldier returning to describe *The Gates Ajar* during the 1870s, for every black martyr returning to Henri Rey's circle in New Orleans, untold numbers fell, and fell silent into the 1870s, the decade of the spirit Indian.[1]

Surveys of the Spiritualist movement have long regarded this decade as a watershed of sorts, a point of divergence between two streams representing the rise and decline of the movement. Before, as the trance medium Nettie Colburn declared, Spiritualists waged a "stern and unyielding warfare against the world without," seeking "to uproot old and stereotyped errors, change ancient ideas, and do battle with school-craft, ignorance and bigotry," but after, they met with a series of setbacks "of a discouraging character which overshadowed believers." For Colburn and many like her, this declension was a product of factors internal to the movement, to the cumulative effect of "debunkers" like the Seybert Commission, to the foibles of the Fox sisters and other alleged confessors to fraud, to the schismatic tendencies of psychic science, occultism, and orientalist Theosophy, or simply to the flaming out of a spectacular fad. But to conclude on a speculative note, I ask whether this Spiritualist watershed might signify larger shifts within American culture, shifts that made the practice of sympathy less engaging, less necessary, and less effective in its scope—shifts that gutted the sympathetic cosmology.[2]

For over a century before Hydesville, sympathy had provided a means for conceiving social relations, bodily relations, and divine relations, and versions of sympathetic theory pulsed through antebellum reform, through discussions of political economy, medicine, psychology, and philosophy, providing a potent framework for understanding the self and society. Though now difficult to recover, the sympathetic worldview was resilient enough to endure for well over a century, thanks in part to an ability to transmute social thought into practical action.

Spiritualists developed a particularly potent version of the sympathetic cosmology. Growing like the mythologies of Friedrich Max Müller by the disease of language, Spiritualist sympathy accumulated shade upon shade, sense upon sense. The concatenation of physiological, occult, and social registers, the admixture of the ecstatic practices of Shakers, the visions of Swedenborg, and the empiricist ethic of natural science helped antebellum Spiritualists to translate sympathy into a social practice that was at once idealist and applied, socially prescriptive and socially poetic. They tapped into the pathologies of walking and preaching in sleep, into mesmeric therapeutics, and into the economies of exchange of Adam Smith, and by hybridizing feeling on several levels, as sensation, sentiment, and social engagement, the sympathetic cosmology drew its practitioners into a laissez-faire of emotion, into the active propagation of sympathetic networks and the promotion of unfettered affective exchange. Sympathy, in short, offered a flexible instrument for healing a wide range of social abrasions, for transcending the separations of life, and for catalyzing the adjustment to the red-shift dislocations of modernity.

But in the watershed of the 1870s, the conjunction of the silence of the Civil War dead and the rise of spirit Indians suggests a continuity that calls for attention. For all their mechanistic, theoretical, and political diversity, during the post–Civil War years white Spiritualists aligned like the magnetic needle of a compass to point toward a single pole: in America, race became ineradicable and eternal, bred into bone and soul, and the heavens themselves cleaved along the biological lines of descent. The shifting content of messages received by whites and Spiritualists of mixed race, the shift away from spirit communion based upon familial and friendly ties and away from a conception of heavenly union toward an eternity of racial segregation, etherealized and essentialized, all point in a common direction. In white Spiritualism and black, the practice and products of spirit communion reinforced the increasing incommensurability of race in American life, shoring up the racial status quo and the increasing tendency to constitute one community, one identity, by the exclusion of others. Although the sympathetic cosmology was never tied firmly to specific discursive ends, its applications were made within a specific logic of social power that underwrote the new political shape of the nation and that suggests that far more than sects or death, the American practice of race had emerged center stage.[3]

For white Americans turning away from carnage and fratricide (Spiritualist and not), the wartime dead passed into silence and public commemorations that so celebrated union that by the 1880s a young Woodrow Wilson could write that "North and South are becoming daily more alike and hourly growing into a closer harmony of sentiment." As the "northern" industrial economy began slowly to expand southward, and the "southern" system of racial ordination became ingrained in northern life, demanding new racial solutions, whites the nation over discovered that "northern interests became southern interests," and sectional strife began to evaporate into a "strange but effective memory community" based upon political and social harmony and industrial and commercial development.[4]

Resurrecting the shards of the white nation by expelling blacks from their emotional orbit, white Spiritualists (like their non-Spiritualist counterparts) did not so much abandon sympathy as transform it, emphasizing its power to cohere over its power to transcend. For them, the lines of human heredity became an architectonic condition, constitutive of a spiritual self and cosmic order. By the time that Wendell Newhall waxed nostalgic over his youthful experiences (in his letter that opens this book), emotional effort and emotional exchange could no longer be held out as the universal emancipator but had become the source of the sometimes conflicting topologies governing nation and race. Trekking from a philosophy of social transcendence founded in unfettered exchange to a world of social cohesion bounded by race, Spiritualists completed a definitively American circuit.

For longtime believers like Wendell Newhall, Spiritualism was re-created as a private, internal discipline, shared only within the most intimate circle. "I do not dare tell folk's what I know," Newhall lamented, whispering, "I keep the secret in my own bosom." In the thirty years between that rapturous night when the spirits first apprehended him and the dim, nostalgic days of 1881, he had never forgotten the sensation of having his tongue seized against his will and turned against him, telling him with his own breath who he had become. Three decades on, the spirit that "waged" his tongue so fluently, so glibly, still stunned him speechless, the synesthetic collision of physical sensation and emotion and the "association of congenial minds" that formed in that encounter with the dead still overwhelming in its power. Soon, he predicted, he would reach his goal and would be greeted in a new world by "loving companions," leaving the mortal world of strife behind.[5]

NOTES

ABBREVIATIONS

APS   American Philosophical Society, Philadelphia

BPL   Department of Rare Books, Boston Public Library

MHS   Massachusetts Historical Society, Boston

SLRI   Schlesinger Library, Radcliffe Institute, Harvard College

UNO   University of New Orleans

WLCL   William L. Clements Library, University of Michigan

INTRODUCTION

1. Newhall to Asa Smith, May 1, 1881, D. N. Diedrich Collection, WLCL. Jesse Hutchinson's cottage was an early site for spiritual manifestations near Lynn, Mass. During the summer of 1852, the Spiritualist seer Andrew Jackson Davis experienced a series of important visions there (A. J. Davis, *The Present Age and Inner Life: A Sequel to Spiritual Intercourse* [Hartford: Charles Partridge, 1853]).

2. Contemporary estimates of spiritualist membership range from 1,037,500 (in 1857), to 2,000,000 (1854), 3,000,000 (1858), or 11,000,0000 (1867), the latter figure approaching one-third of the nation. Because there were no formal criteria for Spiritualist membership, all figures are necessarily speculative. Spiritualists debated to various ends whether Spiritualism constituted a religion, and despite some substantial disagreement, the majority accepted Spiritualism either as a religion in itself or as a philosophy sustaining religious belief. It would seem to qualify under Clifford Geertz's influential definition of religion as "a system of symbols which acts to establish powerful, pervasive, and long-lasting moods and motivations . . . by formulating conceptions of a general order of existence and clothing these conceptions with such an aura of factuality that the moods and motivations seem realistic." Although Geertz has been much criticized for failing to incorporate social experience and "power" in his definition, modifications to Geertz's basic proposal do not substantially alter the interpretation of Spiritualism as religion (New England Spiritualists' Association, *Constitution and By-Laws, List*

of Officers, and Address to the Public [Boston: George K. Snow, 1854]; Uriah Clark, *The Spiritualist Register, with a Counting House and Speakers' Almanac Containing Facts and Statistics of Spiritualism* [Auburn, N.Y.: U. Clark, 1857]; Allen Putnam, *Mesmerism, Spiritualism, Witchcraft, and Miracle* [Boston: Bela Marsh, 1858]; Emma Hardinge, *Modern American Spiritualism: A Twenty Years' Record of the Communion between Earth and the World of Spirits* [N.Y.: The Author, 1870]; Clifford Geertz, *The Interpretation of Cultures* [New York, 1973], 90; Talal Asad, "Anthropological Conceptions of Religion: Reflections in Geertz," *Man* 18 [1986]: 237–59; see also Bret E. Carroll, *Spiritualism in Antebellum America* [Bloomington, Ind., 1997]).

3. Werner Sollors, "Dr. Benjamin Franklin's Celestial Telegraph, or Indian Blessings to Gas-Lit American Drawing Rooms," *Social Science Information* 22, 6 (1983): 995; Carroll, *Spiritualism in Antebellum America,* 142; Lydia Maria Child to Parke Goodwin, Jan. 20, 1856, Child Papers, WLCL. Martha Garland concludes simply that Spiritualism was ineffective relative to "Christian" alternatives for "solving" grief (Martha McMackin Garland, "Victorian Unbelief and Bereavement," in *Death, Ritual, and Bereavement,* ed. Ralph Houlbrooke [London, 1989], 151–70).

4. Putnam, *Mesmerism, Spiritualism, Witchcraft, and Miracle,* 67–68; Ruth Richardson, "Why Was Death So Big in Victorian Britain?" in Houlbrooke, *Death, Ritual, and Bereavement,* 105–17; S. E. Park, *Instructive Communications from Spirit Life* (Boston: William White, 1869), 104.

5. Mike Hawkins, *Social Darwinism in European and American Thought: Nature as Model and Nature as Threat* (Cambridge, 1997), 17. Hawkins employs the term *world view,* rather than *cosmology.* Although both terms leave something to be desired for their inexactitude and for the freight of different meanings they have acquired, cosmology seems more appropriate for a movement that offered its adherents a "Stellar Key" and "Celestial Telegraph" and that stressed its scientific credentials so heavily (A. J. Davis, *The Stellar Key to the Summer Land* [Boston: William White, 1868]; Louis Alphonse Cahagnet, *The Celestial Telegraph; or Secrets of Life to Come, Revealed through Magnetism* [New York: Redfield & Clinton, 1851]). Examining Social Darwinism, Hawkins suggests that any complex cosmology conceivably supports a "whole spectrum of ideological positions" precisely because the cosmology is "not itself a social or political theory" (17).

6. Hudson Tuttle, *An Outline of Universal Government, Being a General Exposition of the Plan of the Universe, by a Society of the Sixth Circle* (Cincinnati: Stebbins & Watkins, 1854), 20.

7. Clarke Garrett, *Spirit Possession and Popular Religion: From the Camisards to the Shakers* (Baltimore, 1987). I use the term *spirit communion* to refer both to possession, in which a spirit controls the body, and communication more generally.

8. Hardinge, *Modern American Spiritualism*, 29, 556; Eliab W. Capron, *Modern Spiritualism: Its Facts and Fanaticisms, Its Consistencies and Contradictions* (Boston: Bela Marsh, 1855). Geoffrey K. Nelson, *Spiritualism and Society* (London, 1969); R. Laurence Moore, *In Search of White Crows: Spiritualism, Parapsychology, and American Culture* (New York, 1977); Janet Oppenheim, *The Other World: Spiritualism and Psychical Research in England, 1850–1914* (Cambridge, 1985); Logie Barrow, *Independent Spirits: Spiritualism and English Plebeians, 1850–1910* (London, 1986); Alex Owen, *The Darkened Room: Women, Power, and Spiritualism in Late Nineteenth-Century England* (Philadelphia, 1989); Ann Braude, *Radical Spirits: Spiritualism and Women's Rights in Nineteenth-Century America* (Boston, 1989); Carroll, *Spiritualism in Antebellum America*. Emma Hardinge is equally well known under her married name, Emma Britten.

9. Hardinge, *Modern American Spiritualism*, 50. Early accounts of the "Rochester knockings" include Eliab W. Capron, *Singular Revelations: Explanation and History of the Mysterious Communion with Spirits* (Auburn, N.Y.: Finn & Rockwell, 1850) and *History of the Mysterious Noises, Heard at Rochester and Other Places, Supposed to Be Spirit Communications, Together with Many Psychological Facts and New Developments* (Rochester, N.Y.: D. M. Dewey, 1850); J. B. Campbell, *Pittsburgh and Allegheny Spirit Rappings, Together with a General History of Spirit Communications* (Allegheny, Pa.: Purviance & Co., 1851).

10. Although the *Oxford English Dictionary* traces Spiritualist use of the term *medium* to the Englishman Henry Spicer in 1853, the term is clearly older. See Isaac Post, *Voices from the Spirit World, Being Communications from Many Spirits by Isaac Post, Medium* (Rochester, N.Y.: Charles H. McDonell, 1852); Henry Spicer, *Sights and Sounds: The Mystery of the Day, Comprising an Entire History of the American "Spirit" Manifestations* (London: Thomas Bosworth, 1853). My definition of *medium* is derived from the *OED*.

11. Post, *Voices from the Spirit World;* Charles Hammond, *Light from the Spirit World, Comprising a Series of Articles on the Condition of Spirits, and the Development of Mind in the Rudimental and Second Spheres,* 2d ed. (Rochester, N.Y.: D. M. Dewey, 1852).

12. Andrew Jackson Davis, *The Magic Staff: An Autobiography* (New York: J. S. Brown & Co., 1857); A. J. Davis, *Principles of Nature: Her Divine Revelations and a Voice to Mankind* (New York: S. S. Lyon and Wm. Fishbough, 1847). For similar and nearly contemporary somnambular experiences, see Cahagnet, *Celestial Telegraph.*

13. Hudson Tuttle, *Arcana of Spiritualism: A Manual of Spiritual Science and Philosophy* (London: James Burns, 1876), 428; Hardinge, *Modern American Spiritualism*, 365; A. J. Davis, *The Approaching Crisis: Being a Review of Dr. Bushnell's Course of Lectures, on the Bible, Nature, Religion, Skepticism, and the Supernatural,*

2d ed. (Boston: William White, 1870), 62; Davis, *Present Age and Inner Life,* 24. See also Nathan O. Hatch, *The Democratization of American Christianity* (New Haven, 1989).

14. Davis, *Stellar Key to the Summer Land,* 72; Davis, *Present Age and Inner Life,* 33.

15. Davis, *Present Age and Inner Life,* 35; Uriah Clark, *Plain Guide to Spiritualism: A Handbook for Skeptics, Inquirers, Clergymen, Believers, Lecturers, Mediums, Editors, and All Who Need a Thorough Guide to the Phenomena, Science, Philosophy, Religion, and Reforms of Modern Spiritualism,* 3d ed. (Boston: William White, 1863), 98, 97; G. A. Redman, *Mystic Hours, or, Spiritual Experiences* (New York: Charles Partridge, 1859), 106.

16. Robert Dale Owen, *The Debatable Land between This World and the Next* (New York: Carleton, 1872). 221; Giles B. Stebbins, *Upward Steps of Seventy Years* (New York: Lovell, 1890), 134; Braude, *Radical Spirits;* Carroll, *Spiritualism in Antebellum America.* Quakers were notable in the early Spiritualist community in New York State, but less so elsewhere. Many Progressive Friends did show an interest in spirit communion, but it is unclear how many considered themselves Spiritualists.

17. See, e.g., Allen Putnam, *Bible Marvel Workers* (Boston: Colby & Rich, 1870); Eugene Crowell, *The Identity of Primitive Christianity and Modern Spiritualism,* 2d ed. (New York, 1875).

18. Hardinge, *Modern American Spiritualism,* 27; Allen Putnam, *Flashes of Light from the Spirit-Land, through the Mediumship of Mrs. J. H. Conant* (Boston: William White, 1872), 61. For a Spiritualist view of the connection, see T. L. Nichols, *Supramundane Facts in the Life of Rev. Jesse Babcock Ferguson, A.M., LL.D., Including Twenty Years' Observation of Preternatural Phenomena* (London: F. Pitman, 1865); see also Stephen J. Stein, *The Shaker Experience in America: A History of the United Society of Believers* (New Haven, 1992); Garrett, *Spirit Possession and Popular Religion;* Phyllis Mack, *Visionary Women: Ecstatic Prophecy in Seventeenth-Century England* (Berkeley, Calif., 1992); Ann Taves, *Fits, Trances, and Visions: Experiencing Religion and Explaining Experience from Wesley to James* (Princeton, N.J., 1999); Stephen Marini, *Radical Sects in Revolutionary New England* (Cambridge, 1982). For "fanaticism," see Francis H. Smith, *My Experience, or Foot-Prints of a Presbyterian to Spiritualism* (Baltimore, 1860), 39.

19. Leigh Eric Schmidt, *Hearing Things: Religion, Illusion, and the American Enlightenment* (Cambridge, 2000), 222; see also Taves, *Fits, Trances, and Visions;* Clarke Garrett, "Swedenborg and the Mystical Enlightenment in Late Eighteenth-Century England," *Journal of the History of Ideas* 45 (1984): 67–81; Colleen McDannell and Bernhard Lang, *Heaven: A History* (New Haven, 1988); Carroll, *Spiritualism in Antebellum America.*

20. Carroll, *Spiritualism in Antebellum America*, 17; Schmidt, *Hearing Things*, 201.

21. Smith, *My Experience*, 213; Abram Pierce, *The Revelator, Being an Account of the Twenty-One Days' Entrancement of Abraham P. Pierce, Spirit-Medium*, 2d ed. (Boston: Adams & Co., 1870), 39.

22. Hardinge, *Modern American Spiritualism*, 102; Post, *Voices from the Spirit World;* John W. Edmonds and George T. Dexter, *Spiritualism*, 2 vols. (New York: Partridge & Brittan, 1853, 1855).

23. James M. Peebles, *Seers of the Ages: Embracing Spiritualism Past and Present* (Chicago, 1903), 174. With Swedenborg, of course, progress began with his new revelations, while for most antebellum Spiritualists progress was an intrinsic part of nature and irresistible, at least in the long run.

24. Schmidt, *Hearing Things*, 221, 222.

25. Thomas Lake Harris to George Bush, Nov. 10, 1853, George Bush Papers, WLCL.

26. A similar response can be seen among Mormons when spirit communion began to spread in Utah: for a time the practice was tolerated by the church hierarchy; however, the tension between divine access and divine control eventually led to its suppression (John L. Brooke, *The Refiner's Fire: The Making of Mormon Cosmology, 1644–1844* [Cambridge, 1994]; Michael W. Homer, "Spiritualism and Mormonism: Some Thoughts on Similarities and Differences" *Dialogue* 27, 1 [1994]: 171–91; Ronald W. Walker, "When the Spirits Did Abound: Nineteenth-Century Utah's Encounter with Free-Thought Radicalism," *Utah Historical Quarterly* 50 [1982]: 304–24; Walker, "The Commencement of the Godbeite Protest: Another View," *Utah Historical Quarterly* 42 [1974]: 227–88; Davis Bitton, "Mormonism's Encounter with Spiritualism," *Journal of Mormon History* 1 [1974]: 39–50).

27. Smith, *My Experience*, 39; Elizabeth Sweet, *The Future Life: As Described and Portrayed by Spirits* (Boston: William White, 1870), 426; Putnam, *Flashes of Light from the Spirit Land*, 245.

28. Epes Sargent, *Planchette; or, The Despair of Science* (Boston: Roberts Brothers, 1869), 323.

29. H. G. Wood, *The Philosophy of Creation: Unfolding the Laws of the Progressive Development of Nature, and Embracing the Philosophy of Man, Spirit, and the Spirit World* (Boston: Bela Marsh, 1864), 103; Davis, *Present Age and Inner Life*, 220; Peebles, *Seers of the Ages*.

30. Whitney Cross, *The Burned-Over District* (Ithaca, N.Y., 1950); Paul E. Johnson, *A Shopkeeper's Millennium: Society and Revivals in Rochester, New York, 1815–1837* (New York, 1974); Mary P. Ryan, *Cradle of the Middle Class: The Family in Oneida County, New York, 1790–1865* (Cambridge, 1981); Michael Bar-

kun, *Crucible of the Millennium: The Burned-Over District of New York in the 1840s* (Syracuse, N.Y., 1986); Hatch, *Democratization of American Christianity;* Jon Butler, *Awash in a Sea of Faith: Christianizing the American People* (Cambridge, 1990); Susan Juster, "The Spirit and the Flesh: Gender, Language, and Sexuality in American Protestantism," in *New Directions in American Religious History,* ed. Harry S. Stout and D. G. Hart (New York, 1997); Brooke, *Refiner's Fire;* Robert H. Abzug, *Cosmos Crumbling: American Reform and the Religious Imagination* (New York, 1994); Nelson, *Spiritualism and Society;* Moore, *In Search of White Crows;* Oppenheim, *Other World.* Spiritualists and Spiritualist ideas flowed in both a national and transnational context, with distinctive national spirit cultures [developing in Britain, Australia, France, Italy, Germany, Brazil, and Iceland. Conceptually and socially Spiritualism assumed distinctive identities in these various national contexts, suggesting the need for careful comparative studies of the differences as well as the commonalties behind these related "movements." Outside of America, the national context has been most thoroughly explored in Britain: see Nelson, *Spiritualism and Society;* Barrow, *Independent Spirits;* Owen, *Darkened Room;* Vieda Skultans, *Intimacy and Ritual* (London, 1974); Oppenheim, *Other World;* Jenny Hazelgrove, *Spiritualism and British Society between the Wars* (Manchester, 2000); Rene Kollar, *Searching for Raymond: Anglicanism, Spiritualism, and Bereavement between the Two World Wars* (Lanham, Md., 2000); but see also William H. Swatos and Loftur Reimar Gissurarson, *Icelandic Spiritualism: Mediumship and Society* (New Brunswick, N.J., 1996); David J. Hess, *Spirits and Scientists: Ideology, Spiritism, and Brazilian Culture* (University Park, Pa., 1991); Hess, *Samba in the Night: Spiritism in Brazil* (New York, 1994); Lynn L. Sharp, "Women in Spiritism: Using the Beyond to Construct the Here and Now," *Proceedings of the Annual Meeting of the Western Society for French History* 21 (1993): 161–68.

31. I. M. Lewis, *Religion in Context: Cults and Charisma* (Cambridge, 1986), 39, 27; Janice Boddy, "Spirit Possession Revisited: Beyond Instrumentality," *Annual Review of Anthropology* 23 (1994): 419; Lewis, *Ecstatic Religion: A Study of Shamanism and Spirit Possession,* 2d ed. (London, 1989); Skultans, *Intimacy and Ritual;* Hess, *Spirits and Scientists;* Hess, *Samba in the Night.*

32. Peebles, *Seers of the Ages,* 357; Barrow, *Independent Spirits;* Braude, *Radical Spirits;* Diana Basham, *The Trial of Woman: Feminism and the Occult Sciences in Victorian Literature and Society* (Houndmills, Eng., 1992); Barbara Goldsmith, *Other Powers: The Age of Suffrage, Spiritualism, and the Scandalous Victoria Woodhull* (New York, 1998); Howard Kerr, *Mediums, and Spirit-Rappers, and Roaring Radicals: Spiritualism in American Literature, 1850–1900* (Urbana, Ill., 1972); Owen, *Darkened Room;* Skultans, *Intimacy and Ritual.* Alex Owen's insightful work suggests that the efforts of women Spiritualists to resist their subordinate status were not highly successful, and may have been self-limiting, a view

now widely held. In contrast, a more optimistic Lynn Sharp argues that even though women Spiritualists did not "radically alter the world in which they lived," they did manage to "create spaces in which women could act more freely . . . act[ing] to build female networks, to express themselves intellectually and physically, and to offer a challenge to the limits of the patriarchal family" (Sharp, "Women in Spiritism," 161–68).

33. Skultans, *Intimacy and Ritual*, 75, 6.

34. Redman, *Mystic Hours*, 107; N. B. Wolfe, *Startling Facts in Modern Spiritualism*, 2d ed. (Chicago: Religio-Philosophical Pub. House, 1875), 75. See also Eugene Crowell, *The Spirit World: Its Inhabitants, Nature, and Philosophy*, 2d ed. (Boston: Colby & Rich, 1880), 149; New England Spiritualists' Association, *Constitution*, 14. Ann Braude's *Radical Spirits* provides the clearest discussion of trance lecturers. Figures for the ratio of male to female Spiritualist lecturers appear in Uriah Clark's *Spiritualist Registers*. In 1857 he recorded ninety lecturers, with males outnumbering females five to one among "normal" lecturers, but females outnumbering males by approximately the same ratio among trance lecturers.

35. Butler, *Awash in a Sea of Faith;* Nell Irvin Painter, *Sojourner Truth: A Life, a Symbol* (New York, 1996), 147; Kerr, *Mediums, and Spirit-Rappers, and Roaring Radicals;* Dorothy Sterling, *Ahead of Her Time: Abby Foster Kelly and the Politics of Antislavery* (New York, 1991), 279. Carleton Mabee mentions a meeting of Progressive Friends in 1857 that was "dominated" by Spiritualists who "were all too often 'morbid' and 'bigoted' and voted Democratic" (Mabee, *Sojourner Truth: Slave, Prophet, Legend* [New York, 1993], 99). See also Hans A. Baer, *The Black Spiritual Movement: A Religious Response to Racism* (Knoxville, Tenn., 1984), and Hans A. Baer and Merrill Singer, "Toward a Typology of Black Sectarianism as a Response to Racial Stratification," *Anthropological Quarterly* 54 (1981): 1–14. I would not wish to set up too strong a dichotomy between public and private with respect to the transformative potential of spirit intercourse. David Hess has shown that spirit possession has the capacity to alter domestic relations, even if it does not affect larger social relations (Hess, *Samba in the Night*).

36. One might begin a critique of the instrumentalist position by questioning the propriety of extending Lewis's observations on contemporary non-Western cultures to the cultures of mid-nineteenth-century America. The direct transference is cast in further doubt by Lewis's focus upon forms of mediumship that are experienced as spiritual attack, very much unlike the mediumship of the Foxes, which was generally experienced by mediums as either benign or a benediction.

37. Sargent, *Planchette*, 300; New England Spiritualists' Association, *Constitution*, 14.

38. Hardinge, *Modern American Spiritualism*, which includes descriptions of all these phases of mediumship; Redman, *Mystic Hours*.

39. Wolfe, *Startling Facts in Modern Spiritualism*, 44; Hardinge, *Modern American Spiritualism*, 196, see also 558. Charles H. Foster displayed skills similar to Comstock's (George C. Bartlett, *The Salem Seer: Reminiscences of Charles H. Foster* [New York: U.S. Book Co., 1891]). Other mediums like the Davenport Brothers were adept at escaping from ropes and chains or enclosure in a box. Late in life Ira Davenport confided in Houdini, passing along his stage secrets (Houdini, *A Magician among the Spirits* [New York, 1924]; see also D. D. Home, *Incidents in My Life* [New York: A. J. Davis, 1864]; Nichols, *Supramundane Facts;* Ken Silverman, *Houdini: The Career of Ehrich Weiss* [New York, 1996]).

40. See, e.g., John Bovee Dods, *Spirit Manifestations Examined and Explained: Judge Edmonds Refuted; or, An Exposition of the Involuntary Powers and Instincts of the Human Mind* (New York: DeWitt & Davenport, 1854); Putnam, *Mesmerism, Spiritualism, Witchcraft, and Miracle;* O. N. Bradbury, Lectures, American Science and Medicine Collection, WLCL; Oppenheim, *Other World.*

I. SLEEPWALKING AND SYMPATHY

1. All quotes in the first two paragraphs are from Samuel Latham Mitchill, *Devotional Somnium: A Collection of Prayers and Exhortations Uttered by Miss Rachel Baker* (New York: Van Winkle & Wiley, 1815), 146–48.

2. Sporadic accounts of sleepwalking as a distinct subject appear well back into the seventeenth century, and of course cognate visionary behaviors have a much longer history still. For a typical pre-Revolutionary account of sleepwalking, see *Gentleman's Magazine* 30 (1760): 236–40.

3. Henry F. May, *The Enlightenment in America* (New York, 1976), 344. A small culling from an immense literature on the filtering of Scots moral philosophy in America includes Morton White, *The Philosophy of the American Revolution* (New York, 1978); Drew McCoy, *The Elusive Republic: Political Economy in Jeffersonian America* (New York, 1980); J. G. A. Pocock, *Virtue, Commerce, and History* (Cambridge, 1985); Graham Richards, *Mental Machinery: The Origins and Consequences of Psychological Ideas, Part I, 1600–1850* (Baltimore, 1992); Joyce Appleby, *Liberalism, Republicanism, and the Historical Imagination* (Cambridge, 1992); S. A. Grave, *The Scottish Philosophy of Common Sense* (Oxford, 1960). John Corrigan's recent exploration of religion, emotion, and commerce in antebellum Boston is an important step toward understanding the experience of sympathetic congress. Although argued on different grounds, Corrigan's stress on the importance of emotion and sympathy as a promoter of social cohesion is largely consistent with mine (Corrigan, *Business of the Heart: Religion and Emotion in the Nineteenth Century* [Berkeley, 2002]). Because I am interested primarily in tracing the general lines of thought as experienced in America, rather than the significant and complex distinctions between individual philosophers, my summaries of Scots moral philoso-

phy remain very general. As should be clear, there are abundant exceptions for individual thinkers and sharp differences, for example, between those more inclined to favor the operation of reason versus those inclined toward sentiment. Though recognizing the pitfalls, I employ the shorthand "Scots" to refer to the abstracted community of ideas encompassed by contributors to the Scots Enlightenment, primarily as interpreted in the United States.

4. May, *Enlightenment in America,* 344.

5. Dugald Stewart, "Account of the Life and Writings of Adam Smith, LLD," in Stewart, *The Works of Dugald Stewart,* vol. 7 (Cambridge: Hilliard & Brown, 1829), 14. Henry May notes that in the American context an emotion-centered ethics was "less useful" to American Presbyterians and Unitarians "who were on the defensive against popular emotions, including religious emotions" (May, *Enlightenment in America,* 406). On the importance of enthusiasm in shaping American evangelical discourse, see Taves, *Fits, Trances, and Visions;* Corrigan, *Business of the Heart,* and J. C. Stewart-Robertson and Davis Fate Norton, "Thomas Reid on Adam Smith's Theory of Morals," *Journal of the History of Ideas* 41 (1980): 381–98 and 45 (1984): 309–21; Elmer H. Duncan and Robert M. Baird, "Thomas Reid's Criticism of Adam Smith's Theory of the Moral Sentiments," ibid., 38 (1977): 509–22.

6. John Abercrombie, *The Philosophy of Moral Feelings* (New York: Harper Brothers, 1837), 28–9, 28; Abercrombie, *Inquiries concerning the Intellectual Powers, and the Investigation of Truth* (New York: Harper & Bros., 1836). Abercrombie's popularity in the United States was enormous; his *Philosophy* went through as many as a dozen American editions before 1840, with his *Inquiries* not far behind.

7. Adam Ferguson, *An Essay on the History of Civil Society* (Edinburgh: Kincaid & Bell, 1767), 31; Henry Home, Lord Kames, *Essays on the Principles of Morality and Natural Religion,* 3d ed. (Edinburgh: John Bell, 1779), 10, 11; "The Theory of Moral Sentiments, . . . by Adam Smith," *North American Review* 8 (1819): 374. Among relevant works discussing Smith's philosophy, are Daniel Walker Howe, *Making the American Self: Jonathan Edwards to Abraham Lincoln* (Cambridge, 1997); Richard B. Sher and Jeffrey Smitten, *Scotland and America in the Age of the Enlightenment* (Edinburgh, 1990); Jean-Christophe Agnew, *Worlds Apart: The Market and the Theater in Anglo-American Thought, 1550–1750* (Cambridge, 1986); Julie Ellison, *Cato's Tears and the Making of Anglo-American Emotion* (Chicago, 1999).

8. James Rodgers, "Sensibility, Sympathy, Benevolence: Physiology and Moral Philosophy in *Tristram Shandy,*" in *Languages of Nature: Critical Essays on Science and Literature,* ed. Ludmilla J. Jordanova (New Brunswick, N.J., 1986), 135; Ruth Leys, "Background to the Reflex Controversy: William Alison and the Doctrine of Sympathy before Hall," *Studies in History of Biology* 4 (1980): 7, 9.

9. Schmidt, *Hearing Things;* Joseph Comstock, *The Tongue of Time, and Star of the States: A System of Human Nature, with the Phenomena of Heaven and Earth* (New York, 1838), 194. See also Brooke, *Refiner's Fire*; Butler, *Awash in a Sea of Faith*. Schmidt was discussing Hermeticism.

10. Agnew, *Worlds Apart*, 178. Agnew and Albert O. Hirschman argue that Smith is in a sense a crypto-Hobbesian; however, his acceptance of a Hobbesian atomism should not obscure his passionate efforts to imagine an alternate moral order. See ibid.; Hirschman, *The Passions and the Interests: Political Arguments for Capitalism before Its Triumph* (Princeton, N.J., 1972).

11. Adam Smith, *The Theory of Moral Sentiments*, ed. D. D. Raphael and A. L. MacFie (Oxford, 1976), 10.

12. Ellison, *Cato's Tears*.

13. Smith, *Theory of Moral Sentiments*, 22, 29. Evan Radcliffe has discussed the implications for the limited extension of sympathy in the context of the late eighteenth-century theories of benevolence: see Radcliffe, "Revolutionary Writing, Moral Philosophy, and Universal Benevolence in the Eighteenth Century," *Journal of the History of Ideas* 54 (1993): 221–40.

14. Smith, *Theory of Moral Sentiments*, 116, 9. William Ian Miller, *The Anatomy of Disgust* (Cambridge, 1997), includes a useful discussion of the shifting nature of the impartial spectator.

15. Smith, *Theory of Moral Sentiments*, 13. Kames also placed an attachment to "objects of distress" (though not specifically death) at the theoretical center of his moral sympathetic system. For Kames, attraction suffering was a necessary part of a divine system to ensure the success of sympathetic bonds in cementing society: sympathetic attraction, he suggested, resulted in pleasure in the act of relieving the sufferer, while the alternative—an aversion to misery—limited the sphere of operation of the sympathetic system (Kames, *Essays on the Principles of Morality*).

16. Adela Pinch, *Strange Fits of Passion: Epistemologies of Emotion, Hume to Austen* (Stanford, Calif., 1996), 24.

17. "On the Pleasure Derived from Witnessing Scenes of Distress," *North American Review* 2 (1815): 65; "Sympathy," *The Cyclopaedia; or, Universal Dictionary of Arts, Sciences, and Literature*, ed. Abraham Rees, vol. 36 (Philadelphia: Samuel F. Bradford, 1810–42), n.p.

18. Abercrombie, *Philosophy of Moral Feelings*, 33.

19. George Combe, *The Constitution of Man, Considered in Relation to External Objects*, 5th Amer. ed. (Boston: Sanborn, Carter & Bazin, 1835).

20. "On the Pleasure," 61–62; "Sketches of Moral and Mental Philosophy . . . by Thomas Chambers," *Princeton Review* 20 (1848): 541; "The Theory of Moral Sentiments, . . . by Adam Smith," 371–96.

21. John Gregory, cited in Christopher Lawrence, "The Nervous System and

Society in the Scottish Enlightenment," in *Natural Order: Historical Studies of Scientific Culture,* ed. Barry Barnes and Steven Shapin (Beverly Hills, Calif., 1979), 27; quote from Leys, "Background to the Reflex Controversy," 7.

22. Lawrence, "The Nervous System and Society in the Scottish Enlightenment," 27; Robert Whytt, *Observations on the Nature, Causes, and Cure of Those Disorders Which Have Been Commonly Called Nervous, Hypochondriac, or Hysteric* (Edinburgh: T. Becket, 1765); Leys, "Background to the Reflex Controversy"; Monfalcon, "Sympathie," *Dictionnaire des sciences médicales,* (Paris: C. L. F. Pancoucke, 1812–22), 543; see also L. S. Jacyna, "Principles of General Physiology: The Comparative Dimension to British Neuroscience in the 1830s and 1840s," *Studies in History of Biology* 7 (1984): 47–92; Karl M. Figlio, "Theories of Perception and the Physiology of Mind in the Late Eighteenth Century," *History of Science* 13 (1975): 177–212.

23. J. R. Park, "On the Laws of Sensation; with a Prefatory View of the Present State of Physiology," *Quarterly Journal of Science and the Arts* 1 (1816): 142; Park, "An Inquiry into the Influence of Corporeal Impressions in Producing Change of Function in the Living Body," *Quarterly Journal of Science and the Arts* 4 (1818): 26; Lawrence, "The Nervous System and Society in the Scottish Enlightenment." On the impact of Hall's theory, see Leys, "Background to the Reflex Controversy."

24. Leys, "Background to the Reflex Controversy," 6. Alison's debt to Reid and Stewart can be seen particularly in his antimaterialism and antiskepticism. Characteristically, William Cullen disapproved of use of the term *sympathy* due to its occult connotations (Lawrence, "The Nervous System and Society in the Scottish Enlightenment").

25. Rodgers, "Sensibility, Sympathy, Benevolence," 120; Lawrence, "The Nervous System and Society in the Scottish Enlightenment"; Leys, "Background to the Reflex Controversy"; see also Roger Cooter's analysis of phrenology, *The Cultural Meaning of Popular Science: Phrenology and the Organization of Consent in Nineteenth-Century Britain* (Cambridge, 1984).

26. "Sympathy," *Cyclopaedia,* 36; J. D. Godman, "On the Doctrine of Sympathy," *Philadelphia Journal of the Medical and Physical Sciences* 6 (1823): 341, 347; Arthur May, *An Inaugural Dissertation on Sympathy* (Philadelphia: Way & Groff, 1799), 13. Trained in Philadelphia, Godman was a major supporter of allopathic orthodoxy and opponent of phrenology and animal magnetism.

27. "Sympathy," *Encyclopaedia; or, A Dictionary of Arts, Sciences, and Miscellaneous Literature,* vol. 18 (Philadelphia: Thomas Dobson, 1798), 251; Charles Caldwell, "Thoughts on Sympathy," *Philadelphia Journal of the Medical and Physical Sciences* 3 (1821): 305, 306, 319. On sympathy and religious enthusiasm, see the exchange of Felix Robertson, "Account of a Singular Convulsive Affection, Which

Prevails in the State of Tennessee, and in Other Parts of the United States," *Philadelphia Medical and Physical Journal* 2, 1 (1805): 86–95, and William Young, "Thoughts on the Exercises Which Have Occurred at the Camp-Meetings in the Western Parts of Our Country," ibid., 3 (1808): 110–18.

28. Caldwell, "Thoughts on Sympathy," 319, 318, 315, 314. Much later in the century, sympathy was still cited as contributing to the formation of sex and gender. An interesting instance of its use is recorded in W. Judkins, "Verbal Report of a Case of Sympathetic Morning Sickness in the Male," *Cincinnati Lancet-Clinic* 28 (1892): 395. The biomedical construction of sexual difference during the late eighteenth and early nineteenth century has been the subject of great historical interest. See Londa Schiebinger, *The Mind Has No Sex: Women in the Origins of Modern Science* (Cambridge, 1989); Cynthia Eagle Russett, *Sexual Science: The Victorian Construction of Womanhood* (Cambridge, 1989); Thomas Laqueur, *Making Sex: Body and Gender from the Greeks to Freud* (Cambridge, 1990); Ornella Moscucci, *The Science of Woman: Gynaecology and Gender in England, 1800–1929* (Cambridge, 1990); Alison Bashford, *Purity and Pollution: Gender, Embodiment, and Victorian Medicine* (New York, 1998).

29. John Mason Good, *The Book of Nature* (New York: J. & J. Harper, 1828), 253, 256.

30. John Bell, *An Essay on Somnambulism, or Sleep-Walking, Produced by Animal Electricity and Magnetism, as Well as by Sympathy &c.* (Dublin: for the author, 1788), 5. The fourfold typology of somnambulism (excluding catalepsy) is that of Alexandre-Jacques-François Bertrand, *Traité du somnambulisme et des différentes modifications qu'il présent* (Paris: Dentu, 1823); see also William Hammond, *Spiritualism and Allied Causes and Conditions of Nervous Derangement* (New York: G. P. Putnam's Sons, 1876). Samuel Latham Mitchill, however, identified twenty-three distinct classes of "somnial" behavior (Mitchill, *Devotional Somnium*).

31. On mesmerism, see Robert Darnton, *Mesmerism and the End of the Enlightenment in France* (Cambridge, 1968); Robert C. Fuller, *Mesmerism and the American Cure of Souls* (Philadelphia, 1982); Cooter, *Cultural Meaning of Popular Science;* A. Wrobel, ed., *Pseudo-Science and Society in Nineteenth-Century America* (Lexington, Ky., 1987); Alan Gauld, *A History of Hypnotism* (Cambridge, 1992); Tony James, *Dream, Creativity, and Madness in 19th Century France* (Oxford, 1995); Alison Winter, *Mesmerized: Powers of Mind in Victorian Britain* (Chicago, 1998).

32. "On Somnambulism," *Littell's Living Age* 63 (1859): 5; Benjamin Rush, *Medical Inquiries and Observations upon the Diseases of the Mind,* 4th ed. (Philadelphia: John Griggs, 1830), 302; John Vaughan, *Observations on Animal Electricity in Explanation of the Metallic Operation of Doctor Perkins* (Wilmington, Del.: Delaware Gazette, 1797), 22. Examples of habitual activity are provided by Robert

Macnish, *The Philosophy of Sleep* (New York: Appleton, 1834); Abercrombie, *Inquiries concerning the Intellectual Powers;* Good, *Book of Nature;* Andrew Carmichael, "An Essay on Dreaming, Including Conjectures on the Proximate Cause of Sleep," *Philosophical Magazine and Journal* 54 (1819): 252–64, 324–35; Benjamin Ridge, "London and Its Vicinity—Somnambulism," *Gentleman's Magazine* 132 (1823): 461–62; "A Case of Somnambulism," *Phrenological Journal* 10 (1848): 101–2, "Somnambulism," ibid., 15 (1852): 135–36; and "Curious Case of Somnambulism," ibid., 24 (1856): 96; as well as its ultimate source, the much cited *Encyclopédie* of Diderot.

33. Lemuel W. Belden, "An Account of Jane C. Rider, the Springfield Somnambulist," *Boston Medical and Surgical Journal* 11 (1834): 53, 54; Belden, *An Account of Jane C. Rider, the Springfield Somnambulist* (Springfield, Mass.: G. & C. Merriam, 1834); Thomas Miner, "The Springfield Somnambulist," *Boston Medical and Surgical Journal* 11 (1834): 73–74; Elisha North, "Remarks on Somnambulism, etc.," ibid., 352–53. Rider's case was widely discussed in other publications.

34. Belden, *Account of Jane C. Rider,* 39, 106; Hammond, *Spiritualism and Allied Causes and Conditions of Nervous Derangement;* Miner, "The Springfield Somnambulist"; M. F. Colby, "Additional Observations on Mrs. Cass, the Stanstead Somnambulist," *Boston Medical and Surgical Journal* 11 (1834): 297–304; M. Carini, J. Visconti, and M. Mazzacorati, "Case of Spontaneous Catalepsy, &c.," *Lancet* 1 (1832–33): 663–65. Belden and Miner agreed that Rider could not see through thick paper or metal, though Miner believed her vision was out of the ordinary only in degree, not nature. Objects translucent to others, he suggested, were transparent to Rider, but she could not see through truly opaque objects, as some popular accounts alleged.

35. "Somnambulism," 192; "On Somnambulism," 9; Bell, *Essay on Somnambulism,* 6; Carini et al., "Case of Spontaneous Catalepsy, &c.," 664.

36. Comstock, *Tongue of Time,* 224; John Fosbroke, "Case of Trance, or Coma Somnolentum," *Lancet* 2 (1835): 349; M. Andral, "Lectures on Medical Pathology," ibid., 1 (1832–33): 769–79; Andrew Ellis, "Clinical Lecture on a Case of Catalepsy," ibid., 2 (1834–35): 129–34; see also the instance of somnambular contagion cited in "Somnambulism," 822. See also James Cowles Prichard, *Treatise on Insanity and Other Disorders Affecting the Mind* (Philadelphia: Carey & Hart, 1839); Joseph Comstock, "Somnambulism and Clairvoyance," *Boston Medical and Surgical Journal* 56 (1857): 389–95; Comstock, "A Case of Very Singular Affection, Supposed to Have Been Occasioned by the Bite of a Tarantula," *Medical Repository* 1 (1803): 1–11.

37. "On Somnambulism," 4; Belden, "An Account of Jane C. Rider," 62; Comstock, "Somnambulism and Clairvoyance," 389. Belden was a lukewarm supporter of phrenology; Carmichael ("An Essay on Dreaming") was warmer.

38. *Littell's Living Age* (1860); Carini et al., "Case of Spontaneous Catalepsy," 665; see also "Somnambulism"; J. C. Colquhoun, "Animal Magnetism," *Lancet* 2 (1832–33): 205–18; cited in "Review of *On Somnambulism and Animal Magnetism,* by J. C. Prichard," *Gentleman's Magazine* 153 (1834): 626. An extended account of the diagnosis of disease by a somnambulist (artificial) is found in an appendix to William Leete Stone, *Letter to Doctor A. Brigham, on Animal Magnetism* (New York: George Dearborn, 1837). The most detailed examples of somnambular social relations are found in the literature on "artificial" somnambulism, where a "community of sensation" might develop between mesmerist and mesmerized, producing a mutuality of sentiment, thought, and action. Alison Winter identifies a series of traits in mesmerism that, not surprisingly, are found as well in natural somnambulism, including "complete catalepsy, lack of sensation and consciousness, mimicry of the mesmerist's sensations" and movements (extending, in natural somnambulism, to other persons), "and a lucid state accompanied by clairvoyance and prescience." "Some patients," she adds, "predicted the progress of their own and others' illnesses and instructed the physician to an appropriate treatment" (Winter, *Mesmerized,* 41).

39. Prichard, *Treatise on Insanity,* 290; "Somnambulism," 199; N., letter to the editor, *Gentleman's Magazine* 130 (1822): 598–99. Clairvoyance and thought transference were more widely encountered in mesmerism, where the connection between operator and operand was one means to mental connection.

40. Colby, "Additional Observations," 301; Belden, *Account of Jane C. Rider.* The public embrace of Rider was sufficiently fond that townspeople volunteered $48 to defray the cost of her treatment at the Worcester Hospital.

41. Carini et al., "Case of Spontaneous Catalepsy," 661; Good, *Book of Nature,* 278–79; Stone, *Letter to Doctor A. Brigham; Journeys into the Moon, Several Planets, and the Sun: History of a Female Somnambulist, of Weilhelm on the Teck, in the Kingdom of Wuertemberg, in the Years 1832 and 1833* (Philadelphia: for Vollmer & Haggemacher, 1837); Justinus A. C. Kerner, *The Seeress of Prevorst* (London: J. C. Moore, 1845). The Spiritualist geologist William Denton and his wife Elizabeth possessed similar space and time transgressive abilities. Elizabeth often indulged herself in visits to foreign planets, while William connected mentally with rocks and fossils to investigate life in the Carboniferous era (William Denton, *The Soul of Things,* 8th ed. [Wellesley, Mass.: Denton Publ. Co., 1888]).

42. Belden, "An Account of Jane C. Rider," 60; Belden, *Account of Jane C. Rider,* 68; H. Dewar, "On Uterine Irritation and Its Effects on the Female Constitution," *Transactions of the Royal Society of Edinburgh* 9 (1823): 366–79; Colby, "Additional Observations on the Case of Mrs. Cass"; Weisten, "Some Remarks on Dreaming, Somnambulism, and Other States of Partial Activity of Other Cerebral Faculties," *Lancet* 1 (1831–32): 919–23; "Somnambulism," *Harper's* 3 (1851):

196–201. Many other cases of enhanced mental powers can be cited: see, e.g., John Elliotson, "Abstract of a Clinical Lecture," *Lancet* 2 (1836–37): 866–73. Like his intellectual forebear David Hartley, John Abercrombie believed that most instances of acquired talents resulted from prior experience recalled through association with current events or emotions, though Abercrombie admitted that some cases simply defied explanation (Abercrombie, *Inquires concerning the Intellectual Powers*).

43. "Somnambulist Story," *Spirit of the Age* 1 (1849): 327.

44. Belden, "An Account of Jane C. Rider," 54, 56, 62, 67.

45. "Somnambulism," 201.

46. J. C. Badeley, "On the Reciprocal Agencies of Mind and Matter," *Boston Medical and Surgical Journal* 45 (1851): 12, 171. See, e.g., "On Somnambulism"; Hammond, *Spiritualism and Allied Causes and Conditions of Nervous Derangement*. Among fictional somnambulists, see Charles Brockden Brown, *Edgar Huntly, or, Memoirs of a Sleep-Walker* (Philadelphia: H. Maxwell, 1799); Henry Cockton, *Sylvester Sound, the Somnambulist* (New York: Burgess, Stringer, & Co., 1844); W. C. Oulton, *The Sleep-Walker, or Which Is the Lady?* (New York: D. Longworth, 1813); W. T. Moncrieff, *The Somnambulist, or, The Phantom of the Village* (London: Moncrieff, 1828).

47. "Somnambulism," 198; Belden, *Account of Jane C. Rider*, 25. A similar claim is made in Carini et al., "Case of Spontaneous Catalepsy."

48. Colby, "Additional Observations," 301; Ellis, "Clinical Lecture on a Case of Catalepsy," 130; Arthur L. Wigan, "The Duality of the Mind," *Lancet* 2 (1845): 366, 367; Wigan, *The Duality of the Mind* (London: Brown, Green, & Longmans, 1844). Wigan's theory enjoyed a revival in the twentieth century: see Basil Clarke, "Arthur Wigan and *The Duality of the Mind*," *Psychological Medicine Monograph Supplement* 1 (1987): 1–52.

49. Belden, "An Account of Jane C. Rider," 55; "On Somnambulism," 6. See Thomas Brown's incisive commentary on mental (personal) identity in Lectures XI–XIV of Brown, *Lectures on the Philosophy of the Human Mind* (Boston: T. Armstrong, 1826).

50. S. W. Mitchell, *Mary Reynolds: A Case of Double Consciousness* (Philadelphia, 1889), 164n; S. W. Mitchell, "Mary Reynolds: A Case of Double Personality," *Transactions of the College of Physicians of Philadelphia* 10 (1888): 366–89; B. W. Dwight, "Facts Illustrative of the Powers of the Human Mind," *American Journal of Science* 1 (1818): 433; Samuel Latham Mitchill, "A Double Consciousness, or A Duality of Person in the Same Individual," *Medical Repository*, n.s., 3 (1817): 185–86; Eric T. Carlson, "The History of Multiple Personality in the United States: Mary Reynolds and Her Subsequent Reputation," *Bulletin of the History of Medicine* 58 (1984): 72–82; J. Goodwin, "Mary Reynolds: A Post-traumatic Rein-

terpretation of a Classic Case of Multiple Personality Disorder," *Hillside Journal of Clinical Psychiatry* 9 (1987): 89–99; Eric T. Carlson, "Multiple Personality and Hypnosis: The First One Hundred Years," *Journal of the History of the Behavioral Sciences* 25 (1989): 315–22; Ian Hacking, "Multiple Personality Disorder and Its Hosts," *History of the Human Sciences* 5 (1992): 3–31; Hacking, "Two Souls in One Body," *Critical Inquiry* 17 (1991): 838–67; Hacking, "Double Consciousness in Britain, 1815–1875," *Dissociation* 4 (1991): 134–46; Michael G. Kenny, *The Passion of Ansel Bourne* (Washington, D.C., 1986). John Corrigan sees double consciousness as a characteristic condition of antebellum America, the product of a state in which emotion was simultaneously a subjective, spiritualized experience and an objectified, commodified thing (Corrigan, *Business of the Heart*, 7).

51. "On Somnambulism," 7; *Annual Register* 57 (1816): 72 and 55 (1814): 101; Bell, *Essay on Somnambulism*, 30. The phrenological explanation that the absence of fear resulted from the inactivity of the corresponding mental organ was very current ("Some Remarks on Dreaming, Somnambulism, and Other States of Partial Activity of the Cerebral Faculties," *Lancet* 1 [1831–32]: 920). On the emergence of a private self, see Karen Lystra, *Searching the Heart: Women, Men, and Romantic Live in Nineteenth Century America* (New York, 1989).

52. Moncrieff, *Somnambulist*, 13; Dewar, "On Uterine Irritation and Its Effects on the Female Constitution"; Macnish, *Philosophy of Sleep;* "Somnambulism"; "Some Remarks on Dreaming, Somnambulism, and Other States of Partial Activity of the Cerebral Faculties," *Lancet* 1 (1831–32): 920.

53. Kames, *Essays on the Principles of Morality*, 197.

54. Cockton, *Sylvester Sound;* Alan Pinkerton, *The Detective and the Somnambulist* (Chicago: Keen, Cooke & Co., 1875); Vaughan, *Observations on Animal Electricity*, 21–22; "The Somnambulist," *Southern Literary Messenger* 3 (1837): 152–54. Grief was a particular interest of J. R. Park; see his "On the Influence of Mental Impressions in Producing Change of Function in the Living Body," *Quarterly Journal of Science and the Arts* 4 (1818): 207–26.

55. "Somnambulism," 200.

56. Mitchill, *Devotional Somnium*, 66; "Review of *Devotional Somnium*," 508.

57. *Trial of Abraham Prescott, for the Murder of Mrs. Sally Cochran, at Pembroke, June 23, 1833* (Concord, N.H., 1834); *Report of the Trial of Abraham Prescott for the Murder of Mrs. Sally Cochran, before the Court of Common Pleas, Holden at Concord, in the County of Merrimack, on the First Tuesday of Sept., A.D. 1834* (Concord, N.H., 1834); S. Estabrook, *Eccentricities and Anecdotes of Albert John Tirrell, the Reputed Murderer of the Beautiful Maria Bickford* (Boston, 1846); Estabrook, *The Life and Death of Mrs. Maria Bickford, a Beautiful Female* (Boston, 1846). The *National Police Gazette* 1 (1845) carried several articles on Tirrell crafted for their working-class audience.

58. The question whether the insane could be held criminally responsibility for their acts was hotly contested during the early nineteenth century. In both Britain and the United States, a defendant could not be held accountable if unaware of the nature of his or her actions (N. Walker, "The Insanity Defence before 1800," *Annals of the American Academy of Political and Social Science* 477 [1985]: 25–30; R. Moran, "The Modern Foundation for the Insanity Defense: The Cases of James Hadfield (1800) and Daniel McNaughtan (1843)," ibid., 31–42; Moran, "The Origin of Insanity as a Special Verdict: The Trial for Treason of James Hadfield," *Law and Society Review* 19, 3 [1985]: 487–519; R. Smith, "The Boundary between Insanity and Criminal Responsibility in Nineteenth-Century England," in *Madhouses, Mad-Doctors, and Madmen*, ed. Andrew Scull [Philadelphia, 1981], 363–84).

59. *Report of the Trial of Abraham Prescott*, 14.

60. Ibid., 18.

61. Daniel A. Cohen, "The Murder of Maria Bickford: Fashion, Passion, and the Birth of a Consumer Culture," *American Studies* 31, 2 (1990): 5–30; Cohen, *Pillars of Salt, Monuments of Grace: New England Crime Literature and the Origins of American Popular Culture, 1674–1860* (New York, 1993); B. Hobson, "A Murder in the Moral and Religious City of Boston," *Boston Bar Journal* 22 (1978): 9–21; Marjorie Carleton, "'Maria Met a Gentleman': The Bickford Case," in *Boston Murders*, ed. Marjorie Carleton (New York, 1948), 15–39.

62. Cohen, *Pillars of Salt*.

63. J. E. P. Weeks, *Trial of Albert John Tirrell for the Murder of Mary Ann Bickford* (Boston: Times Office, 1846), 28, 29, 30.

64. Ibid., 21.

65. Ibid., 39; *The Authentic Life of Mrs. Mary Ann Bickford* (Boston: the compiler, 1846), 4.

66. Lady of Weymouth, *Eccentricities of Albert John Tirrell* (Boston, 1846), 24. Daniel Cohen has suggested that portrayals of Bickford in the yellow press were consumed with images of the pleasures of consumer society, her beauty, fine dresses and expensive possessions, the financial exchanges between Bickford and Tirrell, and, of course, her participation in the commercial sex trade. These, too, reflect the duality and indeterminacy of character when confronted with somnambulism. Bickford was depicted alternately as an innocent victim or as a "depraved seductress" complicit in her own murder through her desire for material goods. She was, in one account, "skilled in all the blandishments of a courtezan, and decked in jewels and silks" who "shone a resplendent meteor [and] . . . was the observed of all observers—praised, petted, admired, by the millionaires of the world" (Cohen, "The Murder of Maria Bickford"; Lady of Weymouth, *Eccentricities of Albert John Tirrell*, 27).

67. "Review of *On Somnambulism and Animal Magnetism*, by J. C. Prichard."

2. CELESTIAL SYMPTOMS

1. John Vaughan, "Remarkable Cases of Madness," *Medical Repository* 5 (1802): 408, 409. The author, John Vaughan, a physician of Wilmington, is often confused with his better known contemporary and colleague John Vaughan the wine merchant of Philadelphia.

2. Ibid., 410–11; David Hume, *Treatise of Human Nature*, ed. Eric Steinberg (Indianapolis, 1977), 576; Pinch, *Strange Fits of Passion*.

3. Vaughan, "Remarkable Cases of Madness," 410–11.

4. Felix Robertson, "Account of a Singular Convulsive Affection, Which Prevails in the State of Tennessee, and in Other Parts of the United States," *Philadelphia Medical and Physical Journal* 2, 1 (1805): 88. In an excellent analysis Ann Taves situates the conceptual linking of mesmeric and revival phenomena in the 1820s; however, through their common origins in sympathetic theory, the theoretical armature was established at least two decades previously (Taves, *Fits, Trances, and Visions*).

5. Young, "Thoughts on the Exercises Which Have Occurred at the Camp-Meetings in the Western Parts of Our Country," 111, 112.

6. William Belcher, *Intellectual Electricity, Novum Organum of Vision, and Grand Mystic Secret* (London: Lee & Hurst, 1798), 24, 20–21.

7. "Sleeping Preacher," *Kirby's Wonderful and Eccentric Museum* 5 (1815): 264–65. Ann Taves's valuable account of the use of animal magnetism as an explanation for false religion in the 1840s draws usefully upon the career of the underappreciated LaRoy Sunderland. She suggests that the reinvigoration of mesmeric practice in America in the 1830s made "armchair comparisons" between the physical phenomena of the revival tent and mesmerism commonplace, but as I will suggest, the comparisons were present from the earliest upwelling of the Second Great Awakening but rooted in the more fundamental phenomena of sympathy (Taves, *Fits, Trances, and Visions*, 131).

8. Mitchill, *Devotional Somnium*, 52; *Gentleman's Magazine* 30 (1760): 236–40; "A Remarkable Nervous Case," *Annual Register* 3 (1760): 68–71.

9. Charles Mais, *The Surprising Case of Rachel Baker, Who Prays and Preaches in Her Sleep*, 2d ed. (New York.: Whiting & Watson, 1814), 5; Ansel W. Ives, "Remarkable Case of Devotional Somnium," *Transactions of the Physical and Medical Society of New York* 1 (1817): 397; "Domestic Literary Iintelligence," 84. The major accounts of Baker's life and ministry are Mais, *Surprising Case;* Mitchill, *Devotional Somnium;* "Domestic Literary Intelligence," *Analectic Magazine* 5 (1815): 84–85; review of *Devotional Somnium, Analectic Magazine* 5 (1815): 497–509; Comstock, *Tongue of Time*. Baker is also discussed in Taves, *Fits, Trances, and Visions*, chap. 4r.

10. Ives, "Remarkable Case of Devotional Somnium," 397; Mais, *Surprising Case*, 5.

11. Ives, "Remarkable Case of Devotional Somnium," 398.

12. Mais, *Surprising Case*, 9. Ives, "Remarkable Case of Devotional Somnium," makes this claim, although the *Analectic*'s anonymous reviewer of *Devotional Somnium* suggests both that Baker "complained of no disorder whatever" and that she "humbly looked upon [her performances] as trials and chastisement" (review of *Devotional Somnium*, 502, 500). The traditional belief in treating insanity by exposure to seawater was seen also in the case of Abraham Prescott described in chap. 1.

13. Mitchill, *Devotional Somnium*, 36, 35; Ann W. G. to Weltha F. Brown, n.d., Hooker Collection, SLRI.

14. W. D. R., *National Advocate*, Mar. 17, 1815. Caroline Walker Bynum, *Fragmentation and Redemption: Essays on Gender and the Human Body in Medieval Religion* (New York, 1991), and Joan Jacobs Brumberg, *Fasting Girls: The Emergence of Anorexia Nervosa as a Modern Disease* (Cambridge, 1998), provide a perspective on the gendered nature of ascetic bodily behavior for periods that were earlier and later, respectively, than Baker's.

15. Mais, *Surprising Case*, 8, 9; Mitchill, *Devotional Somnium*, 47, 42.

16. Mais, *Surprising Case*, 6; "Domestic Literary Intelligence," 84.

17. Ann W. G. to Weltha Brown, n.d., Hooker Collection, SLRI. Other prayers and sermons are recorded in Mitchill, *Devotional Somnium*, and Mais, *Surprising Case*.

18. Ann W. G. to Weltha Brown, n.d. (second letter), Hooker Collection, SLRI. Based upon the chronology provided by Ansel W. Ives, the letter would appear to have been written in the spring of 1816.

19. "Domestic Literary Intelligence," 84.

20. Ibid.; Mais, *Surprising Case*, 12; Comstock, *Tongue of Time*, 414, 415.

21. W. D. R., *National Advocate;* review of *Devotional Somnium*, 499. The issue of private gain in validating spiritual authority was reprised in the early years of the American Spiritualist movement, with Spiritualist mediums condemned as frauds for accepting pay or lauded as authentic for refusing it. See Owen, *Darkened Room*.

22. Mais, *Surprising Case*, 32.

23. Mitchill, *Devotional Somnium*, 49; Mais, *Surprising Case*, 11; Miner, "The Springfield Somnambulist," 74; Dewar, "On Uterine Irritation and Its Effects on the Female Constitution"; Colby, "Additional Observations on Mrs. Cass, the Stanstead Somnambulist"; Fosbroke, "Case of Trance, or Coma Somnolentum," 343–49; MacNish, *Philosophy of Sleep*.

24. Mais, *Surprising Case*, 10, 11, 152.

25. Ann W. G. to Weltha F. Brown, n.d., Hooker Collection, SLRI; Mitchill, *Devotional Somnium,* 42; Braude, *Radical Spirits.* While many contemporaries questioned whether the trance lecturers Braude discussed acted consciously in their own interests, Baker's "transgressions" were interpreted as clearly unconscious manifestations. On the ascetic body, see Steven Shapin, "The Philosopher and the Chicken," *Science Incarnate: Historical Embodiments of Natural Knowledge,* ed. in Christopher Lawrence and Steven Shapin (Chicago, 1998); Bynum, *Fragmentation and Redemption;* Brumberg, *Fasting Girls.*

26. Mais, *Surprising Case,* 31; Mitchill, *Devotional Somnium,* 225, 226, 174, 205, 208.

27. Mitchill, *Devotional Somnium,* 210.

28. Mais, *Surprising Case,* 32; "Domestic Literary Intelligence," 85.

29. Mitchill, *Devotional Somnium,* 42, 47; Mais, *Surprising Case,* 16–17.

30. Ann W. G. to Weltha Brown, n.d. (second letter), Hooker Collection, SLRI.

31. Ives, "Remarkable Case of Devotional Somnium," 404–5, 408–10.

32. Macnish, *Philosophy of Sleep,* 165.

33. review of *Devotional Somnium,* 499, 507.

34. Ibid., 507–8.

35. Ibid., 509.

36. Emerson cited in Wrobel, *Pseudo-Science and Society in Nineteenth-Century America,* 6; Dods, *Spirit Manifestations,* 34, 65. Emerson was speaking of mesmerism, rather than natural somnambulism.

37. Friedrich Fischer, *Der Somnambulismus* (Basel: Schweighauser, 1839), cited in Gauld, *History of Hypnotism,* 262.

38. Lippard, "A Madman's Nightmare," in *George Lippard: Prophet of Protest: Writings of an American Radical, 1822–1854,* ed. David S. Reynolds (New York, 1986), 298.

39. Mitchill, *Devotional Somnium,* 253.

3. TRANSPARENT SPIRITS

1. O. C. S. [i.e., Abby Sewall] to Serena Brown, May 19, 1850, Abby Sewall to Serena Brown, Feb. 7, 1849, Sewall Family Papers, SLRI.

2. Abby Sewall to Serena Brown, Nov. 1850, ibid.

3. Ibid., Apr. 13, 1850.

4. New England Spiritualists' Association, *Constitution,* 11; A. B. Child, *Whatever Is, Is Right* (Boston: Berry, Colby & Co., 1860), 88; Clark, *Plain Guide to Spiritualism,* 270.

5. Edward Whipple, *A Biography of James M. Peebles, M.D., A.M.* (Battle Creek, Mich., 1901), 40; J. O. Barrett, *The Spiritual Pilgrim: A Biography of James M. Peebles* (Boston: William White, 1871); Thomas Richmond, *God Dealing with*

Slavery: God's Instrumentalities in Emancipating the African Slave in America (Chicago: Religio-Philosophical Publishing House, 1870); Stebbins, *Upward Steps of Seventy Years*. Other instructive examples are to be found among ministers who adopted Spiritualist views, including Samuel Watson (Methodist), J. B. Ferguson and Francis H. Smith (Presbyterian), Charles Hammond (Universalism), Thomas Wentworth Higginson, James Freeman Clarke, and Frederick L. H. Willis (Unitarian), and perhaps Isaac Post (Hicksite Quakerism).

6. Richmond, *God Dealing with Slavery*, 41; Donna Hill, *Joseph Smith: The First Mormon* (Garden City, N.Y., 1977), 34; Joseph Smith, *History of the Church of Jesus Christ of the Latter Day Saints*, vol. 1 (Salt Lake City, 1963), 4.

7. William Denton, *Radical Discourses on Religious Subjects* (Boston: Denton, 1872), 176–77; J. B. Ferguson, *Spirit Communion: A Record of Communications from the Spirit-Spheres* (Nashville: Union & American Steam Press, 1854), 191.

8. Josiah Brigham, *Twelve Spirit Messages from John Quincy Adams, through Joseph D. Stiles, Medium* (Boston: Bela Marsh, 1859), 189.

9. Abby Sewall to Serena Brown, July 17, 1853, Sewall Family Papers, SLRI.

10. Ibid., Jan. 13–16, 1851.

11. Augusta Sewall to Thomas Brown, Apr. 6, 1851, ibid.

12. Abby Sewall to Thomas Brown, Apr. 6, 1851, ibid. Karen Lystra ties a growing sense of privacy and separation of space in Victorian America to shifts in the practice of romantic love. The rituals of Victorian courtship, she suggests, revolved around the laying open of hearts, sharing the secret, inward selves and forcing both the prospective bride and groom to cross "gender boundaries" (and, it might be added, interpersonal and other boundaries as well) "by disclosing and sharing what, from the romantic view, was their essence." She further touches on the cross-fertilization between religious and romantic languages, the manner in which the ideal of romantic love involved the subsumption of another subjectivity, and the formation of a self-identity tied to a heightened sense of emotion (Lystra, *Searching the Heart*, 9). As I will suggest, all of these points—adjustments to the concepts of privacy and individuality, the crossing of boundaries, the transparency of the individual in affective relations, the merger of subjectivities, and the intensified emotionality—are central to Spiritualism.

13. Frank Podmore, *Mediums of the Nineteenth Century*, vol. 1 (New Hyde Park, N.Y., 1963), 202; Davis, *Present Age and Inner Life*, 20, 21, 22. The odyllic force of Baron von Reichenbach was likened to mesmeric fluid, a naturally occurring force by which bodies or minds exerted influence upon one another. See Oppenheim, *Other World*.

14. Hardinge, *Modern American Spiritualism;* Hardinge, *Autobiography of Emma Hardinge Britten*, ed. Margaret Wilkinson (London: John Heywood, 1900); Leah Underhill, *The Missing Link in Modern Spiritualism* (New York: Thomas R.

Knox, 1885); A Mystic, "Andrew Jackson Davis, the Great American Seer," *Shekinah* 3 (1853): 4–19. See also Braude, *Radical Spirits,* on the role of mesmerism in preparing Spiritualist trance lecturers.

15. Putnam, *Mesmerism, Spiritualism, Witchcraft, and Miracle,* 6–7; J. J. G. Wilkinson, *A Proposal to Treat Lunacy by Spiritualism* (Boston: Otis Clapp, 1857), 7; Blanchard Fosgate, *Sleep, Psychologically Considered with Reference to Sensation and Memory* (New York: G. P. Putnam, 1850); Cora L. V. Hatch, *Discourses on Religion, Morals, Philosophy, and Metaphysics,* vol. 1 (New York: B. F. Hatch, 1858); Wolfe, *Startling Facts in Modern Spiritualism;* Hardinge, *Modern American Spiritualism;* Crowell, *Identity of Primitive Christianity;* Dods, *Spirit Manifestations.* The conflation of "natural somnambulism" and mesmerism and the union of phrenology and mesmerism in the form of phrenomesmerism underscore the common conceptual foundations of these discourses.

16. Abby Sewall to Serena Brown, Apr. 17, 1853, to Serena and Thomas Brown, Feb. 13, 1854, Sewall Family Papers, SLRI.

17. Abby Sewall to Serena and Thomas Brown, Feb. 13, 1854, ibid.

18. Ibid., Aug. 27, 1854.

19. Ibid., Abby Sewall to Serena Brown, Mar. 12, 1855, ibid.

20. Abby Sewall to Serena Brown, Mar. 17, 1862, ibid. Similar lists of clerical errors are found in many Spiritualist sources. Francis H. Smith, for instance, lists original sin, total depravity, election, reprobation, infant damnation, endless punishment, a personal Devil, and a God of wrath and indignation (Smith, *My Experience,* 10; Samuel H. Terry, *Modern Spiritualism: I—Its Object, II—Its Religion* [Boston: Colby & Rich, 1887]).

21. Herman Snow, *Visions of the Beyond, by a Seer of To-day* (Boston: Colby & Rich, 1877), 30; S. B. Brittan, "Spiritualism: Its Nature and Mission," *Shekinah* 1 (1851): 9–10.

22. Kirk Cunningham to John Cunningham, May 13, 1855, Cunningham Papers, WLCL. Ernest Isaacs has argued for a profound split between "philosophical" and "phenomenal" Spiritualism; however, as seen in the case of Abby Sewall, the two faces of Spiritualism often played a recursive role in sustaining each other (Ernest Isaacs, "The Fox Sisters and American Spiritualism," in *The Occult in America: New Historical Perspectives,* ed. Howard Kerr and Charles L. Crow [Urbana, Ill., 1983], 79–110). Although philosophical Spiritualism was usually held out as the more meaningful, Napoleon Wolfe argued that phenomenal Spiritualism was of a higher order because it provided empirical demonstration acting upon the external senses that confirmed the internal.

23. Kirk Cunningham to John Cunningham, Dec. 26, 1858, Cunningham Papers, WLCL; Davis, *Present Age and Inner Life,* 98.

24. Brittan, "Spiritualism: Its Nature and Mission," 11.

25. James Freeman Clarke to Anna H. Clarke, Apr. 21, 1854, Perry-Clarke Collection, MHS.

26. William Stainton Moses to Epes Sargeant, Sept. 17, 1874, Epes Sargeant Papers, BPL.

27. Printed letter of Alonzo E. Newton, Aug. 12, 1861, laid into A. E. Newton Scrapbook, MHS.

28. Edmonds and Dexter, *Spiritualism* 1:336; Brittan, "Spiritualism: Its Nature and Mission," 11; Davis, *Present Age and Inner Life,* 199; Brigham, *Twelve Spirit Messages,* 95.

29. Davis, *Present Age and Inner Life,* 118.

30. Lystra, *Searching the Heart,* 42. Examining the post–Civil War period, T. J. Jackson Lears, *No Place of Grace: Antimodernism and the Transformation of American Culture, 1880–1920* (Chicago, 1983), offers an extensive analysis of the cultural impact of antimodernism and autonomous individualism, interpreting the former as a hegemonic device by which the elite are able to ensure their continued control of social and political matters and the latter as the center of bourgeois morality. Although Lystra's and Lears's interpretations of the Victorian ethic of self-control (to use Lears's term) are nearly diametrically opposed, both insist upon the centrality of the experience of autonomous individualism in shaping bourgeois values.

31. Abby Sewall to Serena Brown, Mar. 12, 1855, Sewall Family Papers, SLRI.

32. Ibid., July 18, 1859; James Freeman Clarke to Anne H. Clark, Mar. 31, 1854, Perry-Clarke Collection, MHS.

33. Allen Putnam, *Natty, a Spirit: His Portrait and His Life* (Boston: Bela Marsh, 1856), 81.

34. M. T. Shelhamer, *Life and Labor in the Spirit World, Being a Description of Localities, Employments, Surroundings, and Condition in the Spheres* (Boston: Colby & Rich, 1887), 29.

35. H. Link to Mr. and Mrs. Keller, Little Falls, N.Y., June 6, 1852, D. N. Diedrich Collection, WLCL.

36. Abby Sewall to Serena Brown, Apr. 22, 1855, May 11, 1856, Sewall Family Papers, SLRI.

37. James Freeman Clarke, *A Sermon Preached in Amory Hall, on Thanksgiving Day, Nov. 24, 1842* (Boston: Benjamin H. Greene, 1843), 4; Abby Sewall to Serena Brown, May 11, 1856, Sewall Family Papers, SLRI. Elizabeth Clark makes a convincing case that sympathy as practiced by the liberal Protestant denominations such as the Unitarians or Friends was viewed as praxis, not theory. It was something, as Adam Smith would agree, that must be voluntarily assumed by members of society as a means of forging community, and not an innate moral sentiment. For this reason Nina Baym argues that sentimentalism was not "evasive self ab-

sorption" but "a practical philosophy of community" (Elizabeth B. Clark, "'The Sacred Rights of the Weak': Pain, Sympathy, and the Culture of Individual Rights in Antebellum America," *Journal of American History* 82 [1995]: 463–93; Ann Douglas, *The Feminization of American Culture* [New York, 1978]; Nina Baym, *Woman's Fiction: A Guide to Novels by and about Women in America, 1820–1870*, 2d ed. [Urbana, Ill., 1993], xxix–xxx).

38. Abby Sewall to Serena Brown, July 18, 1859, Sewall Family Papers, SLRI.

39. Crowell, *Identity of Primitive Christianity* 1:53.

40. Ibid., 53–54.

41. William Hammond, *Physics and Physiology of Spiritualism* (New York: Appleton, 1871), 13, 14; Richards, *Mental Machinery*. Psychophysiologists and neuroanatomists such as Hammond and William Carpenter were among the harshest critics of Spiritualism.

42. Moore, *In Search of White Crows;* Oppenheim, *Other World;* Nelson, *Spiritualism and Society*. For "Try the spirits," see Epes Sargeant, *The Proof Palpable of Immortality; Being an Account of the Materialization Phenomena of Modern Spiritualism,* 2d ed. (Boston: Colby & Rich, 1876), 46; Sargeant, *Planchette,* 285.

43. Sargeant, *Proof Palpable of Immortality,* 201; Wolfe, *Startling Facts in Modern Spiritualism,* 98; Moore, *In Search of White Crows;* Hardinge, *Modern American Spiritualism;* Shelhamer, *Life and Labor in the Spirit World;* Crowell, *Spirit World;* M. Faraday, *Dissolution, or Physical Death, and How Spirit Chemists Produce Materialization,* 2d ed. (Springfield, Mass., 1887).

44. Putnam, *Mesmerism, Spiritualism, Witchcraft, and Miracle,* 46; Davis, *Present Age and Inner Life,* 16–17; Sollors, "Dr. Benjamin Franklin's Celestial Telegraph."

45. Clark, *Plain Guide to Spiritualism,* 51, 17; Putnam, *Mesmerism, Spiritualism, Witchcraft, and Miracle,* 48; Sarah Moore Grimké to Harriot Kezia Hunt, Apr. 5, 1853, Weld-Grimké Papers, WLCL. The most widely read antebellum Spiritualist newspaper, named the *Spiritual Telegraph,* began publication in Rochester, N.Y., in 1852 and remained in publication for decades.

46. Samuel Watson, *The Clock Struck Three: Being a Review of Clock Struck One and a Reply to It* (Chicago: Religio-Philosophical Publ. House, 1874), 38; Sargeant, *Proof Palpable of Immortality,* 12.

47. Tuttle, *Outline of Universal Government,* 62.

48. Post, *Voices from the Spirit World,* 41, 121–22; Cora Linn Daniels, *As It Is to Be* (Franklin, Mass.: Cora Linn Daniels, 1892), 26–27; Denton, *Radical Discourses on Religious Subjects,* 114–15.

49. Allen Putnam, *Agassiz and Spiritualism: Involving the Investigation of Harvard College Professors in 1857* (Boston: Colby & Rich, 1874), 48; Warren Chase,

Life-Line of the Lone One; or, Autobiography of the World's Child (Boston: Bela Marsh, 1857), 161; "Spirit and Matter," *Shekinah* 1 (1851): 184. See Abraham P. Pierce, *Extracts from Unpublished Volumes,* no. 2 (Boston: William White, 1868), and Denton, *Soul of Things,* for particularly vivid accounts of extracorporeal (extraplanetary) travel.

50. Charles Hammond, *The Pilgrimage of Thomas Paine, and Others, to the Seventh Circle in the Spirit-World* (Rochester, N.Y.: D. M. Dewey, 1852), 236, 237; Sarah Moore Grimké to Catherine Brooks Yale, July 30, 1862, Weld-Grimké Papers, WLCL.

51. Kirk Cunningham to Mary Cunningham, June 29, 1855, Cunningham Papers, WLCL.

52. Ibid., Kirk Cunnigham to John Cunnigham, Aug. 1, 1858, ibid.

53. Brittan, "Spiritualism: Its Nature and Mission," 2; James Freeman Clarke to Anna Clarke, Mar. 31, 1854, Perry-Clarke Collection, MHS.

54. Clark, *Plain Guide to Spiritualism,* 159; James Freeman Clarke to Anna Clarke, Mar. 31, 1854, Perry-Clarke Collection, MHS; Hardinge, *Modern American Spiritualism,* 260.

55. Roy D'Andrade, *The Development of Cognitive Anthropology* (New York, 1995), 131; Lystra, *Searching the Heart;* Lears, *No Place of Grace;* see also the essays in Ronald Hoffman, Mechal Sobel, and Fredrika Teute, eds., *Through a Glass Darkly: Reflections on Personal Identity in Early America* (Chapel Hill, N.C., 1997).

56. Andrew Hedbrooke, "Individual Continuity," *Atlantic Monthly* 58 (Aug. 1886): 263–67, cited in Lears, *No Place of Grace,* 36; Lystra, *Searching the Heart;* David Meredith Reese, *Humbugs of New York, Being a Remonstrance against Public Delusions, Whether in Science, Philosophy, or Religion* (New York: John S. Taylor, 1838).

57. Lystra, *Searching the Heart,* 8, 9, 18.

58. Report of Newton's lecture "Spiritualism as an Agency of Reform," unpaginated, A. E. Newton Papers, MHS; Hammond, *Light from the Spirit World,* 181. Spiritualists advocated a range of reforms in marriage, including the liberalization of divorce laws and the extension of the same "civic privileges" in courtship and marriage to women as men. Opponents of the movement regularly accused Spiritualists of advocating sexual license, free love, or "this theory of religious libertinism," polygamy, provoking outright denials or defensive claims that such views were merely an outgrowth of errant enthusiasm within the movement. Epes Sargeant complained that "free love, pantheism, socialism, &c." were advocated only by "nominal Spiritualists," just as these same views were held by "nominal Christians," while Napoleon Wolfe complained that these views were propagated only among the "crazy sort of spiritualists" (Barrett, *Spiritual Pilgrim,* 143; Capron,

Modern Spiritualism, 380; Sargeant, *Planchette*, 289; Wolfe, *Starling Facts in Modern Spiritualism*, 79). In light of Lystra's work, the presence of deception in the one place where the real self was exposed would seem particularly obnoxious.

59. Clark, *Plain Guide to Spiritualism*, 81; James Freeman Clarke to Anna Clarke, Aug. 15, 1869, Perry-Clarke Collection, MHS; Caroline Healey Dall to Mrs. William Hodge, Dec. 20, 1851, Caroline Wells Healey Dall Papers, MHS.

60. Davis, *Present Age and Inner Life*, 213.

61. A. B. Child, *Soul Affinity* (Boston: William White, 1864), 7, 9, 20.

62. Snow, *Visions of the Beyond*, 98–99. Marital reform and the liberalization of divorce laws were favored topics for Spiritualists, many of whom argued that contemporary marriages were too often made for expediency or for financial betterment, rather than on the basis of soul affinity. "It is an abused custom when minds wed without the wedding ring of circles harmoniously interested in each other's society and welfare" (Hammond, *Light from the Spirit World*, 181). See also William Henry Holcombe, *The Sexes Here and Hereafter* (Philadelphia: Lippincott, 1869), whose Swedenborgian perspective on marriage shares much in common with the Spiritualist, and William Hepworth Dixon, *Spiritual Wives*, 2d ed. (London: Hurst & Blackett, 1868), which analyzes the tendency of Spiritualist views of affinity to weaken the institution of marriage.

63. Joel Tiffany, *Spiritual Manifestations Not Incredible* (New York, n.d.), 164; Herman Snow, *Incidents of Personal Experience; From Notes Taken Whilst Investigating the New Phenomena of Spirit Life and Action, Addressed to Friends by a Minister of the Gospel* (Boston: George C. Rand, 1852), 16.

64. Daniels, *As It Is to Be*, 32.

65. D'Andrade, *Development of Cognitive Anthropology*, 132. Anna M. Speicher, "'Faith Which Worketh by Love': The Religious World of Female Antislavery Lecturers" (Ph.D. diss., George Washington Univ., 1996), writes extensively about the role of intuition among abolitionist women.

66. Hammond, *Light from the Spirit World*, 150.

67. Barrett, *Spiritual Pilgrim*, 207.

68. Post, *Voices from the Spirit World*, 33–4.

69. Agnew, *Worlds Apart*, 181; Smith, *Theory of Moral Sentiments*, 13; Tiffany, *Spiritual Manifestations Not Incredible*, 166, 167.

70. Hammond, *Pilgrimage of Thomas Paine*, 30.

71. Pierce, *Extracts from Unpublished Volumes*, 4–5, 12.

72. Brittan, "Spiritualism: Its Nature and Mission," 9–10.

73. Peebles, *Seers of the Ages*, 13; McDannell and Lang, *Heaven*, 292; Snow, *Visions of the Beyond*, 33; Carroll, *Spiritualism in Antebellum America*. McDannell and Lang suggest that Spiritualist views of heaven did not significantly change until well into the twentieth century, a claim that I address in the final chapter.

74. McDannell and Lang, *Heaven*, 275.

75. Jesse Babcock Ferguson argued typically that the concept of Hell was "founded upon false and superstitious views of the universe. Immature and traditionalised minds, such as we all too willingly possess, readily receive such views, for they save the labor of thought" (Ferguson, *Relation of Pastor and People; Statement of Belief on Unitarianism, Universalism, and Spiritualism* [Nashville: Union & Steam Press, 1854], 8). After the Civil War some Spiritualists developed a Purgatory of sorts and occasionally a geographically distinct hell.

76. Frederick L. H. Willis, *Theodore Parker in Spirit Life: A Narration of Personal Experience Inspirationally Given to Fred. L. H. Willis, M.D.* (Boston: William White, 1868); William Henry Holcombe, *Our Children in Heaven* (Philadelphia: Lippincott, 1875), 72, 216; McDannell and Lang, *Heaven*, 292. Although Holcombe was a Swedenborgian, many of his ideas overlapped with Spiritualist ideas.

77. Pierce, *Revelator*, 74; Pierce, *Extracts from Unpublished Volumes*, no. 2; Davis, *Present Age and Inner Life*, 72–3.

78. R. P. Ambler, *The Birth of the Universe, Being a Philosophical Exposition of the Origin, Unfolding, and Ultimate of Creation* (New York: Harmonial Association, 1853), 107; Peebles, *Seers of the Ages*, 316. In his *Principles of Geology* (Philadelphia: J. Kay, 1837), Charles Lyell popularized the principle of gradualism, the idea that the operation of small forces over long periods of time produced great effects.

79. Post, *Voices from the Spirit World*, 41; Tuttle, *Outline of Universal Government*, 68; Park, *Instructive Communications from Spirit Life*, 16; tombstone, quoting from Hugo, cited in McDannell and Lang, *Heaven*, 294. The quote is drawn from Hugo.

80. A. J. Davis, *Death and the Afterlife* (New York: A. J. Davis, 1873), 90; Tuttle, *Outline of Universal Government*, 67.

81. Park, *Instructive Communications from Spirit Life*, 16; Wood, *Philosophy of Creation*, 89–90, 91.

82. Peebles, *Immortality, or Our Employments Hereafter* (Boston: Colby & Rich, 1880), 110; Post, *Voices from the Spirit World*, 150; Wood, *Philosophy of Creation*, 90, 93; Shelhamer, *Life and Labor in the Spirit World*, 155; Park, *Instructive Communications from Spirit Life*, 16.

83. Snow, *Visions of the Beyond*, 157; Clark, *Plain Guide to Spiritualism*, 177; Davis, *Present Age and Inner Life*, 119. Clark's debt to Quaker theology is particularly strong.

84. B. T. Young, *Scattered Leaves from the Summer Land* (Chicago: C. E. Southard, 1870), 57, 63, 62; John Worth Edmonds, *Uncertainty of Spiritual Intercourse* (n.p., ca. 1856), Boston Public Library, 7; Smith, *My Experience;* Snow, *Visions of Beyond*, 42. One of the best expressions of the passive, neurasthenic type of me-

dium is Frederick Marvin, *The Philosophy of Spiritualism and the Pathology and Treatment of Mediomania* (New York: Asa K. Butts, 1874).

85. Tuttle, *Outline of Universal Government*, 63, 61; Brigham, *Twelve Spirit Messages*, 419; Post, *Voices from the Spirit World*, xviii.

86. Wood, *Philosophy of Creation*, 88, 99; Hammond, *Pilgrimage of Thomas Paine*, 38.

87. Pierce, *Revelator*, 63–64; Holcombe, *Our Children in Heaven*, 172.

4. ANGELS' LANGUAGE

1. I use "opposition" in the sense defined by Michel de Certeau (by way of Richard D. E. Burton) of "forms of contestation of a given system conducted from *within* that system, using weapons and concepts derived from the system itself," while "resistance" refers to "forms of contestation of a given system that are conducted from *outside* that system, using weapons and concepts derived from a source or sources other than the system in question" (Richard D. E. Burton, *Afro-Creole: Power, Opposition, and Play in the Caribbean* [Ithaca, N.Y., 1997], 6; Michael de Certeau, "On the Oppositional Practices of Everyday Life," *Social Text* 3 [1980]: 3–43).

2. Smith, *My Experience*, 87, 164; J. O. Barrett, *Looking Beyond: A Souvenir of Love to the Bereft of Every Home* (Boston: William White, 1871), 16.

3. Denton, *Soul of Things*, 28. Significantly, Andrew Jackson Davis gave the opinion that photography, like telegraphy, clairvoyance, and nervous impulse, was a product of electricity; it was, he wrote, "an electric effect of light—the action of light on metals" (Davis, *Stellar Key*, 105).

4. Denton, *Soul of Things*, 30–31.

5. It may not be coincidental that one of the first American books illustrated with actual photographs was a treatise on fossil footprints in the Connecticut Valley: John Collins Warren, *Remarks on Some Fossil Impressions in the Sandstone Rocks of Connecticut River* (Boston: Ticknor & Fields, 1854).

6. William Henry Holcombe, *A Mystery of New Orleans: Solved by New Methods* (Philadelphia: Lippincott, 1891).

7. James Turner, *Without God, without Creed* (Baltimore, 1985); Michel Foucault, *Discipline and Punish: The Birth of the Prison* (New York, 1977); *Banner of Light*, Oct. 31, 1874.

8. Gary Laderman, *The Sacred Remains: American Attitudes toward Death, 1799–1883* (New Haven, 1996), 57.

9. Laderman, *Sacred Remains;* Jay Ruby, *Secure the Shadow: Death and Photography in America* (Cambridge, 1995); Stanley Burns, *Sleeping Beauties: Memorial Photography in America* (Altadena, Calif., 1990); Floyd and Marion Rinehart, *The*

American Daguerreotype (Athens, Ga., 1981). Marcus Root charged $10 for a single image in 1853 (Root invoice, June 18, 1853, Lamb Papers, WLCL).

10. Among the useful basic histories of the Anglo-American Spiritualist movement are Owen, *Darkened Room;* Braude, *Radical Spirits;* Moore, *In Search of White Crows.*

11. Mumler claimed to have taken his first spirit photograph in March 1861, while Podmore (*Mediums of the Nineteenth Century*) apparently placed the foundational event with the appearance of the spirits of Dr. H. F. Gardner's children in an image taken during the fall of 1862. Early in 1863 Mansfield noted that Mrs. H. F. Stuart was also active in taking spirit photographs (Mumler, *The Personal Experiences of William H. Mumler in Spirit Photography* [Boston: Colby & Rich, 1875], 5). The following description is based mostly upon Mumler's self-justificatory retrospective account written after having been tried for fraud. It differs in many details from other accounts, including his own.

12. Mumler, *Personal Experiences,* 5, 6.

13. Mumler, ibid., 7. Although statistics are unavailable, there appears to be little correlation between the sex of mortals and spirits in Mumler's images, other than a weak tendency for one to be male, the other female.

14. "Spirit-Photographs: A New and Interesting Development," *Journal of the Photographic Society of London* 8 (1863): 214–15; *Boston Almanac* 25 (1860) through 30 (1865); *Boston Directory* 55 (1859) through 61 (1865); James V. Mansfield Letterbook 15:232–38, WLCL.

15. Mumler, *Personal Experiences,* 41, 39, 30. Mary Todd Lincoln's interest in Spiritualism was very active during the winter of 1862–63, when she first contacted James V. Mansfield for a communication from Willie (Mansfield Letterbook 14:165, WLCL). Mumler's image of Mrs. Lincoln with her attendant but very dead husband by her side was widely reprinted and circulated.

16. Mumler, *Personal Experiences,* 41.

17. "Spirit-photographs," 214.

18. Mumler, *Personal Experiences,* 51–52, 66, 41.

19. An interesting series of essays delineating the conjoint histories of photography and the state are found in John Tagg's *The Burden of Representation: Essays on Photographies and Histories* (Amherst, Mass., 1988). The development of cost-effective photomechanical means of reproducing photographs for mass production—particularly the development of the halftone process in 1888—effectively spelled the end of books illustrated with "real" photographs.

20. M. Orvell, "Almost Nature: The Typology of Late Nineteenth-Century American Photography," in Dan Younger, ed., *Multiple Views: Logan Grant Essays on Photography, 1983–89* (Albuquerque, 1991), 139–67. In the later nineteenth

century, images of spirits became common novelty items but clearly did not make the same sort of claims to eyewitness representation of the existence of spirits.

21. Seybert Commission, *Preliminary Report of the Commission Appointed by the University of Pennsylvania to Investigate Modern Spiritualism* (Philadelphia: Lippincott, 1887), 91, 92. In Spiritualist and, more particularly, non-Spiritualist circles, mediums who derived their income from their work were considered suspect, in that the prospect of profit was thought to entice them into fraudulent enhancement of Spiritual phenomena. Alex Owen has highlighted the degree to which this concern operated most powerfully against women.

22. "Spiritual Photography," *Harper's Weekly* 13 (May 8, 1869): 289.

23. Ibid.; *Scientific American* 23 (1870): 360.

24. Podmore, *Mediums of the Nineteenth Century,* 117, 122.

25. William Stainton Moses to Epes Sargent, Apr. 23, 1879, BPL.

26. "Spiritual photography," 289.

27. "Spirit-photographs," 214; Mumler, *Personal Experiences,* 43, 23. Adam Smith's definition of sympathy as "our fellow feeling with any passion whatever" seems particularly appropriate here (Smith, *Theory of Moral Sentiments,* 10).

28. For descriptions of Mansfield's mediumship, see Hardinge, *Modern American Spiritualism;* Hardinge, *Nineteenth Century Miracles* (New York: W. Britten, 1884); Samuel Watson, *The Clock Struck One, and Christian Spiritualist* (Louisville, Ky.: S. R. Wells, 1873) and several articles in *Le Spiritualiste de la Nouvelle-Orléans* 1 and 2 (1857–58) and the *Banner of Light.*

29. Mansfield Letterbook 13:108–11, 2 (17), 53, WLCL. "Bro. Child" may be A. B. Child, a Spiritualist and author of *Whatever Is, Is Right,* which Mansfield found distasteful in its implications.

30. Mansfield Letterbooks 13:66–75, WLCL.

31. Hardinge, *Modern American Spiritualism;* Redman, *Mystic Hours.*

32. Mansfield Letterbook 13:66–75, WLCL.

33. Ibid., 14:16–17, 15:162–66, 232, 238, 14:41. For the implications of counterfeiting, see Brooke, *Refiner's Fire.*

34. Mansfield Letterbook 15:173–78, WLCL.

35. Shelhamer, *Life and Labor in the Spirit World,* 216–17; Mumler, *Personal Experiences,* 67.

36. Mansfield Letterbook 15:112–13, 16:245–47, WLCL.

37. Ibid., 15:162–66.

38. Ibid., 15:232–38, 293, 19:274–76.

39. Several other Spiritualists rejected Mumler's images. Charles Foster, the "Salem Seer," sat for Mumler late in his career and was disimpressed with the result, calling it a "thin fraud": on the back of the spirit image produced by Mumler,

he wrote, "appeared a well-known actress, which of course was no test; and, as plenty of photographers could produce equally as good or better 'spirit' pictures, we came to the conclusion that this phase [of Spiritualism] was not worthy of any further attention" (Bartlett, *Salem Seer*, 46).

40. Dolores A. Kilgo, *Likeness and Landscape: Thomas M. Easterly and the Art of the Daguerreotype* (St. Louis, 1994), 1.

41. Marcus Aurelius Root, *The Camera and the Pencil, or, The Heliographic Art* (Pawlet, Vt., 1971), 26.

42. *Banner of Light*, Nov. 21, 1874, 7. John Pierpont used the term *palimpsest* to describe the traces that an individual possessed of strong "magnetic powers" leaves on an object she or he has handled. Handwriting and hair were among the most common artifacts for psychometric analyses (Pierpont to Miss Tyler, Apr. 10, 1854, John Pierpont Papers, WLCL; Stuart Blersch, "Victorian Jewelry Made of Hair," *Nineteenth Century* 6 [1980]: 42–43; Marion Ruth Yount Sams, "Sentimental and Memorial Jewelry," *Alabama Heritage* 35 [1995]: 28–33; Mrs. Stewart McCormack, "Death and Adornment," *Missouri Historical Society Bulletin* 25, 3 [1969]: 201–6).

43. The identity of the woman in the photograph and whether she was living or dead at the time are unknown. Substitution of a photograph was also a common feature of memorial photography: if the corpse of the deceased could not be photographed, the living relatives might be photographed gathered around an image of the deceased. Other images of photographic substitution for living sitters are provided in John Dobran, "The Spirits of Mumler, Part I," *Northlight* 5 (1978): 47, especially the images on p. 5, and are discussed in Mumler, *Personal Experiences*, 26–29. Photographs of spirit handwriting are mentioned by Mumler, ibid., 28–29, 49, and Arthur Conan Doyle, *The Case for Spirit Photography* (New York, 1923).

44. Examples of their advertisements may be found in issues of the *Banner of Light* for 1874 and 1875.

45. See, for example, the advertisement in *Banner of Light*, Jan. 9, 1875. Conant was one of the better known of the mediums who contributed to the *Banner of Light*.

46. Esther Schor, *Bearing the Dead: The British Culture of Mourning from the Enlightenment to Victoria* (Princeton, N.J., 1994), 5. I take my cue from Richard D. E. Burton's perceptive analysis of the game of cricket, in which former colonies regularly beat English sides. "In classical oppositional style," Burton concludes, cricket "challenges the dominant order on the latter's own terrain . . . and while victory over the other on the other's own terms enables the dominated to get their frustration out of *their* system, *the* System itself survives—strengthened, not weakened by its merely symbolic defeat" (Burton, *Afro-Creole*, 185–86).

47. Shelhamer, *Life and Labor in the Spirit World,* 196.

48. Alfred Russel Wallace to Epes Sargeant, June 9, 1874, Epes Sargeant Papers, BPL.

5. VOX POPULI

1. Edmonds and Dexter, *Spiritualism* 2:261–63.

2. Ibid., 450.

3. Few works deal explicitly with the issue of spirit communication from the illustrious dead. See Sollors, "Dr. Benjamin Franklin's Celestial Telegraph." The celebrity dead were particularly common in Hardinge, *Modern American Spiritualism;* Hammond, *Pilgrimage of Thomas Paine;* Post, *Voices from the Spirit World;* A. E. Simmons, *Spiritualism: Communications, from Daniel Webster and Others* (Woodstock, Vt.: printed for the medium, 1852); Edmonds and Dexter, *Spiritualism.*

4. See, e.g., Brigham, *Twelve Spirit Messages;* Edmonds and Dexter, *Spiritualism;* Peebles, *Immortality;* Hammond, *Pilgrimage of Thomas Paine.*

5. Dods, *Spirit Manifestations,* 70. Hardinge, *Modern American Spiritualism,* reproduces a petition headed "Peace but not without freedom," signed in facsimile by Franklin, Washington, and a host of their deceased colleagues. Ironically, such Spiritualist petitions occasionally appear in library collections as forgeries (see the Forgeries Collection, WLCL, for examples).

6. Lydia Maria Child to Sarah Shaw, Jan. 12, 1859, in *Lydia Maria Child: Selected Letters, 1817–1880,* ed. Milton Meltzer and Patricia G. Holland (Amherst, Mass., 1982), 319–20; Podmore, *Mediums of the Nineteenth Century* 1:268. The book Child alluded to is Brigham's *Twelve Spirit Messages,* which included facsimiles of writing from the spirit and the mortal Washingtons (among others) in order to demonstrate their identity.

7. Post, *Voices from the Spirit World,* 35; Sollors, "Dr. Franklin's Celestial Telegraph." During the Civil War, Elias Brewster Hillard interviewed a handful of surviving veterans, painting them simultaneously as valorous relics and supremely ordinary citizens, tying the Unionist present to the original intent of the Union. The use of photographs in the book—an image of each man tipped in, and sold separately as well—suggests the same pattern of emotional and commercial circulation I have described for spirit photographs (Hillard, *Last Men of the Revolution* [Hartford: N. A. & R. A. Moore, 1864]).

8. Brigham, *Twelve Spirit Messages.*

9. Pierce, *Revelator,* 14, 11.

10. Post, *Voices from the Spirit World,* 32, 50; Brigham, *Twelve Spirit Messages.* Many other spirits employed the same formula of renouncing sin for a new life: in Post, see Calhoun, Webster, John Adams, Elias Hicks, and Swedenborg, among others.

11. Post, *Voices from the Spirit World*, 32.

12. Ibid., 31; Crowell, *Spirit World*, 93.

13. Hammond, *Pilgrimage of Thomas Paine*, 27.

14. Peebles, *Immortality*, 164–65.

15. Post, *Voices from the Spirit World*, 33; Nathan Francis White, *Voices from Spirit-Land* (New York: Partridge & Brittan, 1854), 89.

16. Post, *Voices from the Spirit World*, 36–37; Brigham, *Twelve Spirit Messages*, 317–18; Hardinge, *Modern American Spiritualism*, 492.

17. Brigham, *Twelve Spirit Messages*, 316; Hardinge, *Modern American Spiritualism*.

18. Richmond, *God Dealing with Slavery*, unpag., 94–95.

19. Post, *Voices from the Spirit World*, 52.

20. Jesse Babcock Ferguson, *Address on the History, Authority, and Influence of Slavery* (Nashville, Tenn.: J. T. S. Fall, 1850); William Henry Holcombe, *Suggestions as to the Spiritual Philosophy of African Slavery, Addressed to the Members and Friends of the Church of the New Jerusalem* (New York: Mason Brothers, 1861).

21. Smith, *Theory of Moral Sentiments*, 46–47.

22. Brigham, *Twelve Spirit Messages*, 314.

23. Edgar Fahs Smith, *Life of Robert Hare: An American Chemist, 1781–1858* (Philadelphia: Lippincott, 1917). Smith essentially ignores Hare's involvement in Spiritualism.

24. Robert Hare, *Defence of the American Character: or An Essay on Wealth as an Object of Cupidity or the Means of Distinction in the United States* (Philadelphia, 1819).

25. Ibid., unpag.

26. Robert Hare, *Experimental Investigation of the Spirit Manifestations, Demonstrating the Existence of Spirits and Their Communion with Mortals* (New York: Partridge & Brittan, 1855), 124; Robert Hare to "the Editors," n.d. [ca. 1852], Robert Hare Papers, APS.

27. Hare, *Experimental Investigation*, 428. As a Spiritualist, Hare became a sharp-tongued critic of Christian Spiritualists, informing the publisher Charles Partridge, "I am of opinion that reverence for the Pentateuch, is even among Spiritualists still an incubus upon the free exercise of reason" (Hare to Partridge, Feb. 6, 1857, scroll, Robert Hare Papers, APS); Spicer, *Sights and Sounds*, reported thirty spirit circles in Philadelphia in 1853 and estimated 30,000 mediums in the country at large. Britten, *Modern Spiritualism*, also provides an overview of Spiritualism in Philadelphia and Hare's importance.

28. Hare to Dear Sir, Feb. 8, 1857, Robert Hare Letterbook 8a, Hare-Willing Papers, APS; Hare, *Experimental Investigation*.

29. Hare, *Experimental Investigation*, 92, 98.

30. Hare to Dear Sir, Feb. 8, 1857, Robert Hare Letterbook 8a, Hare-Willing Papers, APS; Hare, *Experimental Investigation*, 125.

31. Hare, "Views respecting Slavery and Peonage, Sanctioned by the Spirits of Washington, Franklin, Calhoun, and Those of Many Distinguished Anti Slavery Philanthropists, Isaac T. Hopper, for Instance," n.d., Robert Hare Papers, APS; Hare to Dear Sir, Nov. 26, 1857, Robert Hare Letterbook 8a, Hare-Willing Papers, ibid. The literature on proslavery argumentation has grown in recent years. See, e.g., Larry E. Tise, *Proslavery: A History of the Defense of Slavery in America, 1701–1840* (Athens, Ga., 1987); John David Smith, ed., *The "Benefits" of Slavery* (New York, 1993); Douglas Ambrose, *Henry Hughes and Proslavery Thought in the Old South* (Baton Rouge, La., 1996).

32. Richard K. Crallé to George Bush, Jan. 3, 1853, George Bush Papers, WLCL; Hare to T. W. Dunbar Moodie, July 15, 1857, Robert Hare Letterbook 8a, Hare-Willing Papers, APS.

33. Hare, "Views respecting Slavery and Peonage" n.d., and Hare, "On Slavery," n.d., scroll (addressed "To the North American"), Robert Hare Papers, APS; Holcombe, *Suggestions*, 10.

34. Ferguson, *Address on the History, Authority, and Influence of Slavery*, 4. This quote antedates Ferguson's conversion to Spiritualism, but as I have argued, his conversion did little to alter his proslavery views.

35. Nichols, *Supramundane Facts*, 46.

36. Ferguson, *Address on the History, Authority, and Influence of Slavery*, 28.

37. Nichols, *Supramundane Facts*, 37.

38. Ibid., 45; Jesse Babcock Ferguson, *Nationality versus Sectionalism: An Estimate of the Political Crisis* (Washington, D.C.: McGill and Witherow, 1866).

39. Ferguson, *Address on the History, Authority, and Influence of Slavery*, 16, 6, 4.

40. Holcombe, *Suggestions*, 4.

41. Ibid., 4–5, 7.

42. Ibid., 10, 7, 5.

43. Hare, "Views respecting Slavery and Peonage," n.d., Robert Hare Papers, APS.

44. Ferguson, *Address on the History, Authority, and Influence of Slavery*, 23; Hare, "On Slavery," no. 2, n.d., scroll, Robert Hare Papers, APS; Hare, *Defence of the American Character*.

45. Hare to T. W. Dunbar Moodie, July 15, 1857, Robert Hare Letterbook 8a, Hare-Willing Papers, APS; Hare, "Views respecting Slavery and Peonage," n.d., scroll, Robert Hare Papers, APS.

46. Ferguson, *Address on the History, Authority, and Influence of Slavery*, 26; Nichols, *Supramundane Facts*, 43.

47. Hare, *Defence of the American Character,* unpag.; Hare, "On Slavery," no. 2, n.d., scroll, Robert Hare Papers, APS.

48. Hare, "On Slavery," no. 2, n.d., scroll, and "On Slavery," n.d. [ca. 1854], scroll (addressed "To the North American"), Robert Hare Papers, APS.

49. Hare, "On Slavery," n.d. [ca. 1854], scroll, Robert Hare Papers, APS.

50. Hare, "Views respecting Slavery and Peonage," n.d., scroll, Robert Hare Papers, APS.

51. Barrett, *Spiritual Pilgrim,* 143.

52. Smith, *Theory of Moral Sentiments,* 139.

53. Hare, *Experimental Investigation,* 240.

54. Ibid., 241.

55. Nichols, *Supramundane Facts,* 45.

56. Davis, *Present Age and Inner Life,* 115, 116.

57. Ferguson, *Address on the History, Authority, and Influence of Slavery,* 27.

6. INVISIBLE WORLD

1. New York *Herald,* Sept. 4, 1866, 4; "Spiritualism and Dietetics," *New Era,* Dec. 28, 1853, A. E. Newton Scrapbook, MHS.

2. William Lloyd Garrison to Lydia Maria Child, Feb. 6, 1857, Garrison Papers, BPL.

3. Citizen of Ohio, *Interior Causes of the War: The Nation Demoralized, and Its President a Spirit-Rapper* (New York: M. Doolady, 1863), 6, 94, 28; Richmond, *God Dealing with Slavery;* Nettie Colburn Maynard, *Was Abraham Lincoln a Spiritualist? Or, Curious Revelations from the Life of a Trance Medium* (Philadelphia: Rufus C. Hartranft, 1891); see also William Ramsey, *Spiritual Manifestations: Their Nature and Significance* (Boston: Scriptural Tract Repository, 1888) and *Spirit Workings in Various Lands and Ages* (Boston: Scriptural Tract Repository, 1888), in which he argued for the reality but diabolical nature of spiritual manifestations, and hence their contribution to the moral decline of America. In 1863 medium James V. Mansfield claimed that he had telepathically answered sealed letters from Mrs. Lincoln (James V. Mansfield Letterbook 14:165, 19:299–302, WLCL).

4. John Patrick Deveney, *Paschal Beverly Randolph: A Nineteenth-Century Black American Spiritualist, Rosicrucian, and Sex Magician* (Albany, N.Y., 1997), 10.

5. Anna W. Weston to Mary Ann Estlin, Oct. 26, 1852, Charles Fox Hovey to Anna W. Weston, June 28, 1852, Weston Sisters Papers, BPL. See, e.g., Speicher, "Faith Which Worketh by Love"; Speicher, *The Religious World of Antislavery Women: Spirituality in the Lives of Five Abolitionist Lecturers* (Syracuse, N.Y., 2000).

6. David R. Roediger, *The Wages of Whiteness: Race and the Making of the*

American Working Class (New York, 1991); Alexander Saxton, *The Rise and Fall of the White Republic: Class Politics and Mass Culture in Nineteenth-Century America* (London, 1990).

7. Caryn Cossé Bell, *Revolution, Romanticism, and the Afro-Creole Protest Tradition in Louisiana, 1718–1868* (Baton Rouge, La., 1997); James H. Dorman, *Creoles of Color of the Gulf South* (Knoxville, Tenn., 1996); Arnold R. Hirsch and James Logsdon, *Creole New Orleans: Race and Americanization* (Baton Rouge, La., 1992); Virginia R. Domínguez, *White by Definition: Social Classification in Creole Louisiana* (New Brunswick, N.J., 1986). *Creole* has numerous denotations and connotations, but here I use it in one of its most common meanings in the 1850s and 1860s to refer only to Francophones of mixed race.

8. Hatch, *Discourses on Religion, Morals, Philosophy, and Metaphysics,* 22.

9. *Banner of Light,* Sept. 24, 1857, 4; Tiffany, *Spiritual Manifestations Not Incredible,* 169. As many historians have noted, antislavery writing in general was deeply imbued with the language of sentiment. Although some argue that sentimental works like *Uncle Tom's Cabin* remained content with appeals to emotional identification (i.e., empathy, rather than sympathy), Elizabeth Clark suggests that sympathy entailed "praxis, not theory," requiring the active engagement of the reader in lessening that suffering. As such, she concludes that the sympathetic antislavery literature "played a positive role, forming conduits for arguments about the extension of individual rights to suffering others" (Clark, "The Sacred Rights of the Weak," 479, 486; Gregg D. Crane, "Dangerous Sentiments: Sympathy, Rights, and Revolution in Stowe's Antislavery Novels," *Nineteenth Century Literature* 51 [1996]: 176–204).

10. See Baer, *Black Spiritual Movement;* Baer and Singer, "Toward a Typology of Black Sectarianism as a Response to Racial Stratification."

11. Deveney, *Paschal Beverly Randolph.*

12. "Spiritual Mountebanks," *Spiritual Telegraph,* Nov. 6, 1858, 277, cited in Deveney, *Paschal Beverly Randolph;* Hardinge, *Modern American Spiritualism,* 242–43. The connection between the representations of African Americans in Spiritualism and on the minstrel stage seems a fruitful topic for further exploration, and Eric Lott's hypothesis that such representations represent . On minstrelsy, see Eric Lott, *Love and Theft: Blackface Minstrelsy and the American Working Class* (New York, 1993).

13. Painter, *Sojourner Truth;* Hardinge, *Modern American Spiritualism,* 498.

14. Smith, *My Experience,* 101.

15. *Banner of Light,* Nov. 7, 1857, 7.

16. Frances E. Hubbard Journal, Apr. 9, 1836, WLCL. The appearance of a French-language journal, *Le Spiritualiste de la Nouvelle-Orléans* edited by Joseph Barthet (1857–58), bespeaks a substantial support for Spiritualism among the

French in the city, despite the fact that the journal soon folded for lack of financial support. It was not, as has sometimes been assumed, a Kardecist journal, following in the philosophical footsteps of the French Spiritualist Alain Kardec, who profoundly influenced Spiritualist thought in France, Brazil, and other places. Barthet's spirits investigated Kardec's belief in reincarnation and concluded with a spirit who wrote that from their vantage point, "we have not seen a single reincarnation," though keeping open to the possibility that it might occur on a voluntary basis (*Spiritualiste de la Nouvelle-Orléans* 1 [1857]: 212 [translated from French]). The histories of the French- and English-speaking white Spiritualist communities remain to be explored.

17. Clark, *Spiritualist Register*. While Clark's raw figures are undoubtedly unreliable, or at least open to dispute, the statistics are probably more robust with respect to assessing the comparative strength of Spiritualism in different states: strong in New England and the upper Midwest, weak in the South. In 1859 he listed only 15,000 Spiritualists in Louisiana, ranking it in raw score below Tennessee, Texas, and Missouri and equal to Mississippi. The significance of the change is unclear.

18. Britten, *Autobiography*, 146.

19. Hardinge, *Modern American Spiritualism*, 425; René Grandjean Séance Register 64, 16 (n.d.), Grandjean Collection, ser. 9, UNO. Unless otherwise noted, I have translated all messages from the séance Registers from the original French. Like many trance lecturers Hardinge often relied upon the magnetism of strong clairvoyants to aid her in descending into trance. Valmour may have been J. B. Valmour, a blacksmith, listed in the New Orleans city directory for 1858–59. His address is given as the corner of Toulouse and C——, just north of the French Quarter and only four or five blocks from the address at which Rey indicates the circle met, Rue St. Louis, between Miro and Galvez. Valmour's date of death is unknown, but he appears as a spirit in the late 1860s.

20. Hardinge, *Modern American Spiritualism*, 428–29.

21. Dormon, *Creoles of Color of the Gulf South;* Joseph Logsdon and Caryn Cossé Bell, "The Americanization of Black New Orleans, 1850–1900," in Hirsch and Logsdon, *Creole New Orleans*, 200–261; Domínguez, *White by Definition;* Rodolphe Lucien Desdunes, *Our People and Our History* (Baton Rouge, La., 1973).

22. Rodolphe Lucien Desdunes, *A Few Words to Dr. DuBois: "With Malice toward None"* (New Orleans, 1907), 13; Logsdon and Bell, "The Americanization of Black New Orleans."

23. Grandjean Séance Register 30:44 (Dec. 1, 1858), UNO; Hardinge, *Modern American Spiritualism;* Mansfield Letterbooks, WLCL. *Le Spiritualiste de la Nouvelle-Orléans* regularly reprinted notices culled from northern publications.

24. Grandjean Séance Register 30:44 (Dec. 1, 1858), UNO.

25. Ibid., 31:20.

26. James G. Hollandsworth, *The Louisiana Native Guards: The Black Military Experience during the Civil War* (Baton Rouge, La., 1995); Howard C. Westwood, *Black Troops, White Commanders, and Freedmen during the Civil War* (Carbondale, Ill., 1992); Mary F. Berry, "Negro Troops in Blue and Gray: The Louisiana Native Guards, 1861–1863," *Louisiana History* 8 (1967): 165–90; testimony of Charles W. Gibbons, Dec. 25, 1866, *House Reports,* 39th Cong., 2d sess., no. 16.

27. Berry, "Negro Troops in Blue and Gray"; *New York Times,* Nov. 5, 1862, quoted in Hollandsworth, *Louisiana Native Guards,* 6.

28. Grandjean Séance Register 31:124, UNO; Desdunes, *Our People and Our History,* 114; Hollandsworth, *Louisiana Native Guards.*

29. Joseph T. Wilson, *The Black Phalanx* (Hartford: American Publ. Co., 1890), 195; Westwood, *Black Troops, White Commanders, and Freedmen during the Civil War.*

30. *L'Union,* Oct. 18, 1862, translated and reprinted in Logsdon and Bell, "Americanization of Black New Orleans," 220–21.

31. "The Funeral of Captain Cailloux," *Harper's Weekly* 7 (Aug. 29, 1863): 551; Hollandsworth, *Louisiana Native Guards;* Joseph T. Glatthaar, "The Civil War through the Eyes of a Sixteen-Year-Old Black Officer: The Letters of Lieutenant John H. Crowder of the 1st Louisiana Native Guards," *Louisiana History* 35 (1994): 210–16.

32. Desdunes, *Our People and Our History; Acts Passed by the General Assembly of the State of Louisiana* (New Orleans, 1870).

33. In their perceptive article Logsdon and Bell trace the transition of the antebellum three-tiered system of race ordination, in which nonwhites were divided by "color, culture, law, occupation, and neighborhood," to the starkly dualistic two-tiered "American" system. Marked by legal milestones such as the Redeemer Constitution of 1879 that effectively reinstated the antebellum white leadership, the disfranchising constitution of 1898, and the Jim Crow legislation that followed, the process was one of a constant reduction in political power and diminishment of social mobility for persons of mixed race. At the same time the transition was accompanied by an increasing awareness of common racial concerns and the development of an assertiveness, defiance, and resistance to the harshest aspects of racial domination (Logsdon and Bell, "The Americanization of Creole New Orleans").

34. Grandjean Séance Register 30:156 (July 1, 1863), UNO.

35. "The Funeral of Captain Cailloux," 551; Hollandsworth, *Louisiana Native Guards,* 27. The best accounts of Cailloux are found in ibid.; William Wells Brown, *The Negro in the American Rebellion: His Heroism and His Fidelity* (Boston: Lee & Shepard, 1867); Wilson, *Black Phalanx;* Felix James, "Andre Callioux," in

A Dictionary of Louisiana Biography, ed. Glenn R. Conrad, vol. 1 (New Orleans, 1988), 147. See also Glatthaar, "The Civil War through the Eyes of a Sixteen-Year-Old Black Officer" and Berry, "Negro Troops in Blue and Gray."

36. Grandjean Séance Register 31:228–29 (Apr. 18, 1869), UNO.

37. Ibid., 25 (Dec. 23, 1869).

38. Ibid., 20 (Dec. 2, 1865).

39. Ibid., 33 (Jan. 27, 1866), original in English, 109 (Feb. 18, 1869).

40. Ibid., 33:22 (July 22, 1871), 35:146 (Dec. 22, 1871).

41. This concept can be found in northern Spiritualism, but in Creole New Orleans it was almost inevitably strictly enmeshed with ideas of racial inequality.

42. Grandjean Séance Register 35:152 (Dec. 23, 1871), 36:55 (Feb. 9, 1872), UNO.

43. Ibid., 32:50 (Aug. 4, 1870). For other examples of other fallen Guards, see ibid., 10–11.

44. Ibid., 33:55 (June 10, 1871), 32:96 (Nov. 9, 1870), message in English. Toussaint appears in ibid., 34:83 (Nov. 4, 1871); "American Jesus" in ibid., 32:52 (Aug. 5, 1870).

45. Ibid., 31:9–10 (Dec. 7, 1865).

46. Ibid., 34:154–55 (Nov. 28, 1871), message in English.

47. Ibid., 35:212 (Dec. 27, 1871).

48. Ibid., 66 (July 19, 1872), message translated by Grandjean into English.

49. Ibid.

50. Ibid., 32:77 (Oct. 26, 1870), message in English.

51. Ibid., 30:53 (Oct. 6, 1871), 38:398–99 (Feb. 8, 1872).

52. Ibid., 32:40–41 (July 14, 1870), message in English.

53. Ibid.

54. Ibid., 35:2–3 (Dec. 11, 1871).

55. Ibid., 63:34–35 (May 18, 1877). "Luminous society" (*société lumineuse*) might also be translated as "enlightened society"; however, when it appears in English in the Grandjean registers, it is usually written as "luminous."

56. Ibid., 57:37 (Sept. 14, 1874).

57. Ibid., 67 (June 9, 1874), message in English.

58. Ibid., 38:401 (Feb. 8, 1872); see also ibid., 57 (Sept. 4, 1874), 4.5, for Abraham Lincoln's claim to know of such a spiritual army.

59. Ibid., 57:12.5 (Sept. 6, 1874).

7. SHADES

1. J. M. Roberts, "The National Developing Circle," *Spirit Voices* 1, 1 (Jan. 1885): 23.

2. Ibid., 21, 22; National Developing Circle, *How to Become a Medium* (Boston[?], 1885), 13.

3. Seybert Commission, *Preliminary Report*, 151–52. Peebles's quixotic self-appointed mission to assist in peace negotiations with Plains Indians is described in *Immortality*.

4. Brigham, *Twelve Spirit Messages;* Allen Putnam, *Biography of Mrs. J. H. Conant, the World's Medium of the Nineteenth Century* (Boston: William White, 1872).

5. Philip Deloria, *Playing Indian* (New Haven, 1998), 129; Robert F. Berkhofer, *The White Man's Indian: Images of the American Indian from Columbus to the Present* (New York, 1979); Richard Slotkin, *Regeneration through Violence* (Middletown, Conn., 1975); Roy Harvey Pearce, *The Savages of America* (Baltimore, 1953); Eve Kornfeld, "Encountering the 'Other': American Intellectuals and Indians in the 1790s," *William and Mary Quarterly* 52 (1995): 287–314.

6. Wolfe, *Startling Facts in Modern Spiritualism*, 91; Sargent, *Proof Palpable of Immortality;* Henry S. Olcott, *People from the Other World* (Hartford: American Publ. Co., 1875); Lott, *Love and Theft;* Noel Ignatieff, *How the Irish Became White* (New York, 1995); Michael Rogin, *Blackface, White Noise: Jewish Immigrants in the Hollywood Melting Pot* (Berkeley, Calif., 1996); William J. Mahar, *Behind the Burnt Cork Mask: Early Blackface Minstrelsy and Antebellum American Popular Culture* (Urbana, Ill., 1999); David R. Roediger, "The Pursuit of Whiteness: Property, Terror, and Expansion, 1790–1860," *Journal of the Early Republic* 19 (1999): 579–600. The Eddys specialized in producing a rapid succession of spirits, including a number of Indians "differently clad in true Indian costume," from a materialization cabinet while the medium was seated within (Mary Dana Shindler, *A Southerner among the Spirits: A Record of Investigations into the Spiritual Phenomena*, 2d ed. [Boston: Colby & Rich, 1877], 43).

7. Seybert Commission, *Preliminary Report*, 151–52.

8. Putnam, *Flashes of Light from the Spirit Land*, 373.

9. J. W. Hurlbut, "The Mystic Wheel: A Vision," *Shekinah* 3 (1853): 149–50.

10. Smith, *My Experience*, 172–73; Young, *Scattered Leaves from the Summer Land*, 57. Late nineteenth-century race concepts are summarized in George Stocking, *Victorian Anthropology* (New York, 1987); Stocking, *Delimiting Anthropology: Occasional Inquiries and Reflections* (Madison, Wis., 2001); William Stanton, *The Leopard's Spots: Scientific Attitudes toward Race in America, 1815–1859* (Chicago, 1960).

11. Peebles, *Immortality*, 155–56, 103; Crowell, *Spirit World*, 50; Pierce, *Revelator*.

12. Crowell, *Spirit World*, esp. p. 67. It is probably significant that Crowell reports that when the Winnebagos boarded the boat for their first ride, the boiler exploded, scattering and causing pain (though of course not death) to the Indians. The implication that Indians and modern technology were immiscible was a common one in Spiritualist writing.

13. Crowell, *Spirit World*, 49; Hammond, *Light from the Spirit World*, 96–97; Snow, *Visions of the Beyond*, 91; Brigham, *Twelve Spirit Messages*, 417.

14. Terry, *Modern Spiritualism*, 15; Nichols, *Supramundane Facts*, 84; Watson, *Clock Struck Three*, 123; see also Ferguson, *Relation of Pastor and People;* Ferguson, *Address and Correspondence, Delivered Dec. 30, 1855, in the "Christian Church," Nashville, Tennessee* (Nashville: Smith, Morgan & Co., 1856).

15. Ferguson, *Spirit Communion*, 102; "Churchianic" was a neologism employed by Peebles, *Seers of the Ages*. On the Primitive Church and Spiritualism, see Carroll, *Spiritualism in Antebellum America*.

16. Brigham, *Twelve Spirit Messages*, 416–17; Shelhamer, *Life and Labor in the Spirit World*, 86, 85.

17. Davis, *Present Age and Inner Life*, 277; S. G. Horn, *The Next World Interviewed* (Chicago: Progressive Thinker, 1896), 51, 121.

18. Crowell, *Spirit World*, 51, 55, 57. Similarly, James B. Ferguson reported that the higher Indian spirits no longer wore Red Men's clothes, although they appeared that way to mortals so they might be recognized. Robert Dale Owen reported a séance in which a "dark-bronze hand" appeared to whiten progressively until at last "it was as fair as any Caucasian hand," symbolically recapitulating the whitening of the body in the afterlife (Ferguson, *Spirit Communion*, 91; Owen, *Debatable Land*, 507).

19. Carrie E. S. Twing, *Contrasts in Spirit Life; and Recent Experiences of Samuel Bowles . . . in the First Five Spheres* (Springfield, Mass.: Star Publ. Co., ca. 1881), 43.

20. Horn, *Next World Interviewed*, 194.

21. Denton, *Soul of Things*, 217–19, 242.

22. Davis, *Death and the Afterlife*, 90–91.

23. Hardinge, *Modern American Spiritualism*, 481, 382. See, for a different example, the "Indian remedies" advertised by Dr. R. Green in Adin Ballou's Christian Spiritualist newspaper, the *Practical Christian*, during 1856. "Not himself an Indian," Green claimed his remedies came from study of Indian medicine and "by actual experience with the Indians themselves" (*Practical Christian* 16, 23 [Mar. 8, 1856]).

24. Brigham, *Twelve Spirit Messages*, 233. Although Brigham was not specifically referring to Indian spirit physicians in this passage, Indians played an important role in his larger view of healing.

25. Peebles, *Immortality*, 106. For Burr, see Davis, *Death and the After-Life;* for Arnold and André, see Brigham, *Twelve Spirit Messages;* for Lincoln and Booth, see Twing, *Contrasts in Spirit Life.*

26. Hardinge, *Modern American Spiritualism*, 482; Putnam, *Natty, a Spirit*, 93, 94, 91.

27. Snow, *Visions of the Beyond*, 60–61.

28. Shindler, *Southerner among the Spirits*, 100; *Spirit Voices* 1, 1 (Jan. 1885): 20; Stebbins, *Upward Steps of Seventy Years*, 204; Tuttle, *Arcana of Spiritualism*, 442–43. Consideration of the depth of religious sentiment in other cultures led some Spiritualists, like the notoriously impious William Denton, to argue for a form of religious relativism, placing Christianity as a source of knowledge on par with the Juggernauts of India, the Muslims of Turkey, and Chinese believers in Confucius, as well as a source of criticism for evangelical Christian claims to truth (Denton, *Common Sense Thoughts on the Bible for Common Sense People*, 4th ed. [Wellesley, Mass.: Denton, 1871]; Denton, *Radical Discourses on Religious Subjects*). The disdain expressed by Tuttle for non-Christian religions in calling them "poisonous nightshade," even while offering them as sources of inspiration, was common even in the less-impious Spiritualist literature. Napoleon Wolfe, for example, reported that when the spirit Mohammed had come to enlist "in the great work of opening communication between the two worlds," he renounced the "error of his teachings" and the "debasing effects they exert upon the lives of his followers" (Wolfe, *Startling Facts in Modern Spiritualism*, 278).

29. Brigham, *Twelve Spirit Messages*, 83.

30. Ibid., 420.

31. Ibid., 422, 419, 427, 428, 429. Franklin and other spirits were busily engaged in devising new machines for the benefit of humanity, but the particular construction of the machine described by Brigham bears a resemblance to a physical machine constructed by John Murray Spear that attempted to harness the harmonial power of men and women in concert. See, among other sources, Wolfe, *Startling Facts in Modern Spiritualism;* Hardinge, *Modern American Spiritualism;* Crowell, *Spirit World;* Shelhamer, *Life and Labor in the Spirit World;* Pierce, *Revelator;* and in the secondary literature, Oppenheim, *Other World;* Moore, *In Search of White Crows.*

32. Crowell, *Identity of Primitive Christianity* 1:50; Crowell, *Spirit World*, 148, 149. The most thorough contemporary summary of early materialization séances is Sargent, *Proof Palpable of Immortality*. Leah Underhill, one of the Fox sisters, popularized but probably did not originate materialization séances in 1860 when she materialized a full spirit for the benefit of Robert Dale Owen. See also Capron, *Modern Spiritualism;* Podmore, *Mediums of the Nineteenth Century;* Underhill, *Missing Link in Modern Spiritualism;* Owen, *Debatable Land.*

33. E. A. Atwell, "The Transparent Crown; or, The Angel's Offering," *Shekinah* 3 (1853): 287. I would not wish to concede that all mediums were self-conscious frauds; some, James V. Mansfield among them, appear to have believed sincerely in the phenomena they manifested.

34. Roediger, *Wages of Whiteness*, 104.

35. Michael Taussig, *Mimesis and Alterity: A Particular History of the Senses* (New York, 1993), 75, 16, xiii.

36. Lepore, "Remembering American Frontiers," 345–6.

37. Crowell, *Identity of Primitive Christianity* 1:333.

38. Barrett, *Spiritual Pilgrim*, 175. Whether Black Hawk represents a means of promoting resistance to oppression or, on the contrary, displaces resistance by postponing equilibration to the afterlife is an open question. For various perspectives, see Baer, *Black Spiritual Movement;* Baer and Singer, "Toward a Typology of Black Sectarianism as a Response to Racial Stratification"; Claude F. Jacobs and Andrew J. Kaslow, *The Spiritual Churches of New Orleans: Origins, Beliefs, and Rituals of an African-American Religion* (Knoxville, Tenn., 1991); Jason Berry, *The Spirit of Black Hawk* (Jackson, Miss., 1995); George Lipsitz, *Time Passages: Collective Memory and American Popular Culture* (Minneapolis, 1990); Painter, *Sojourner Truth;* Sherry Sullivan, "The Literary Debate over "the Indian" in the Nineteenth Century," *American Indian Culture and Research Journal* 9 (1985): 13–31; Gregory Dowd, *A Spirited Resistance: The North American Indian Struggle for Unity, 1745–1815* (Baltimore, 1992).

39. Hardinge, *Modern American Spiritualism*, 481.

40. Barrett, *Spiritual Pilgrim*, 174–75.

41. Deloria, *Playing Indian*, 65; Ferguson, *Relation of Pastor and People*, 12; A. F. C. Wallace, *Thomas Jefferson and the Indians: The Tragic Fate of the First Americans* (Cambridge, 1999); Lepore, "Remembering American Frontiers," 327–60; Brian W. Dippie, *The Vanishing American: White Attitudes and U.S. Indian Policy* (Middletown, Conn., 1982). Christopher Densmore, *Red Jacket: Iroquois Diplomat and Orator* (Syracuse, N.Y., 1999) provides a perspective on the historical (and to a lesser degree, fictional) Red Jacket.

42. Crowell, *Identity of Primitive Christianity* 1:318, 319.

43. Ferguson, *Spirit Communion*, 91; Nichols, *Supramundane Facts*. Frank Podmore concluded that Ferguson "did much to advance the propaganda of Spiritualism in the South" (Podmore, *Mediums of the Nineteenth Century* 1:208).

44. Of course Ferguson had argued that Christianity and civilization were compensation for enslavement.

45. Ferguson, *Spirit Communion*, 158, 134–35, 156.

46. Ferguson, *Relation of Pastor and People*, 18.

47. Ibid., 17.

48. Shindler, *Southerner among the Spiritualists*, 117; Ferguson, *Spirit Communion*, 134–35, 156. On Garrison in heaven, see Shelhamer, *Life and Labor in the Spirit World*, 341, who witnessed the ranks of "poor despised negroes" presenting themselves to Garrison, "kneeling before their benefactor." In a more palatable, satiric guise, see William Denton, *Garrison in Heaven* (Wellesley, Mass.: E. M. F. Denton,

ca. 1880?), who joked of establishing an underground railroad from Hell to smuggle abolitionists denied entry into the Christian heaven.

49. Ferguson, *Address on the History, Authority, and Influence of Slavery,* 27; Nichols, *Supramundane Facts,* 45.

50. Adrian Desmond, *The Politics of Evolution: Morphology, Medicine, and Reform in Radical London* (Chicago, 1989); Desmond, *Archetypes and Ancestors: Palaeontology in Victorian London, 1850–1875* (Chicago, 1982); Peter Bowler, *The Non-Darwinian Revolution: Reinterpretation of a Historical Myth* (Baltimore, 1988); James R. Moore, "Geologists and Interpreters of Genesis in the Nineteenth Century," in *God and Nature: Historical Essays on the Encounter Between Christianity and Science,* ed. David C. Lindberg and Ronald L. Numbers (Berkeley, 1986), 322–50; Frederick Gregory, "The Impact of Evolution on Protestant Theology in the Nineteenth Century," ibid., 369–90; Jon Roberts, *Darwinism and the Divine in America: Protestant Intellectuals and Organic Evolution, 1859–1900* (Madison, Wis., 1988). Spiritualist perspectives include James M. Peebles, *The Conflict between Darwinism and Spiritualism* (Boston: Colby & Rich, 1876); William Denton, *Is Darwin Right? or, The Origin of Man* (Wellesley, Mass.: Denton, 1881); S. F. Coues, *Possibilities of Organism* (Washington, D.C.: Mohun Brothers, 1878); Hudson Tuttle, *The Origin and Antiquity of Physical Man Scientifically Considered* (Boston: William White, 1866); Tuttle, *Arcana of Spiritualism;* Davis, *Death and the Afterlife;* Stebbins, *Upward Steps of Seventy Years;* Sargent, *Proof Palpable of Immortality;* Owen, *Debatable Land;* Horn, *Next World Interviewed.* On Wallace, see Joel Schwartz, "Darwin, Wallace, and the Descent of Man," *Journal of the History of Biology* 17 (1984): 271–89; Malcolm J. Kottler, "Alfred Russel Wallace, the Origin of Man, and Spiritualism," *Isis* 65 (1974): 145–92; Michael Shermer, *In Darwin's Shadow: The Life and Science of Alfred Russel Wallace* (New York, 2002).

51. Stocking, *Victorian Anthropology;* Stocking, *Delimiting Anthropology,* Stanton, *Leopard's Spots;* Desmond, *Politics of Evolution;* Desmond, *Archetypes and Ancestors;* Bowler, *Non-Darwinian Revolution;* Moore, "Geologists and Interpreters of Genesis in the Nineteenth Century"; Gregory, "The Impact of Evolution on Protestant Theology in the Nineteenth Century"; James A. Second, *Victorian Sensation: The Extraordinary Publication, Reception, and Secret Authorship of Vestiges of the Natural History of Creation* (Chicago, 2000).

52. Stocking, *Delimiting Anthropology,* 15. The Spiritualists in this work, like the majority of anthropologists at the time, typically employed the fivefold racial typology of J. F. G. Blumenbach, including Caucasians, Malays, Mongolians, Africans, and Americans.

53. Stebbins, *Upward Steps of Seventy Years,* 210, 293.

54. Sargent, *Proof Palpable of Immortality,* 156.

55. Peebles, *Conflict between Darwinism and Spiritualism*, 3, 5, 7.

56. Peebles, *Around the World*, 29–30.

57. Peebles, *Conflict between Darwinism and Spiritualism*, 14, 13; Peebles, *Around the World*, 103.

58. Peebles, *Conflict between Darwinism and Spiritualism*, 15.

59. Ibid., 18; Peebles, *Around the World*, 256.

60. Peebles, *Around the World*, 185–86, 278, 186.

61. Peebles, *Conflict between Darwinism and Spiritualism*, 22; Peebles, *Around the World*, 254.

62. Tuttle, *Origin and Antiquity of Physical Man*, 17.

63. Ibid., 22.

64. Ibid., 34–35, 129, 134.

65. Ibid., 35–36, 91. James Cowles Prichard, *Researches into the Physical History of Man* (London: Sherwood, Gilbert & Piper, 1841–51); Prichard, *The Eastern Origin of the Celtic Nations Proved by a Comparison of Their Dialects with the Sanskrit, Greek, Latin, and Teutonic Languages* (London: Sherwood, Gilbert & Piper, 1841–51); Friedrich Max Müller, *Lectures on the Science of Language*, 7th ed.(London: Longmans, Green & Co., 1878); Stocking, *Victorian Anthropology*.

66. Tuttle, *Origin and Antiquity of Physical Man*, 109, 110–11.

67. Ibid., 93.

68. Ibid., 94.

69. Ibid., 95–96.

70. Ibid., 95–96, 98–99, 100, 97.

71. Ibid., 184; Tuttle, *Outline of a Universal Government*, 61.

72. Tuttle, *Origin and Antiquity of Physical Man*, 237, 67, 242, 88, 258.

73. Ibid., 62, 212, 231, 258.

74. Denton, *Garrison in Heaven*, 35.

75. Denton, *Is Darwin Right?* 16.

76. Ibid., 167, 178–79; *The Word*, July 20, 1892, 3.

77. Davis, *Morning Lectures* (New York: C. M. Plumb, 1865), 11, 15.

78. Ibid., 212.

79. Davis, *Death and the Afterlife*, 179.

80. Ibid., 179, 180.

81. Ibid., 181, 182.

82. Ibid., 183, 184.

83. Ibid., 184.

84. Davis, *Morning Lectures*, 263, 264.

85. Hudson Tuttle, *Mediumship and Its Laws: Its Conditions and Cultivation* (Chicago: Progressive Thinker, 1900), 174.

CONCLUSION

1. Houdini, *Magician among the Spirits*, xvi.

2. Maynard, *Was Abraham Lincoln a Spiritualist?* 126.

3. Eckard V. Toy, "Silver Shirts in the Northwest: Politics, Prophecies, and Personalities in the 1930s," *Pacific Northwest Quarterly* 80 (1989): 139–46.

4. Wilson cited in Michael Dennis, "Looking Backward: Woodrow Wilson, the New South, and the Question of Race," *American Nineteenth Century History* 3 (2002), 81, 98; Nina Silber, *The Romance of Reunion: Northerners and the South, 1865–1900* (Chapel Hill, N.C., 1993); David Blight, *Race and Reunion: The Civil War in American Memory* (Cambridge, Mass.: 2001), 139.

5. Wendell Newhall to Asa Smith, May 1, 1881, D. N. Diedrich Collection, WLCL.

INDEX